Cheating Death

Cheating Death

COMBAT AIR RESCUES IN VIETNAM AND LAOS

GEORGE J. MARRETT

Smithsonian Books

Collins
An Imprint of HarperCollinsPublishers

In
memory
of all the rescue crews,
especially the Skyraider pilots,
who paid the supreme price to rescue
American aviators shot down over Vietnam and Laos;
this book is dedicated to them
and to their
families.

For permission to reproduce the photographs appearing in this book, please correspond directly with the owners of the works, as listed in the individual captions. Smithsonian Books does not retain reproduction rights for these photographs or illustrations individually, or maintain a file of addresses for photo resources.

HarperCollins books may be purchased for educational, business, or sales promotional use. For information please write: Special Markets Department, HarperCollins Publishers, 10 East 53rd Street, New York, NY 10022.

First Collins trade paperback edition 2006

Designed by Brian Barth

Library of Congress Cataloging-in-Publication Data
Marrett, George J.
    Cheating death : combat air rescues in Vietnam and Laos / George J. Marrett.
        p. cm.
    ISBN-13: 978-0-06-089157-2
    ISBN-10: 0-06-089157-2
    Vietnamese Conflict, 1961–1975—Search and rescue operations—Vietnam. 2. Vietnamese Conflict, 1961–1975—Search and rescue operations—Laos. 3. Vietnamese Conflict, 1961–1975—Aerial operations, American. 4. Vietnamese Conflict, 1961–1975—Personal narratives, American. 5. Marrett, George J. I. Title.

DS559.8.S4M37 2006
959.704'348092—dc22

06 07 08 09 10 RRD 10 9 8 7 6 5 4 3 2 1

Poor is the country that has no heroes, but beggared is
that people who, having them, forgets

*quoted from an unknown source by A-1 Sandy pilot Col. William
A. Jones III*, Maxims for Men at Arms

CONTENTS

ACKNOWLEDGMENTS

Special recognition and thanks go to my wife Jan for taking care of the home front while I was at war. She has also been my copilot for forty-four years and provided love, encouragement, and helpful suggestions as I brought these words to print. To my older son Randy, thanks for suggesting that I interrupt my test pilot writing to concentrate on completing my war memoirs. To my younger son Scott, who told Jan, "Dad must have been the only pilot to eat as he flew on a combat mission," thanks for reading and reviewing these words.

I am deeply grateful to my father, George Rice Marrett, who taught me a sense of patriotism, and to my mother, Julia Etta (Rachuy) Marrett, who at age ninety-two has a wonderful memory. She taught me faith and persistence, traits I needed to both survive combat and to write this book.

To George Larson, senior editor of *Air* & *Space* magazine, thanks for recommending the Smithsonian Institution Press (SIP) for publication of my manuscript. SIP acquisitions editor Mark Gatlin, his assistant Nicole Sloan, and the staff of the press are a very professional organization and have been a joy to work with. Copy editor John Raymond has been extremely helpful in turning my "pilot talk" manuscript into a readable human-interest story.

I owe a great deal to Darrel D. Whitcomb, author of the book *The Rescue of Bat 21* (Naval Institute Press, 1998), for encouraging me to write a first-person account of a Sandy rescue pilot at war and for reviewing the manuscript.

To Richard Hallion, Historian of the U.S. Air Force, thanks for having confidence that a pilot who had flown for forty-three years could transition from the cockpit to the typewriter.

William Forsyth, the Laotian specialist from the Joint Task Force–Full Accounting, located in Camp H. M. Smith, Hawaii, generously provided me with compass maps, SAR (search-and-rescue) logs, and results of government searches for missing airmen and crash sites in Laos.

In chapter 9 I relied heavily on information from Maj. Jimmy W. Kilbourne. I thank him for his generous permission to quote from and paraphrase some of his chapter about Col. William A. Jones III ("Sandy One: You're on Fire!") from his book *Escape and Evasion* (New York: Macmillan, 1973). Kilbourne's chapter originally appeared in *Airman* magazine in the late 1960s.

I also wish to thank John L. Frisbee, contributing editor of Air Force online magazine (published by the Air Force Association), for permission to quote from his January 1986 story about Colonel Jones called "A Triumph of Will."

The story in chapter 8 about my dead-stick landing in Laos was first published in a similar form in *Wings* magazine in April 2000. I wish to thank *Wings* for their permission to use it here.

I am grateful to Louie F. Alley, the Freedom of Information Act manager at the Headquarters Air Force Safety Center at Kirtland AFB, New Mexico, for providing releasable portions of Maj. Jerry J. Jenkinson's accident in the T-37B on December 17, 1969.

I wish to acknowledge Curly J. Putnam, author and publisher of "The Green, Green Grass of Home," for the portion of his song quoted in chapter 16.

In addition I wish to thank A-1 pilot Byron Hukee, who created and maintains the Web site: www.skyraiders.org.

The following individuals, some of whom provided photographs, kindly agreed to be interviewed for this publication: Gordon Breault (June 18,

2002), Bill Buice (March 24, 2001), Mel Bunn (April 1998), Tom Campbell (April 1998), John Carlson (April 1998), Don Dineen (April 1998), Don Dunaway (April 8, 2001), Harry Dunivant (April 3, 2001), Kenny Fields (April 1998), Ron Furtak (April 17, 2001), Jim George (April 28, 2001), Doug Horka (April 16, 2001), Don Johnson (July 21, 2001), Elizabeth Jones (April 8, 2001), Bob Kraus (March 11, 2001), Pete Lappin (April 1998), Fred Lentz (August 31, 2001), Ed Leonard (April 1998), Gene McCormack (April 19, 2001), John McMurtry (April 1998), Tom O'Connor (April 18, 2001), Bill Palank (March 15, 2001), Dave Richardson (April 1998), Walt Stueck (March 31, 2001), Darryl Tripp (April 29, 2001), Wayne Warner (April 1, 2001), and Darrel Whitcomb (November 13, 2001).

REUNION

Sometimes I still hear the call I made on the UHF (ultrahigh frequency) radio. It does not come to me in a dream, but it's entrenched in my mind.

"Sandy 7, this is 8."

I repeat it over and over.

"Sandy 7, this is 8. . . . Sandy 7, this is 8."

The guns are silent now, the Laotian jungle regrown and green. The American air warriors from the Vietnam era are back home again; that "secret" war is long over. Instead, the call must be a memory resounding in my head, a frantic call I repeat, echoing unanswered across all these years.

Tchepone was only a spot on a map, a tiny village near the intersection of dirt roads and a narrow river in central Laos. In the early evening of May 31, 1968, the men of the 602nd Fighter Squadron flew cautiously over that intersection. A short time earlier, a Navy Corsair A-7 attack jet from the carrier USS *America* had been shot down. A rescue force of four Sandy A-1 propeller-driven Skyraiders ("Sandy" was the call sign our squadron used for rescue missions) and two Jolly Green HH-3 jet helicopters (Jolly Greens had a specific call sign for each of their aircraft, JG 07, for example) arrived to extract the downed pilot from this enemy-infested area. The rescue force entered slowly. It was a clear, hot day—the sun beat down incessantly. The road below was hard packed from the thousands of North Vietnamese who carried arms and supplies southward over a route called the Ho Chi Minh Trail.

Leading the rescue force was Air Force Maj. William Palank and his wingman, Maj. Eugene McCormack Jr. The second flight of Skyraiders was led by Capt. Edward Leonard Jr., a combat veteran who had just completed a one-year tour but had extended for six more months. I was his wingman, a new guy, just three weeks from the States, flying my first rescue mission over unfamiliar country. Ed Leonard and I were escorting two of the Jolly Green helicopters to a safe area—awaiting the call from Bill Palank to attempt the rescue of Streetcar 304, Lt. Kenny W. Fields, the downed Navy pilot.

The men of the rescue force were hot, sweating profusely from the steaming jungle air. They wore survival vests, web belts with knife and pistol, helmets, oxygen masks, and gloves—all their exposed skin was covered to protect them from the rigors of flight and perhaps the fear of the unknown that confronted them. A few miles to the east were the steep karst mountains of North Vietnam. Below was a winding river, a network of trails, and an American pilot in trouble.

The enemy, cool in their camouflaged trenches in the jungle, watched and waited. They could both see and hear the single-engine propeller aircraft that was orbiting overhead, looking for the missing airman. All at once the guns opened fire on the lead Sandy plane, striking the Skyraider's left wing and the huge Pratt & Whitney radial engine. Palank pushed his throttle full forward and climbed westward into the setting sun toward his home base, Nakhon Phanom (known to us as NKP), located about a hundred miles away across the Mekong River in friendly Thailand. I watched Palank's aircraft gradually disappear into the golden glow of approaching night, leaving a trail of smoke marking his route to safety.

Then Leonard and I left the safety of our orbit and descended into the twilight to search for Streetcar 304. The gunners were waiting. They had shot up two American planes so far—more would surely follow.

Meanwhile, commanders of the air war headquartered in Saigon realized we were being outgunned over Tchepone. They ordered several flights of heavily loaded jet fighters into the fray. These fighters were on the way, they told me on my radio—a Gunfighter flight (fighter aircraft used call signs like Gunfighter, Hellborn, Panda and so on) of four F-105 Thunderchiefs would be with us in five minutes. Scuba, Spitfire, and Hot Rod flights would follow. I hurriedly copied the information of radio frequencies and ordnance load on my five-by-seven mission card while banking back and forth, keeping Leonard's Skyraider in sight. The sun was long gone, leaving only a ghost-like aura of trees blending into the dark abyss. An explosion near the burning wreckage of Streetcar 304's A-7 caught my attention. The white canopy of a parachute drifted into the darkness of the jungle.

"Sandy 7, this is 8," I called. "Sandy 7, this is 8."

Silence.

Darkness.

I was the last of four Sandy pilots and looking down at the chaos of war. Now two pilots were in the jungle, and only I and the two slow-moving Jolly rescue helicopters remained in the air. I was stunned to watch this rescue attempt fall apart so quickly. The image of that parachute sinking into the darkness of Tchepone is still indelible in my mind thirty-three years later. The gunners on the trail thirsted for more prey.

The battle to rescue Streetcar 304 lasted three days and two nights. In the end we rescued Lieutenant Fields, but six American aircraft careened into the dense jungle, and one went down at sea. It took 189 sorties to finally get Streetcar 304 out of the jungle. It was an unrelenting fight, such as none of us had seen—or would see again.

Like most airmen who meet at war, we were comrades of the moment, companions of the sky, flying for a common purpose. As time went by, one by one we returned to the United States, to our families, to our jobs and careers. I was not, as some men say of themselves, reborn in war. When I returned I tried to forget my year of toil and torment and go on with my life. But I had roots of restlessness that went deep within. I held a great deal of anger and hostility toward anything Asian.

I was also sure that I walked off the battlefield a more knowing man. Those who survive such a long and lethal assault emerge with at least a small piece of truth, some little lesson, a sliver of light. Across the years—starting a new career flying as a civilian test pilot, raising a family, buying a house—the emotions of my year of combat were partially submerged. But years later, I still had feelings of loss and unanswered questions.

So, in the fall and early winter of 1997, I set out to find the men I once held close, intimates who had been side by side under a flaming-white jungle sun and who had spent nights flying formation, dodging enemy tracers. Those men had been a mirror of me; likely they too carried home some doubts. Perhaps my flight mates had answers to the unanswerable.

My search began in an old, faded-blue Air Force briefcase that I had carried with me in Vietnam. It was a repository of crinkled black and white photographs, all 188 of my mission cards, and several soft-covered books about men at war. I also found a pencil outline drawing of my two sons' feet—used by Thai shoemakers to make two pairs of children's combat boots. Several cases of military medals were in the briefcase along with one new leather flight glove. The missing glove must have had a story to tell—but after all the years I drew a complete blank. In other places I found letters to my wife, my jungle survival boots, an olive-drab cotton flight suit, a box of 35-mm color slides, and a set of wings. Most items were useless, simple reminders of time spent 8,000 miles from home and over thirty years in the past. The faded black and white photographs were a rich vein of remembrance. Some of the pilots were smiling or mugging for the camera. Others were hollow-eyed, as though wondering what would be their fate. The Skyraider always sat as a backdrop to the photos, oil running down its exhaust stacks, drenching the centerline fuel tank and ramp.

I made a few phone calls, placed an ad in the River Rats Association magazine, and worked the Internet. A few weeks later, I had the names of nine of the men from the rescue of Streetcar 304.

Ed Leonard (Sandy 7) had a "What me worry?" grin like Alfred E. Newman's in *Mad* magazine. He was from the state of Washington and was shot down in a burst of 37-mm ground fire. An Air Force captain, he was captured by the North Vietnamese on the third day of the rescue of Streetcar 304 and held as a prisoner of war for five years. His personal story is a remarkable saga of courage, selflessness, and survival.

Kenny Fields (Streetcar 304) was a short, snuff-chewing Navy lieutenant from West Virginia. He was shot down by 37-mm ground fire over Tchepone and became the focus of a three-day battle to free him from enemy-occupied jungle. While on the ground he was wounded by falling ordnance from an Air Force fighter and infected with malaria, but he survived to fly a second combat tour in Southeast Asia.

Bill Palank (Sandy 5) was a bald-headed air commando major, a B-26 combat veteran of the Korean War. After he was hit by ground fire over Tchepone, I flew in close formation and watched him eject from his stricken Skyraider.

Pete Lappin (Nail 69—Nail forward air controllers had their own personal call signs) was a smooth-talking Air Force captain, who was called back from a vacation in Bangkok to serve as a forward air controller (or FAC, pronounced "Fack") to rescue Streetcar 304. He probably had the best eyesight of any American pilot flying over Vietnam.

John Carlson (deputy commander of 602nd Fighter Squadron) was a tall, white-haired lieutenant colonel, nicknamed "The Mad Bomber." He absolutely loved the Skyraider and rescue missions.

Gene McCormack (Sandy 6) was a wisecracking Air Force major from Florida, who kept me in laughs for the entire year. Full of war stories, he wrote a song about the Sandys and Jollys, "Sandy Cannon Ball," that was tape-recorded at a squadron party . He was one of the gutsiest pilots ever to strap into a Skyraider.

Mel Bunn (Sandy 3) was a tall and extremely thin Air Force major, who looked as if he spent his year of combat at Auschwitz.

Tom Campbell (Sandy 9) was an Air Force major, who, as Sandy lead conceived of a master plan to rescue Streetcar 304, which worked flawlessly. He was one of the coolest pilots ever to fly a Skyraider under fire.

Dave Richardson (Jolly Green 9) was a no-nonsense Air Force captain, who, as a rescue helicopter pilot, had only a week left in his year tour when he was called to rescue Streetcar 304. He hovered his Jolly Green helicopter, which was enveloped in a spiritual white light, as Kenny Fields was hoisted aboard. His faith in God allowed him to perform a miracle.

After a month and a half of inquiries, I had phone numbers and addresses. I called former POW Ed Leonard, who was living in his home state of Washington. He retired from the Air Force in 1978 as a lieutenant colonel. Each year he was given a POW physical examination by the military at the Naval

Air Station in Pensacola, Florida. His next exam was scheduled for April 1998—nearly thirty years from the date he parachuted into the jungle of Laos and became a prisoner of war. Because Ed sacrificed so much to rescue Streetcar 304, we held our first reunion in nearby Fort Walton Beach, Florida the weekend before his medical evaluation.

Kenny Fields lived in North Carolina, only a day's drive from Florida. Fields had never met Leonard and wanted a chance to thank him for his sacrifice. Every member of the rescue team I contacted about the reunion didn't ask about the location or date of the get-together. They simply said, "I'll be there."

Most men had changed little, though all had gray hair and wore glasses. Most had gained a few pounds except for Mel Bunn, who still looked like he needed a good square meal. We have drawn close to one another again, just as we did when danger was at hand. We are linked forever by events that altered all our lives. There are moments when this attachment is as fierce as a blood bond, as enduring as a kinship. We don't pretend to understand the forces that held us together, or why, across all these years, they awaken us still, make us stir. We have spent long hours telling war stories, drinking beer, laughing and crying about our experiences so many years ago. I'm not sure even now that it is possible to convey the whole story of what happened between us—what is happening still—or to explain the longing we felt, the desire, at least one more time, to be close together.

Here, however, is how it began for me.

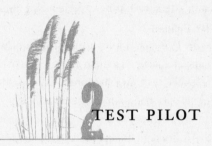

TEST PILOT

During the late fall of 1967, I was making a grand tour of Europe. Although I was only a captain in the Air Force, an eight-passenger T-39 Sabreliner jet, usually reserved for generals, was my private mode of transportation. I was flying in glorious style.

The previous three years, I had been a fighter test pilot assigned to the Air Force Flight Test Center located at Edwards Air Force Base in California, flying the F-4C Phantom, F-5A Freedom Fighter, F-104A Starfighter, and F-111A Aardvark. I wore an orange flying suit, a bright blue custom flight helmet, and high-speed ejection spurs as I accelerated to Mach 2 in my silver beauties over the Mojave Desert.

I had recently completed several extremely dangerous test flights in the F-4C trying to determine why eight aircraft flown by Tactical Air Command pilots had crashed while maneuvering at low altitude. In preparation for flying combat, F-4C aircraft were loaded with twenty-five-pound smoke bombs, and pilots dropped them on simulated targets in Air Force gunnery ranges. With a full load of fuel, the aircraft was being flown out of balance. As a result, the flight controls were so light that some pilots maneuvered the F-4C through airframe buffet and into a full stall, ending in loss of control and a crash. At Edwards I came up with a method to move the aircraft into balance. Test engineers and I also modified systems to alert the pilot when he was nearing a dangerous condition. After my testing experiences, I didn't think much of the F-4C as a fighter-bomber.

Senior officers in Tactical Air Command were anxious to hear the results of my flight tests. I gave a detailed briefing to them at their headquarters at Langley Air Force Base in Virginia. Fearing that more F-4Cs would be lost, the commanders asked me to give presentations to operational F-4C units in the United States. Interest in my Phantom flight test results also came from the headquarters of the U.S. Air Force in Europe. A request came for me to brief the European headquarters staff and all the F-4C squadrons in England, Germany, and the gunnery range at Wheelus AB in Libya. So a T-39 and pilot was made available to transport me in high fashion.

During a refueling stop in Germany, I made a phone call to my boss back at Edwards. He had news for me. I had received military orders to go to war in Vietnam and would be required to start combat crew training in the Douglas A-1 Skyraider at Hurlburt Field, Florida in a little over a month. The Skyraider was a tail-wheeled propeller aircraft that cruised at 165 knots and flew at very low altitude. It was painted in jungle camouflage markings and resembled the old P-47 Thunderbolt of World War II fame. I thought there must have been a mistake in those military orders—I was a *jet pilot!*

When I first entered military service in February 1958, the Air Force was quickly transitioning into an all-jet fighting force. The only propeller-powered aircraft I had flown was a T-34—and that was only for thirty flight hours as a student pilot. Then I graduated and was assigned to the first class to fly the twin-jet T-37. From there I went to Air Force basic flight training in Texas to fly the T-33 jet, the trainer version of the F-80 Shooting Star that saw action in Korea. After earning my silver wings, I went to advanced flying school in Georgia where I flew the illustrious MiG-killing North American F-86 Sabre jet. Next, I spent four years as a jet interceptor pilot flying the supersonic twin-engine F-101B Voodoo from Hamilton AFB, California. During the Cuban missile crisis I carried two nuclear rockets inside the Voodoo as I orbited over the Pacific Ocean waiting for Soviet bombers to appear over the horizon. Now I couldn't believe I was going to war in a propeller aircraft—let alone a tail-wheeler.

My interest in fighter aircraft started during World War II when I was a six-year-old boy living in Nebraska. I heard reports over the radio about aerial dogfights in Europe and dreamed of becoming a fighter pilot. I spent hours and hours shooting my BB gun at paper airplanes set up in my parents' basement. Later, my dad took me pheasant hunting through the cornfields of the Midwest, and I became what he called a good shot.

At Edwards I got the opportunity to fire the Gatling gun that was scheduled to be installed in the newest and most advanced version of the Phantom: the F-4E. After returning from Europe, my next flight test assignment had been to fly all the stability and control tests on the F-4E, an aircraft expected to be the best jet fighter in the Air Force.

But by receiving these military orders I was now going to war in a tail-wheeled, propeller-powered aircraft, leaving Edwards and the best job a junior captain in the Air Force could have. My wife Jan reminded me that I would also be leaving her and our two sons, age three and seven, for my year of combat. Secretary of Defense Robert S. McNamara said the war would be over in six weeks. Being optimistic, I thought maybe the war would be won even before I got to Vietnam.

Escape and Evasion School

My first official training prior to going to war was attending the Air Force Escape and Evasion School taught at Fairchild AFB near Spokane, Washington. I left Edwards on temporary duty to attend the school. Even though it was December and the terrain and weather in the northern part of the United States was not even remotely similar to the jungle of Southeast Asia, the techniques of being captured and escaping could still be taught. During the course of training for aircrew, we were subjected to conditions we could expect if we were shot down and captured. Our captors seemed very authentic but were actually American servicemen dressed in Russian uniforms. We were given a small taste of the horrors that could be inflicted upon us if we were unfortunate enough to be imprisoned by the North Vietnamese or the Laotian Pathet Lao.

Each of us was placed in a windowless box about the size of a telephone booth. We were instructed to be quiet, wear a burlap sack on our head, and remain standing. If a guard pulled the door open and we were found to violate any of these rules, we would be taken outside and placed in the hole. The hole was a five-foot-deep opening in the soil covered by a sheet of metal. The outside temperature was slightly above zero. For the better part of a day each of us endured this treatment. Sometime during this affair a small eight-by-eight-inch opening at the base of the door was opened from the outside and a bowl of soup pushed inside. It was a temptation to eat it, but I could tell that it had been oversalted. Its nutritional value was probably not worth the unpleasant aftertaste and increased thirst.

Everyone got the opportunity to spend some time in another box. This box, made of wood, was about fourteen inches wide, thirty inches high, and thirty-six inches long. You got down on your knees, lowered your head, and scooted slowly forward to get inside. Then the door behind you was closed and locked. The guard started beating the box with a stick. In this position you were totally confined, unable to readjust your limbs, or scratch your nose. Soon discomfort turned to pain. My mind told me a real enemy could leave me in the box for hours, days, or even weeks. It was both a physical and a mental torture.

The most interesting part of the instruction for me was interrogation both alone and in a group setting. The primary technique taught was to evade, not confront. If you chose to stand up directly to the enemy, you would certainly be physically beaten. To prevent this, the idea was to evade, plead sickness, answer another question, or take the interrogation on another path. Children use this technique instinctively. As prisoners we needed to be subtle in our evading; there was a fine line to tread, but it was our only hope.

One on one, the interrogator would invade your space like a baseball manager in an argument with an umpire. Nose to nose, with spit flying, we would be called every name in the book. Most military officers hadn't experienced this treatment since being hazed in flight school.

In a group setting, the interrogator was very aggressive and looked for weakness. While about ten of us sat on the floor, he asked a black airman why he was willing to die for the United States when his race was discriminated against and denied freedom. An enlisted airman was asked why he was willing to fight for the United States when his military pay was so low. I could tell that if I were injured, suffered from lack of sleep, and was worried about my family and future that keeping mentally sharp would be very difficult.

Each person was asked what he liked best about America. Again words and thoughts were twisted to give the captors a verbal advantage. I answered, "Fireworks." The captor said I was stupid to select something so irrelevant and frivolous, something that was a waste of a country's resources and didn't help the starving children in America. But to me, fireworks were simply a symbol of the Fourth of July and, above all, freedom. I got my point across to the other captives. While being verbally degraded, I placed one flight glove on top of my knee, folded and balanced in such a way that only the middle finger was sticking straight up. The guard couldn't see my glove, but the other prisoners did. I could see smiles on their faces; my subtle message had been sent and received.

HURLBURT FIELD, FLORIDA

So after four years as a test pilot, it was time to pack up and leave Edwards to start training to become a combat pilot. Jan and I loaded our sons into the station wagon and drove from California to Florida during the Christmas holidays of 1967. We rented an apartment near Hurlburt Field. Hurlburt was Eglin AFB auxiliary field number 9. The field had first been used back in 1942 when Col. James "Jimmy" Doolittle trained his B-25 crews for the "secret" raid on Tokyo. As I would find out later, we would be trained to fight the "secret" war in Southeast Asia.

Over the next two and a half months, instructors from the 4410th Combat Crew Training Wing would train ten pilots in my class to fly and fight in the A-1 Skyraider. My class was made up of one full colonel, four lieutenant colonels, two majors, and three captains. Although no one had flown the Skyraider before, we were all experienced pilots with years in the cockpit and thousands of hours of flying time. After completion of the school, four of us (Lt. Col. William A. Jones III, Maj. Thomas O'Connor, Maj. Alan Hale, and I) would be transferred to the 602nd Fighter Squadron located at Udorn Royal Thai Air Force Base (RTAFB) in Thailand. The other six pilots would go to two A-1 squadrons in South Vietnam.

My instructor for the training was Capt. James Thomas. Jim Thomas had just returned from a year tour in the 602nd and had applied for entry into the Air Force Test Pilot School. It was ironic: I was being assigned where Thomas had been stationed, and he wanted to go to Edwards, the base I had come from. Needless to say, we had a lot in common and became instant friends.

Jim Thomas gave me a description and a first look at the plane I would be flying in combat. Designed at the end of World War II, the Douglas Aircraft Company's A-1 Skyraider was never used in that conflict. It quickly picked up the nickname Spad, the endearing name of a classic World War I aircraft. Some in the Air Force called it the Super Spad. The Navy called it "AD" for Attack Douglas or its phonetic alphabet name, Able Dog. All Skyraiders were built in El Segundo, California. The chief designer, Ed Heinemann, had created a sturdy and rugged warplane. It was a tail dragger, thirty-eight-feet-ten-inches long, with a fifty-foot wingspan. With a maximum speed of 310 knots, a service ceiling of 25,000 feet, and a range of 1,100 nautical miles, the Skyraider could carry not only four wing-mounted 20-mm cannon (with 200 rounds each) but up to 12,000 pounds of fuel, napalm, bombs, or rockets parceled out on fifteen underwing positions. The A-1 could carry as much ordnance as the B-17 Flying Fortress. It was the undisputed world champion at carrying ordnance. It was called by some a "flying dump truck."

With its huge four-bladed propeller hanging out in front and a tail wheel in back, the Skyraider was less an aircraft than a collection of heavy metal— a relic of the piston-engine prop age somehow surviving into the jet age. Its big 2,500-horsepower Wright Cyclone R-3350 piston engine smoked, belched, and wheezed on start up. The eighteen-cylinder radial was the biggest and most powerful engine ever put in a single-engine prop aircraft. It had to be to pull the Skyraider through the air at gross weights of up to 25,000 pounds. Rated at 2,700 horsepower for takeoff, the engine was the same as the one used on the Douglas DC-7C airliner.

Firing ordnance from an aircraft would be a new experience for me. During four years as an F-101B interceptor pilot I carried live air-to-air heat-seeking missiles on many occasions. However, I never intercepted a hostile aircraft where I would be required to shoot at another plane. Also, I flew with two nuclear rockets during the Cuban missile crisis, but the confrontation with the Soviets was settled before anyone fired. At Edwards, I tested the F-4C Phantom, carrying dummy loads that simulated the weight and shape of actual rocket pods and bombs. The tests did not require me to actually launch live ordnance. When I fired the Gatling gun from an F-4E prototype at Edwards, the firing was a test of the gun, not of its accuracy on a real target. So even though I had been a fighter pilot for seven years, I had never fired a shot in a wartime environment. This fact was soon to change.

Midway through my training at Hurlburt, the North Vietnamese made a surprise attack on South Vietnam, the Tet Offensive. It was clear that if the enemy could carry armament and supplies all the way to Saigon and mount such a severe assault, the war was far from being won. From that time on, I never heard Secretary of Defense McNamara say the war would be won in the next six weeks. As history now shows, he believed the war was lost.

Even though my classmate Al Hale was a bomber-transport test pilot at Edwards during the time I was stationed there, we hadn't known each other very well. We were just two of about forty pilots assigned to the Flight Test Center and had tested entirely different aircraft. During the course of our instruction at Hurlburt we became friends and decided to room together when we were finally sent to Udorn.

On one occasion Hale and I scheduled a Skyraider for a weekend cross-country flight together. Since all of our instruction at Hurlburt consisted of flying formation and launching ordnance in the nearby weapons range, we didn't get the opportunity to fly the A-1 for long distances. Pilots were encouraged to plan a flight where the Skyraider would be flown at high altitude and a distance of several hundred miles to familiarize themselves with its navigational capabilities.

Al Hale and I were given A-1E, serial number 132649, for a weekend trip to North Carolina to visit some of his friends. Actually, that particular aircraft was a very historic Skyraider. Just one year earlier, on March 10, 1967, Maj. Bernard Fisher landed the aircraft on an abandoned airfield in the A Shau Valley of South Vietnam while it was under attack. He rescued another pilot, Lt. Col. Wayne "Jump" Myers, who, by coincidence, was the commander of the 602nd. During the pickup of Myers, Fisher's A-1 was hit nineteen times by ground fire. For that daring rescue, Bernie Fisher was awarded the Medal of Honor. Shortly thereafter, the aircraft was scheduled to be transferred to the United States Air Force Museum at Wright-Patterson AFB in Dayton, Ohio. It seemed strange to me to fly an aircraft that had been in such a hostile situation that the pilot was awarded the Medal of Honor. It brought home to Hale and me how risky the next year of our life could be.

SNAKE SCHOOL

With Skyraider training completed at Hurlburt, I departed from Travis AFB in California in a Boeing 707 bound for Southeast Asia. In April 1968 I attended the Air Force Jungle Survival School at Clark Air Base in the Philippines; it was commonly referred to as the snake school. The course at Clark consisted of about three days of classroom instruction followed by a couple of nights in the jungle using our newly learned skills to survive. Most of us pilots had never been in a jungle before and assumed it would be like the Tarzan movies we had seen in our youth.

After we completed the classroom instruction, late one afternoon our group was loaded in the back of several trucks. Rain was coming down in bucket loads, as the monsoon season struck the Philippine Islands with full force. Sitting with a plastic poncho wrapped tightly around my body, I was one cold and wet fly-boy. Several other pilots and I were being transported into the jungle for several days to use our newly learned knowledge to actually survive. We would have no food, no tent, no bedding, just as it would be if we were shot down over Vietnam. Not only was I cold and wet, I was irritated. Military tradition was to "hurry up and wait." We had been waiting a long time with the sound of the rain roaring in our ears, preventing us from even grumbling to one another.

When I had departed from Travis AFB only a few days before, spring was in full bloom. The sky had been sparkling clear with a warm, balmy wind. Now I was sitting in the chilly rain, 8,000 miles from home and only four days into a 365-day combat tour. It occurred to me again how long and difficult this next year could be. In the best case, I would return home a year from now uninjured. Or I could be shot down but rescued without injury. Worst case, I could be shot down and captured or killed. Suddenly the cold and rain did not seem so bad. I was wasting my energy letting something as small as this inconvenience cause me to become so upset that I couldn't think straight. Maybe really bad days were ahead. My anger subsided—a calm set in. It didn't make sense to think about how comfortable the past had been, nor to be overly concerned about the unknowable future. As a recovering alcoholic might have put it, only today was important. I reminded myself to live in the present as well as I could. The rain continued.

As the truck bounced along a dirt road in the jungle, two of us at a time were dropped off and warned to stay close together. But not so close as to make the capture of us likely. Who was going to capture us? The Air Force hired a group of natives, called Negritos, to find and capture us. Our job was to get from where the truck dropped us off back to the base without being detected by the Negritos. The Negritos were natives of the Philippines, about four feet tall and black as the ace of spades. They lived in the jungle all of their lives and had played this survival game many times. They wore nothing but a G-string—not even shoes. If they captured us, they were rewarded with a chit. The chit could be cashed in for rice, so they took their part of this game very seriously. We were captured once on the first day and twice on the next by two different groups of Negritos. The last group took us to an assembly where we got more jungle training.

Air Force instructors let us taste bananas just picked from a tree. They were small, very green, and tasted extremely bitter. We were warned that animals in the wild eat fruit that is not ripe by human standards. So if we planned to wait for it to ripen, it would most likely be gone by then. We were shown how to eat monkey meat raw, because a fire would give away our position to the enemy. It was all very valuable instruction, but I came away deciding it was better not to get shot down.

Udorn Royal Thai Air Force Base

After attending the snake school, I flew as a passenger in a C-141A Starlifter to Tan Son Nhut Air Base outside of Saigon for a refueling stop. Those of us going on to Thailand were asked to stay aboard because a rocket attack was imminent. All I could see out of a small passenger window was gunfire damage to the corner of one building.

Compared with the three flights totaling twenty-two hours to cross the Pacific Ocean, the flight from Tan Son Nhut to Don Muang Airport in Bangkok was short, just about an hour. Arrival at Don Muang was probably like any arrival in Saigon or the cities of Thailand for an American. A putrid odor and boiling heat hit me when the jet transport's door was opened. Then the sound of the Thai language confirmed I was in a foreign country far from home. "*Sawadee*" greeted me when I stepped from the plane to start my year tour of

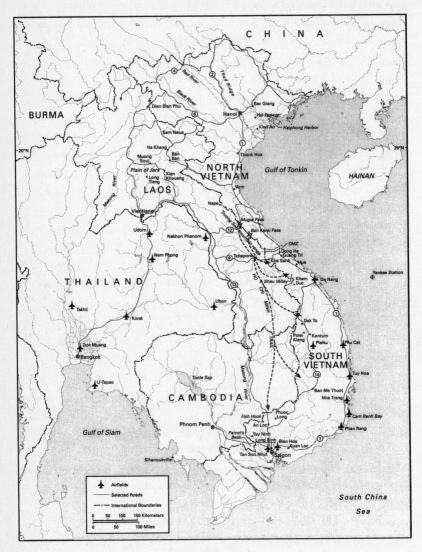

Southeast Asia (Courtesy Darrel Dean Whitcomb)

duty. *Sawadee* was the Thai way of saying *hello* or *welcome;* the same expression was used for *good-bye* or *so long*.

In Bangkok I stayed in a hotel awaiting the "klong" flight for the trip up-country the next day. In 1968 the only way up-country from Bangkok to my new duty station at Udorn was by way of the klong flight. Klongs were ditches filled with dirty, green slime-colored water and sewage, a terrible sight and smell for newcomers to Asia. Several C-130 Hercules cargo ships flew a round-robin circuit to all of the five Thai bases every day. These trash-littered, smelly aircraft were more like cattle cars. Fully loaded with supplies, mail, and military personnel, the C-130 limped off the runway at Don Muang and turned north.

Without air conditioning in the cargo hold, the half-hour flight to Takhli RTAFB seemed much longer. At least when the rear ramp was opened after we landed, I got a breath of air. But it still smelled like the klong. Takhli was the home of the Air Force 355th Tactical Fighter Wing. The wing was composed of three tactical fighter squadrons, all flying the F-105 Thunderchief. My Thai booklet on Takhli said that the king cobra snake was indigenous to the area, hence the nickname, "Land of the King Cobra." These and other varieties of poisonous snakes were a hazard to the unwary. We halted without shutting down the engines, and about twenty passengers were unloaded; it seemed as if even more people got back on. We were packed in tight.

Our next stop was Korat RTAFB about a hundred miles east of Takhli. Korat was the home of the 388th Tactical Fighter Wing, which also had three fighter squadrons of F-105s. At Korat we went through the same ritual: land, unload, and reload again. The next leg would be two hundred miles to Ubon RTAFB. The heat, humidity, and vibration were starting to take a toll on me; I tried to close my eyes and sleep. Between the summer afternoon turbulence and the excitement of getting close to the base where I would be spending a year flying combat, I got little rest.

We landed at Ubon RTAFB, home of the illustrious MiG-killing 8th Tactical Fighter Wing nicknamed Wolf Pack. Three squadrons of F-4 Phantom jets sat on the flight line. Just as occurred at Takhli and Korat, supplies and personnel were exchanged for the next leg to Udorn.

After another bumpy flight of about an hour, the C-130 started its descent into Udorn. I tried to get a quick peek at the jungle of Thailand through a small window. Several minutes later the Hercules transport touched down and the rear cargo door was lowered. I got my first view of the flight line with aircraft packed in tight. After about five hours trapped in the back of the klong aircraft, I had finally arrived at Udorn RTAFB.

The base was just a mile or two south of the town of Udorn in the northeastern section of Thailand. Udorn was the third-largest city in Thailand with about 80,000 people, only twenty-five miles from Laos and 320 miles from Hanoi. Those of us getting off were new guys fresh from the States. The six-month rainy season had just started; a light sprinkle added to the oppressive heat and my mental outlook of the moment. As a citizen soldier, I had not volunteered to go to war. I went because I was given the assignment and was not particularly happy about it. But as a good soldier, I followed orders and planned to make the best of it. Now, everything I looked at was red. Red mud, red dust, redwood buildings, and red rain: it reminded me of Oklahoma. Soon I would go off to war; red was an ominous color.

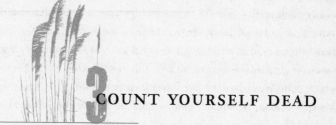

3 COUNT YOURSELF DEAD

As I deplaned from the C-130, I took a quick look around the Udorn flight line. The ramp was full of F-4 Phantoms and aircraft operated by Air America, a civilian-run flying operation funded by the CIA that carried out classified missions not appropriate for the U.S. military. Two Skyraiders were in the landing pattern. I knew I was at the right base.

Carrying my bulging military B-4 bag off the C-130, I looked for someone from the 602nd Fighter Squadron. An airman met me on the ramp and drove a jeep to the Skyraider pilots' living quarters called hooches. We went on a dusty road past many aircraft hangars until we arrived at a long wooden building with a sign that announced: "602nd Fighter Squadron (C), 'Home of the Sandys.'"

The squadron had a long and illustrious history. The 602nd Fighter Squadron (C) (C for Commando) had been stationed in Southeast Asia long before the Vietnam War. Formed in 1942 as the 2nd Fighter Reconnaissance Squadron, it soon picked up the "commando" designation and saw action in India, Burma, and Thailand in 1944 and 1945. Flying P-51 Mustangs, the commandos provided close air support to ground forces attacking Japanese-held airfields and other targets along the Irrawaddy River. On other missions they struck Japanese supply routes, truck parks, and bridges—missions similar to those I would fly in Southeast Asia.

Ironically, it was a strike into Thailand that brought the highest praise to the early commandos. The P-51 was a long-range aircraft that enabled the commandos to strike Don Muang Airfield, near Bangkok. Flying from Burma, 780 miles from their target, the commandos were in their single-seat cockpits nine hours for the round-trip. The raid on Don Muang caught the Japanese completely by surprise. Seventeen aircraft were destroyed on the ground, three more in the air. In addition, the commandos chalked up four probable kills and eighteen enemy aircraft damaged. At the end of World War II, having compiled an impressive record after only three months in combat, the 2nd Fighter Squadron (Commando) was deactivated.

But history was to bring the squadron back to fly a similar aircraft under similar circumstances in the same part of the world nearly a quarter century later. Re-designated the 602nd Tactical Fighter Squadron, the unit was re-activated on October 14, 1964 at Bien Hoa Air Base in the Republic of Vietnam. Its early mission in Vietnam was training Vietnamese pilots to fly the Skyraider. But the pilots of the 602nd were also combat trained and often flew close air support for ground forces in South Vietnam.

In December 1966 the 602nd was reassigned to Udorn RTAFB and soon was re-designated the 602nd Fighter Squadron (Commando), the only fighter squadron in the Air Force to fly a propeller aircraft. With the move came a change of role: the training mission was eliminated. The pilots found themselves flying strike missions, reconnaissance missions, as well as escort, where they used the call sign "Firefly." But their most important new mission was the search and rescue of downed American aircrew, where the call sign was "Sandy." The squadron's operations officer first came up with the call sign Sandy. He had a dog by that name and used the name for the rescue mission. The name stuck.

As I unloaded my bag from the truck, I spotted a familiar face. Maj. David Thomas, a classmate of mine from the Air Force Test Pilot School at Edwards AFB, came over and shook my hand. Dave Thomas helped me carry my gear to his room, where we piled it in a corner. His roommate was temporarily gone, he said. I could bunk down with him for a few days until I got assigned a permanent room. Typically, two pilots shared a small room. Each room had two beds, two metal lockers, a desk, a chair, and a noisy air conditioner that ran day and night. The room looked small and cramped, but it was better than spending the night in the jungle. Thomas interrupted my daydreaming, saying, "Come on down to the Sandy Box and meet the guys. Let's have a beer."

After our graduation from test pilot school, Dave Thomas and I were assigned to Test Operations at Edwards. Thomas was a helicopter test pilot and had flown many test missions, including support of the X-15 rocket ship. When I was a member of an accident board trying to determine why a rocket-powered F-104 Starfighter had caught fire, Thomas flew me in an H-21 helicopter over the Mojave Desert. As we flew, I looked for a metal panel that had exploded off the F-104 during the fire. Now Dave Thomas was coming to the end of his year tour; he had only a few more combat missions before returning to the States.

We walked up elevated wooden steps to a bar at the end of the building. The Sandy Box was the local watering hole, a room exactly the size of the other standard two-person living quarters. The Box was the meeting and lounging place for all the pilots in the squadron. Inside, it was very crowded, elbow to elbow, with pilots drinking beer and talking about the missions of the day with their hands duplicating aerial maneuvers. The walls of the Sandy Box were covered with photographs of crashed Skyraiders, of pilots who had completed their tour and gone home, and an assortment of pornographic material. The room was filled with the acrid smell of cigarette smoke and reeked of liquor. Everyone was in a flight suit. Many had returned from combat missions just moments before, and their suits were wet from perspiration; there were white stains around their arms and on their backs. A white refrigerator packed with beer stood in the corner.

I was introduced to the squadron pilots, took a can of beer, smiled, and lied that I was happy to be at Udorn. The pilots all appeared to me to be rugged individualists. Certainly no two were alike in personality or mannerisms. Around twenty-five pilots were assigned to the 602nd; most were senior captains or majors with a couple of lieutenant colonels thrown in. It was a gung ho group. I immediately liked all of them.

It seemed to me that I was being sized up—the new guy in the crowd, someone who would soon be their wingman. The experienced Skyraider pilots had been in the thick of battle day after day; they knew what it was like to be shot at and had nothing to prove. I was the outsider, an unknown quantity yet to be tested under fire. I listened to war stories in the Sandy Box that night for hours and hours. I had nothing to say. I didn't speak their language yet; I was not a brother in arms. I nodded my head in agreement and flashed a dumb smile every now and then. I knew I had a lot to learn.

The squadron was assigned twenty-four Skyraider aircraft. About half were single-seat H or J models called Spads; the other half were side-by-side–seated E or G models called Fat-face. Usually, several aircraft would be out of commission for scheduled maintenance or battle-damage repair. I was told that I could expect to fly every day. The squadron flew missions seven days a week, thirty days a month. Every day was the same; it was hard to tell one day from the next; there was no such thing as a weekend. Most pilots purchased a self-winding Japanese Seiko watch that showed the hour, day of the week, and date of the month. Sunday was displayed in red, so it was referred to as a red-letter day.

Standing with a beer in my hand, I listened to the many war stories. I tried to ask intelligent questions, but my mind wandered off. I was also posing questions to myself. What would combat really be like? Would I ever learn to be a rescue pilot? Would I be scared? Would I ever be accepted? I guessed that every pilot had faced the same questions. We had all been trained to fly the Skyraider at Hurlburt and had spent time in the jungle at survival school in the Philippines. Air Force training was considered to be top-notch. But would I remember all my training? Would I measure up?

I assumed I would be shot at every time I flew. The enemy on the ground would be trying to hit my Skyraider, shoot me down, and either capture or kill me. In a year of flying they would have plenty of opportunity to hit me. Would I end up in Hanoi, beaten up, broken down, and a disgrace to my country and myself?

I thought that this was going to be a long year, and I would probably use every bit of aeronautical knowledge I had learned in my nine years in the cockpit. I would be facing perils I had never experienced before, even in flight test. The odds were low that a pilot could fly a year of combat unharmed. There was no guarantee I could avoid ground fire, severe monsoon weather, and engine malfunction. These uncertainties were simply a fact of life for Skyraider pilots flying combat missions over enemy territory.

In the Sandy Box you could boast, exaggerate, and tell a good story. Once airborne, your true talent would come to the surface. Flying a single-seat, single-engine Skyraider, you would be alone and totally responsible for your own actions. That was the acid test, not talking big in the Sandy Box.

While eating dinner in the Udorn Officers Club the following night, I saw Capt. James Hurt. Jim Hurt was also in my class at the test pilot school at Edwards. Before attending the school, he was a T-38 flight instructor in Air Training Command. After graduation he was assigned to the Air Force Special Weapons Center at Kirtland AFB in Albuquerque, New Mexico. There he flew the F-105 Thunderchief, testing different munitions that could hold a nuclear bomb. Now he was finishing his year tour in the F-4 Phantom and would return to Edwards as a fighter test pilot. I envied him and his new assignment.

While both Thomas and Hurt were nearly through with their tour, Capt. Terry Uyeyama was just starting. Terry Uyeyama was in the bar in the Udorn Officers Club the same night I saw Jim Hurt. He was an RF-4 reconnaissance pilot flying out of the 14th Tactical Reconnaissance Squadron located at Udorn. We were classmates in Air Force Primary Flying School back in 1958 at Bainbridge, Georgia. At the time we were both second lieutenants.

Uyeyama was Japanese by ancestry but grew up in New Jersey before joining the Air Force. On one of his solo flights as a student flying the T-37, he forgot to monitor the amount of jet fuel remaining in his aircraft. He finally landed after using 300 gallons of the 311 onboard. This was an extremely low fuel state, especially for a student. After receiving hours and hours of reeducation from his instructor, he was scheduled for another solo flight. The following day, ignoring the pleas of the fainthearted, Uyeyama successfully proved that the T-37 could and would fly on fumes, this time landing with only two gallons remaining. Another student pilot asked him if his father had been a kamikaze pilot in World War II, who didn't have to worry about the fuel on board his aircraft. Uyeyama didn't think the comment was funny, but we may have been correct.

Uyeyama disappeared on a night mission over North Vietnam on May 18, 1968, only a few days after I saw him at Udorn. Fortunately, he was captured and returned to the United States during Operation Homecoming in 1973. I always wondered if he had really been shot down or had just run low on fuel again like he did in flying school.

War Theater Briefings

The water drops, the ants eat the fish.
The water rises, the fish eat the ants.
So it is better to love than to hate.

—LAOTIAN PROVERB

I had little time to question my flying abilities after that first night in the Sandy Box. Before flying combat every Skyraider pilot was required to sit in on extensive briefings about the country of Laos, the location of the battle areas, and the rules of engagement in conducting the war. Over the course of the next several days, intelligence officers briefed me about the "secret" war being conducted in the northern half of Laos, an area given the code name Barrel Roll. The southern half of Laos was code named Steel Tiger.

Laos, once known as Lane Xong, "the land of a million elephants," was the Shangri-la of Southeast Asia. It was mountainous, covered with tiger-haunted jungle and elephant-inhabited rain forest. It could only be reached by air, by traversing two very primitive dirt roads, or by sailing up the mighty Mekong River. The kingdom of Laos was about the size of Great Britain but was land-locked and so primitive that the adjective "underdeveloped" would be a com-pliment. A U.S. survey disclosed that 90 percent of Laotians thought the world was flat—and populated mainly by Laotians.

It was less a single country than an archipelago of small, lush river valleys, cut off from each other by sharp limestone mountains, separated by plateaus where the tigers and elephants roamed. In winter the hills of Laos were alight with opium poppies, and in summer the floods brought by the monsoon rains flowed over the five hundred or so miles of meandering dirt roads.

The Mekong River swiftly flowed down from China's Yunnan Province and then was slowed by silt and sewage on its 1,600-mile run to the South China Sea. In prewar times it was the principal means of transportation. The river was known as "the soul of Laos" and was the border with Thailand.

Strange pinnacles of rock, called karst, soared thousands of feet above the valleys of jungle. Fog often filled these valleys and drifted past the rocky cliffs. Caves dotted the karst—some big enough to hide large pieces of artillery or enough fuel and supplies for an army. For Skyraider pilots, finding their way through clouds that were often filled with peaks was always dangerous and sometimes fatal.

Laos lies in the shape of a lamb chop among quarreling neighbors. To the North Vietnamese and Chinese Communist countries in the north, Laos was a vital corridor that could fuel guerrilla warfare against South Vietnam and a country to be captured by the Pathet Lao. To Cambodia, Laos was a buffer that permitted it to be neutral. To firmly anticommunist Thailand on the western border, Laos was a geographic and ethnic neighbor, and, if the communists should ever take it over, a potential threat. To the United States, Laos was primarily a supply line to deny to the enemy and about as inconvenient a place to conduct a war as could be found.

The war over the mountains in Laos was an almost perfect mirror image of the war being waged in Vietnam. In Vietnam the war was public, vividly portrayed on nightly television across the world. The war in Laos was a carefully guarded secret. Even after the broad outlines of what was going on became public, details remained classified.

In Vietnam, the U.S. military took over the biggest burden of fighting the war. In Laos, all the ground fighting—and dying—was done by a group of mountain people known as the Hmong. Early in the war they provided much of their own air support, flying mission after mission until they died.

In Laos, the American involvement was masterminded by the U.S. ambassador in Vientiane, the capital, and was carried on by a strange collection of CIA agents and contract Air America personnel, who masqueraded as soldiers of fortune.

In another important aspect this "secret" war was different. In Vietnam, the South Vietnamese and U.S. military held the big, valuable targets—the cities and large military bases—while the enemy flowed through the villages and hamlets, able to pick the time and place for combat. In Laos the situation was the opposite. The Hmong held the mountaintops, while the North Vietnamese and Pathet Lao allies were tied to the cities, to vulnerable supply depots, and to trails where they were subject to attack.

In the northern part of the country, near the border with North Vietnam, was a large, relatively flat area covered with what looked like large jars, left behind by some ancient civilization. It was known by its name in French, the Plaine des Jarres (Plain of Jars). American pilots simply called it the PDJ, for the French initials. The PDJ was a 500-square-mile, diamond-shaped region in northern Laos that was covered with rolling hills, high ridges, and grassy flatlands. The average altitude was about 3,000 feet. Hundreds of huge gray stone jars, about five feet high and half again as broad, dotted the landscape. These containers were created by people with a megalithic iron-age culture and probably served as burial urns. Exactly who these people were, and why their culture disappeared, was not known.

During the long Southeast Asian war, all sides found the PDJ to be situated in a highly strategic location. The area had several Laotian dirt airfields and contained a limited road complex that connected various sectors of the country and the outside world. This crossroads had been a battleground for centuries but never so intensively as in the conflict between North and South Vietnam.

The struggle for the PDJ in 1968 and 1969 was a mysterious and tragic affair, wrapped up in confusion and obscured by years of falsehoods and half-truths. It was a sideshow to the main war in Vietnam, but it was ennobled by some of the finest and most heroic flying in the history of the Air Force. These valiant efforts were designed to support U.S.-backed forces and to destroy Communist North Vietnamese units that opposed them.

The many campaigns in the PDJ were fought parallel with a continuing bombing effort against the Ho Chi Minh Trail. The latter campaign would prove to be futile, for enemy activities in South Vietnam could be sustained on as little as sixty tons of supplies a day—the equivalent of about thirty trucks' worth of matériel.

Although the formal American presence in Laos could be observed in the capital of Vientiane, the military focal point of U.S. activity in Laos was in a compound in the hills to the west of the PDJ known as Long Tieng. It was also known as Lima Site 20 Alternate. We commonly called it Alternate. Although the American press was barred from visiting, they came to refer to it as the CIA's secret headquarters. Long Tieng was actually more of a military outpost and staging area. The CIA had its truly secret administrative base at Udorn.

Lima was the phonetic alphabet for the letter *L*. Lima sites were military outposts, sometime with dirt airstrips, located in the country of Laos. "Lima site" was easier for American pilots to pronounce than the names of the nearby Laotian villages. Likewise, military outposts in Vietnam were called Victor sites.

The central figure at Long Tieng was the charismatic Hmong general named Vang Pao. Although he did not have a high school education, Vang Pao had a natural flair for guerrilla warfare that impressed the French, with whom he fought against the Viet Minh. In 1952, when he was eighteen, the French sent him to a military academy in Vientiane. He emerged as a second lieutenant in time to help lead a rescue force of Hmong resistance fighters on a forced march through the jungles when a large French garrison was trapped at Dien Bien Phu in 1954. But they arrived on the scene the day after the French surrendered and turned around to retrace their steps back to Laos.

Vang Pao was a type-A personality, an enthusiastic and demanding leader, willing to do the dirty work himself and more than willing to lead in combat. He was trusted by the Americans, who delivered to him something no Laotian leader had ever possessed: massive logistical support and air power. He expanded the number of Hmong personnel under arms until they eventually numbered some 40,000. He saw to it that they were trained and well equipped and led them first in guerrilla warfare and finally in conventional warfare against the North Vietnamese. Vang Pao was always proudly conscious that he was a Hmong who had made good in competition with the lowland Laotians.

His leadership style led to some monumental victories but also caused some heavy defeats. His tactics resulted in heavy casualties over the years, so much so that eventually only preteen-age children and men over forty-five remained to serve as soldiers. Everyone else had been killed, captured, or wounded. To spur recruitment, he would withhold rice from communities that sought to shield their young from joining his armies. Nonetheless, in a country where fighters were few and fighting leaders almost nonexistent, Vang Pao established himself as the man to deal with. He was generally admired by the Americans who flew in his support, whether with the CIA-operated airlines or with the Ravens, the covert Air Force FACs.

By 1968, Laos was swarming with about 40,000 North Vietnamese troops and about 35,000 Pathet Lao. The Royal Lao Army was characterized at the time as overweight in generals and underweight in fighting. It had 60,000 troops but still had a preference for leaving the real fighting to the Hmong.

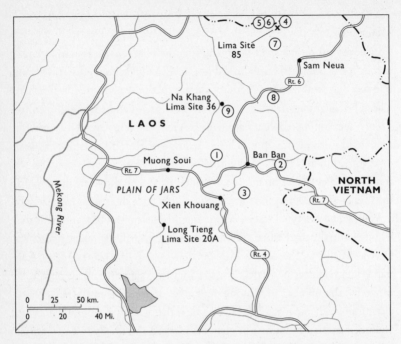

Plaine des Jarres (PDJ), Laos, with crash sites: (1) Sandy 6 (Maj. J. B. East lost); (2) Firefly 20 (Capt. Clint Ward lost); (3) Firefly 26 (Capt. "Bat" Masterson lost); (4) Sandy 1 (Maj. Don Westbrook lost); (5) Sandy 6 (Capt. Joe Pirruccello lost); (6) Firefly 34 (Maj. Tom O'Connor rescued); (7) Firefly 22 (Capt. Jerry Jenkinson rescued); (8) Sandy 3 (Maj. Charlie Kuhlmann lost); (9) Firefly 24 (Capt. Clyde Campbell lost).

Lima Site 85

One of the intelligence officers explained that friendly forces had suffered a horrible defeat just a little over a month before I arrived. For the Americans, the loss of Lima Site 85 on March 11, 1968 was a terrible blow. Although kept secret for many years, the fall of this little mountaintop position in northeast Laos was one of the most crucial and devastating defeats of the entire war in Southeast Asia.

Lima Site 85, called "the Rock," was located on a 5,800-foot mountain ridge known as Phou Pha Thi, about thirty miles from the border with North Vietnam and only about 150 miles from Hanoi. Partway up the mountain was a short, 600-foot airstrip. At the top was a tactical air navigation (TACAN) station and radio beacon. It was much like the other Lima sites; then in 1967 it took on a new role and became much more important than the other sites. Prefabricated buildings and tons of electronic equipment were plunked down on the top of the mountain by helicopter.

It was manned on a rotating basis by fifteen Air Force technicians, who were "sheep-dipped," or secretly removed from the military to appear as civilians. Their job was to operate Commando Club, a system that promised a dramatic improvement in the accuracy of fighter-bomber attacks against North Vietnam. The system, called TSQ-81 (a portable version of the MSQ-77, an extremely sophisticated radar-navigational device), was based on the Strategic Air Command's Combat Skyspot radar-scoring system. But instead of calculating where simulated bombs had fallen, it was used in this case to guide where real bombs would fall. It was needed for precision bombing of targets in North Vietnam north of Vinh at night and in inclement weather.

Although the North Vietnamese probably didn't know just what the activity at Phou Pha Thi was all about, they saw enough to decide it was worth knocking out. The U.S. military, whose job it was to defend the site, was alarmed to see aerial photos of a new road snaking through the jungle toward Lima Site 85. They called for air strikes to stop the road. Enough air strikes were obtained to annoy the road builders, but not enough to stop them.

If an attack were to come, the defenders—a mixed force of Hmong and Thai soldiers—couldn't hold the site. The hope was that air power could hold off the attackers long enough to permit an evacuation of the Americans and many of the Thai, while the Hmong melted into the jungle to regroup elsewhere. Before abandonment, they also planned to destroy the radar-bombing equipment, codes, and encryption systems.

The North Vietnamese assault on the site began in a bizarre way on January 12, 1968, when two 1930s-era Soviet-built single-engine AN-2 Colt biplanes made a bombing attack on the new installation atop the mountain. They dropped about fifteen 120-mm mortar shells from a hole in the bottom of the aircraft. The attack was basically ineffective. Three Laotian soldiers and one technician were wounded. The TACAN station was down for a few days and a few power cables had to be repaired. The radar site was unharmed.

The AN-2 planes were so slow that an Air America helicopter was able to pull alongside one of them while a sharpshooter, Glen Woods, shot the plane down with an M-16 rifle. (Woods was killed later in 1969.) The other Colt was hit by small-arms fire and crashed in the jungle. There were two other

AN-2s in the area, orbiting at a higher altitude, but they made no attempt to attack the site.

When the attack by North Vietnamese infantry came on March 11, it was more sophisticated than the assault by the two old biplanes. Heavy artillery and mortars hammered the mountain, smashing defenses and destroying electronic equipment. Under cover of darkness, three teams of enemy commandos scaled the cliffs of Phou Pha Thi. Although armed with M-16s, grenades, and a few hand weapons, the noncombatant technicians were no match for the enemy commandos.

The defenders pleaded for air support. On the second morning of the assault, the air was filled with planes, but the battle was already lost. A full-scale evacuation was then attempted, but of the sixteen Americans at the site only six survived, and five of them were wounded. Many of the Thai and Hmong defenders were also evacuated by helicopter, and the remainder showed up at Lima Site 36 thirty miles south a few days later.

A flight of F-4s from the 555th Tactical Fighter Squadron at Ubon was sent to destroy the radar equipment and other facilities to keep it from getting into enemy hands. Every one of their bombs missed the mountain entirely.

Finally, one of the pilots in the 602nd, Major Palank, was sent to lead a flight of four A-1s to accomplish the objective. Palank told me later that he was armed with napalm and instructed to dive bomb it at the installation. Normally napalm was delivered in a shallow dive angle and released at a very low altitude. But in this case, the military leadership believed that the enemy would have great firepower and that a low pass would be too hazardous. Palank said he ignored orders and decided to deliver the napalm at low altitude. On his first pass, his Skyraider's engine air scoop, located on top of the engine and directly in front of the windscreen, was hit by ground fire. After that close call, Palank now agreed with his former order and dropped the napalm in a dive. He was very successful and set the radar vans on fire. Air Force Gen. Richard V. Secord described Palank's attack in his 1992 book, *Honored and Betrayed*, as "blowing the top off the mountain." Palank said the general's description was an overstatement, but his flight did destroy all the classified equipment still on the mountain. However, the North Vietnamese had already acquired a gold mine of secret technology and top-secret code systems.

The day after Palank's flight, on March 13, forty-two-year-old Maj. Donald Westbrook from the 602nd was in a flight of four A-1s looking for survivors of Lima Site 85. According to Palank, Westbrook was flying below the top of the mountain and banking back and forth, attempting to spot friendly troops. An enemy gun near the top of the mountain actually fired down at Westbrook, hit him, and he crashed. None of the other Skyraider pilots saw Westbrook get hit. Observers said there was no parachute seen, no emergency beeper went off, and no radio contact made over Westbrook's survival radio. The wreckage of Westbrook's smoking aircraft was seen scattered over a wide area. Maj. Donald Westbrook was declared missing.

The loss of Lima Site 85 came in the aftermath of the enemy's Tet Offensive and the assault on Khe Sanh in South Vietnam. Although the destruction of the site—which had controlled a quarter of the bombing missions against North Vietnam—was kept secret from the public, it weighed heavily on the minds of officials in Washington, D.C. A few days after the fall of Lima Site 85, President Lyndon Johnson called a halt to bombing in North Vietnam, and, on March 31, announced that he would neither seek nor accept his party's nomination to run for reelection.

First Combat Flight

The day finally came—on May 8 I would fly my first combat mission in a two-seated A-1E model. We had the flight call sign Firefly 17; Maj. Glede Vaughn would sit in the right seat as my instructor pilot. Vaughn was nearing the end of his year tour; I figured he would watch me very carefully to make sure I didn't get us both killed. He was a soft-spoken pilot, seemed rather fidgety, and was constantly rearranging his flight suit, his survival equipment, and other flight gear. I detected a bit of nervousness, but maybe he had doubts about how I would perform in combat.

We gathered in the 602nd squadron briefing room and discussed the upcoming mission. I prepared my maps and charts, folding them in such a way that I could easily refer to them in flight. I filled in a five-by-seven-inch mission card listing my ordnance, scheduled time on target, weather, and emergency procedures. Vaughn and I talked about the route to the target area, the weather conditions, and possible enemy gun positions.

By then I felt overloaded with information. Just like I did at the start of a sports competition, I felt very apprehensive and questioned whether I was really ready to go. Fortunately, the Skyraider's big radial engine started without backfiring—I was off to a good start. We taxied to the arming area located next to the end of Udorn's 10,000-foot concrete runway. With both canopies open, we placed our hands on top of our helmets, signaling to the armament crew that our hands were off the gun trigger and weapon-release buttons. We were ready for the crew to pull the safety pins on our ordnance. My bombs and rocket pods were painted olive drab, blending into the camouflage paint of my Skyraider. When the weapons were armed, it was at that moment I fully realized I was going to war.

Soon we were airborne, heading north to the Mekong River. Even with climb power, the old A-1, now fully loaded with weapons of destruction, staggered in the hot and humid air. It would take forty-five minutes to reach the PDJ. Vaughn recommended I compare the outside terrain we were flying over with my map.

Our target was a troop storage area north of the PDJ and south of Lima Site 36. I made contact with our FAC, Raven 17, who was flying an O-1 Bird Dog. As we approached, Vaughn called for me to "push-em-up and set-em-up." This meant I should increase engine power, pre-arm the four 20-mm guns, and select a pair of bombs. All that was left now was to turn the master arm switch to "On" and confirm that the optical gun sight was illuminated with the proper mil setting. Now I would have to fly the Skyraider with just the palm of my right hand—keeping my thumb and fingers slightly off the trigger and weapon-release buttons so as not to accidentally fire any armament.

Raven 17 marked a target and cleared me in for my first pass. I saw white phosphorus smoke coming up from the jungle but could see nothing of the enemy or gun positions. I rolled in, praying I wouldn't get shot down on the first pass of my first mission. It was a ragged delivery; I wasn't sure if the dive angle and release airspeed were correct—I just pickled (dropped) two bombs and pulled up. I forgot to jink (maneuver vigorously) until reminded to do so by Vaughn.

The FAC seemed satisfied, so I made several more bomb drops and then fired my rockets. By then I was boiling hot, both from the afternoon jungle air and my concern about getting hit by ground fire. At no time did I see anyone firing at me, but I didn't really know what it would look like if they were. If shots hit the A-1, I don't think I would have known unless it was a large shell.

The FAC cleared me to go home; I scrambled to figure out what heading to take. We had gone around in a left-hand circle for several minutes, and I was completely confused as to the direction to take to return to Udorn. Raven gave me my bomb damage assessment. He had to repeat the information; I couldn't find my pencil to copy it down. As Air Force flight instructors used to say to student pilots, I was mentally behind the aircraft.

After landing, we debriefed and went to the Sandy Box to have a beer. Now I finally had something to talk about.

What, Me Worry?

The instructor pilot for my next three missions was Capt. Edward W. Leonard III. Ed Leonard was a big man, six foot three, and moved with an easy grace. His blue eyes suggested his Danish heritage, and the twinkle in them confirmed a zest for life. Ed Leonard, the ultimate in combat bravado, was absolutely invincible.

Leonard, who was thirty-one, was born and raised in Winlock, Washington. He graduated from the Air Force Academy in 1959. During one summer break from the academy in 1957, Leonard met a young woman, Suzanne Edgell. Although the spark of romance was there, she attended the University of Hawaii, and he was a cadet in Colorado Springs, Colorado. Because of the distance involved they lost track of each other over the years.

Earlier in 1968, after a particularly bad string of missions over North Vietnam, Leonard was given rest and recuperation (R and R). All military pilots received one free five-day trip to any of the major cities in Asia or Hawaii during the year of combat; they could choose from among exotic places like Bangkok, Hong Kong, or Sydney. Leonard said he spent the time drunk as a skunk in the Officers Club in Bangkok. While there, Leonard wrote to Suzanne in care of her parents back in the States.

When he returned to Udorn, Leonard came down with hepatitis after eating native food in a restaurant downtown. He was sent to a military hospital at Clark AB in the Philippines. While there, a letter was forwarded to him from the 602nd at Udorn. The letter was from Suzanne and said, "I'm teaching kindergarten at San Miguel Naval Station, a couple of hours north of Clark. If you ever get to the Philippines, look me up." Leonard picked up the phone and called her. The old spark was still alive. They began to make plans for the time when Leonard's tour would be over. He planned to visit her in the Philippines in early June 1968.

At the time Ed Leonard and I met, he had flown combat in the squadron for thirteen months, one month longer than required. A pilot was required to fly for twelve months before rotation back to the States, but Leonard had extended or agreed to fly for another six months. If a pilot extended, he was given a couple of weeks vacation and could fly, space available, to Hong Kong or other exotic locations. Leonard was in the process of getting a divorce, so going home to the United States held no special attraction. In addition, he had been given an assignment to fly Boeing B-52s in the Strategic Air Command. He was not pleased at the thought of flying bombers. By extending, he could get out of the B-52 assignment, travel to the Philippines to see Suzanne, and receive combat pay for another six months. A perfect combination, he said.

By the end of May 1968, Leonard had flown just over 250 combat missions and rescued seventeen pilots from behind enemy lines. He had been awarded three Silver Stars for heroism. He was a character larger than life, a superb storyteller, and a great wit.

Over the course of the next week, I spent hours and hours listening to Ed Leonard talk about the Skyraider, the tactics used to fly combat, and the close calls he had had during his earlier missions. Being a test pilot, I was accustomed to long, involved planning sessions and briefings before flying a test flight. Leonard took briefing to an entirely new level.

Leonard told me that the majority of strike missions in Barrel Roll, the nickname for the northern Laos, were just milk runs. Any pilot could fly up there, dump a few bombs, fire his rockets, and come home safely. He said Barrel Roll was a good place to practice weapon delivery and operational tactics without the threat of heavy enemy gunfire. The real mission of the 602nd was the rescue of downed American aircrews. The real challenge for a Skyraider pilot was to find and safely recover every airman shot down, no matter where they were located on the dangerous Ho Chi Minh Trail.

Leonard said he would never be awarded an Air Force Cross or Medal of Honor because he would never do something stupid enough to deserve the commendation. In his estimation, the hazards of rescuing a downed pilot were severe enough—a pilot didn't need to take extra risks. To emphasize the point, he said, "Just count yourself dead now. Figure you will be killed some-time over the next twelve months." It was a sobering pronouncement, and I took it seriously.

Leonard explained that an awards and decorations officer wrote a narra-tive on each rescue. He said it was a fine line between writing a story that could be used for submission for a combat award and one for a court martial. It all depended upon the direction the squadron commander wanted to take. There was a political component to every award.

He cautioned me about getting complacent flying the Firefly missions in Barrel Roll. "You could develop bad habit patterns," he said, "and not be ready for the really hazardous rescue missions." Leonard also made a remark that I didn't take seriously at the time but was a theme I remembered in the months to follow. He said, "Every Skyraider pilot in the 602nd will have a real bad day sometime in their year tour." Leonard emphasized "real bad." He added, "You might fly missions for weeks, or even months, and everything will work like clockwork. But eventually the day of reckoning will arrive, and you will need everything you ever learned about aviation to survive." He told me about his bad day.

Six weeks before I arrived at Udorn, on March 18, 1968, Leonard was scheduled to fly a Firefly mission. It was his fourth mission after release from the Clark AB hospital. Leonard flew to northern Laos, and during the return to Thailand his engine quit. He started to look ahead for a remote part of the jungle to spend the night in when the engine started again. Leonard climbed back to cruising altitude, and then the engine quit again. After losing about 5,000 feet in altitude, the engine started again. He continued this fly versus glide scenario for nearly an hour, slowly getting lower on each cycle. Once he called "May Day, May Day, May Day!" on the UHF radio; then the en-gine started again.

Leonard ran his engine on the fuel primer button for some time, but even-tually that method also failed. After crossing the Mekong River back into Thailand and twenty-two miles from Udorn, it quit for the last time. Avoid-ing several villages, he selected a rice paddy and set up for a belly landing. He had plenty of time to prepare, went through his checklist three times, tight-ened all his straps, and lastly locked the shoulder harness. When he touched down, the right strut pylon dug into a ridge, whipping the fuselage to the left, but the high-powered radial engine kept going straight. Leonard said he was thrown around the inside of the cockpit like a Ping-Pong ball inside an empty coffee can. His helmet smashed against the gun sight, and his left shoulder hit the throttle quadrant. When he came to a stop, his straps still held him so tight he could scarcely move. He even had trouble releasing the straps so he could exit his smashed A-1.

Leonard's wingman was Maj. Albert Roberts Jr. Al Roberts, from San Jose, California, was a new guy in the 602nd and had just completed his five combat sorties with an instructor pilot. He was flying his first solo combat mission. Like me, Roberts was a former F-101B Voodoo jet pilot with little propeller aircraft experience.

Roberts saw Leonard touch down in a cloud of dust, and he set up in an orbit around him. He saw a village nearby where a group of people was getting on a truck. Roberts was concerned for Leonard's safety but only had 20-mm ammunition left to protect him. He had expended all of his bombs and rockets earlier on the target in Laos. As the villagers approached, Roberts made a warning pass down the road, not knowing whether the people were friendly or enemy.

Leonard ran away from his demolished Skyraider, sat down, and wondered why his A-1 was pointing in two directions. The Wright Cyclone engine was bent nearly 90 degrees to the left, immediately in front of the cockpit. Miraculously, he was uninjured, but he was shaken.

Leonard drank water from a baby bottle he had secured in his flight suit pocket as an emergency ration. Thai villagers arrived, talking excitedly. They saw him drinking from his bottle, and a villager brought a kettle of water and offered him a cup. He didn't want to offend them but didn't want to drink it either after the case of hepatitis he had earlier. So he poured the water over his head and thanked them as best he could. He got out his survival radio and started talking to Roberts. The radio died when the villagers poured the entire kettle of water over Leonard's head. Leonard told me he thought this dunking predated NFL sideline celebrations.

Roberts remarked in a humorous tone that he became technically search-and-rescue qualified on his first solo combat mission.

The squadron commander told the operations officer to take his .38 caliber pistol to Leonard's crash site and look for battle damage to the A-1. If there wasn't any, the officer was to shoot bullet holes in the plane so that official squadron records would record it as a "combat loss" rather than an "accident"—which it probably was. This would make the squadron leadership look better.

Leonard was lucky to live to tell me about his bad day.

Sometimes my briefing for a combat mission with Ed Leonard would take well over an hour. He would go on and on with don'ts. Don't fly at a very low altitude; don't fly directly over big guns; don't fly straight and level; don't fly slow; don't, don't, don't. . . . Most of the information was important, but Leonard would go on and on. I began to think he just liked to hear himself talk.

Leonard's debriefings after a mission were just as long as the briefings. I got extremely tired listening to him talk about every conceivable problem or difficulty we could encounter on a mission. After all, there were an infinite number of situations we might encounter. I started to daydream, my mind thinking about other times and places. Then it dawned on me that I was trapped in Thailand and that I was going to spend twelve months flying combat in Southeast Asia. It didn't really matter whether I spent the time listening to Leonard, sleeping in bed, or sitting on the toilet. I might as well listen to Leonard the yarn spinner; he did have a unique perspective and interesting stories. I might actually learn something useful. Little did I know then how right I was.

4 TCHEPONE

During early May I flew three more dual combat missions with Ed Leonard sitting in the right seat as my instructor pilot. As each flight went by, my ability to mentally keep up with activity surrounding combat improved, my bombs were getting closer to the target, and I felt more comfortable that I understood and performed the duties of a strike wingman. Leonard said I was ready to get my strike wingman check flight after I got a training flight in a single-seat A-1H model. Until that time, all my Skyraider flights at Hurlburt and Udorn had been in either a side-by-side A-1E or A-1G model. On May 16, I flew an unarmed A-1H model in the local Udorn flying area. Leonard watched from the ground as I made a couple of touch-and-gos on the Udorn runway and came back for a full-stop landing. I was ready for my check flight the next day.

On May 17, 1968, I flew wing on Maj. Thomas Campbell as Firefly 15 with Maj. George Duffy as my evaluation pilot. We flew north, back again to Barrel Roll, and put in a strike near Lima Site 36. After all the hours of briefing and combat discussion I sat through with Leonard during the previous week, flying the check flight was a piece of cake. I passed with flying colors and landed back at Udorn with a total of fifteen hours and forty-five minutes of combat time during my first five missions.

Over the next week I flew a Firefly strike flight every day in either an A-1E or an A-1H. Soon I had ten missions under my belt and was now qualified to advance to the rescue role as a Sandy wingman. Again I was teamed with Leonard, and his exhaustive briefings continued. We would fly from Udorn to NKP (Nakhon Phanom), land, and sit rescue alert with the Jolly Green helicopters stationed there. All the time we were on the ground at NKP, Leonard would talk about the rescues he had made. By then I just wanted to lay on a bunk bed and take a nap. After all, I had been a test pilot at Edwards AFB for four years; I did know something about aviation. I just didn't want to listen to him anymore.

If aircrew were not shot down by mid-afternoon, the Sandy alert flight would take off and orbit near where strikes were taking place. That way if a plane was shot down, we could quickly get to the scene before darkness and hopefully make a rescue attempt before the enemy could marshal their forces to resist us. By the end of May I had flown a total of eighteen combat missions during fifty-nine hours of flight. I could hold my own at the Sandy Box, I had not been hit by enemy ground fire yet, and I was beginning to feel comfortable and relaxed flying the Skyraider.

Meanwhile, back at the hooch in Udorn a controversy was coming to the surface. Because we did not have a way to wash our clothes, Thai maids were hired to perform that function. They would place our clothing on the floor of our shower stall (six shower heads in a stall next to a large common bathroom), sprinkle soap on them, and scrub the clothes with a bristle brush. In addition, they would remove the mud from our jungle survival boots and shine them. Usually each maid worked for four to six pilots for about 120 *baht* (U.S.$6) per pilot per month. Bill Jones's maid wanted to be paid more. Jones got a Thai employee of the Officers Club, who spoke English, to explain his position. He thought some maids were worth more but only if they did good work. The maid would have to bargain with each pilot and not expect an automatic increase for all the maids if one maid got a raise. Jones said a dollar or two per month increase made little difference to each pilot, but he wanted to hold the line against inflation. He thought it would disrupt the local economy if we overpaid them and wanted to keep the increase small. Such was the focus of discussion and debate in the Sandy Box. I felt it was a trivial matter and was much more interested in the fact that there were rumors that the 602nd Squadron would move to NKP.

On Friday, May 31, 1968, four Sandy aircraft departed Udorn for a three-day alert at NKP. The flight lineup was: Sandy 5—Maj. William Palank flying an A-1G (odd number call sign was a flight lead); Sandy 6—Capt. William Groff an A-1E (even number was a wingman); Sandy 7—Capt. Edward Leonard in an A-1E; Sandy 8—Capt. George Marrett in an A-1E.

Because Groff felt ill, Gene McCormack flew in a helicopter from Udorn to NKP to replace him. Groff always seemed to be sick with what some called an imaginary illness.

Around 4:45 p.m. we were notified that a Navy A-7 Corsair light attack aircraft with the call sign Streetcar 304 had been shot down on the 120 degree radial, 98 nautical miles from the NKP TACAN. The location was near the town of Tchepone, a tiny village near the intersection of several dirt roads and a narrow river in central Laos. This area was part of the Ho Chi Minh Trail, about twenty-five miles west of Khe Sanh, South Vietnam. I had never flown in this area before; it was going to be new to me.

Our Sandy flight got airborne in about ten minutes and headed southeast for Tchepone. Palank and McCormack went directly to Streetcar 304's position, and Leonard and I escorted Jolly Green 20 and 37 to a safe area a few miles southwest of Tchepone.

Flying as Streetcar 304 was Lt. Kenny W. Fields, who, at twenty-seven, had 600 total flying hours, 400 in the A-7. His wingman, flying as Streetcar 307, was twenty-four-year-old Lt. (jg) Frederick Lentz Jr., a 1965 graduate of the Naval Academy and a young, inexperienced pilot right out of flying school. Both were launched off the carrier USS *America* in the Gulf of Tonkin and were on their first combat mission.

It was a completely clear day over South Vietnam and Laos as they crossed over land at 16,000 feet, just south of the demilitarized zone (DMZ), checked in with a ground radar controller, and asked for target assignment. They were passed over to Nail 66, Capt. John McMurtry, flying an O-2. McMurtry was a FAC assigned to the 23rd Tactical Air Support Squadron at NKP. The O-2 was the military equivalent of the civilian Cessna 337. It was a high-wing aircraft with two reciprocating engines, one on the nose and one on the tail of the fuselage. Cruising at only 120 mph, around 1,000 feet above the jungle, it carried two

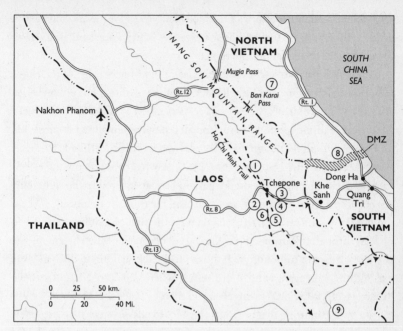

Tchepone, Laos, with crash sites: (1) Panda 1 (Maj. Richard Brownlee and PJ Sgt. Charles King lost); (2) Streetcar 304, Sandy 7, and Sandy 1 (Lt. Kenny Fields rescued, Capt. Ed Leonard captured, and Maj. Bill Palank rescued); (3) Stormy 2 (Capt. Victor Smith lost and Lt. Jim Fegan rescued); (4) Sandy 2 (Lt. Col. Pete Morris rescued); (5) Sandy 10 (Capt. Robert Coady lost); (6) Jolly Green 67 (Sgt. Don Johnson, Sgt. Tom Pope, and Lt. Col. Pete Morris rescued); (7) Roman 2 (Lt. Charles Mosley and Lt. Don Hallenbeck rescued); (8) Carter 2 rescue (Lt. Col. William Jones injured); (9) Pintail 1 rescue (Lt. Col. Richard Walsh lost).

pods of white phosphorus marking rockets. Usually the enemy gunners did not fire on the O-2 because the pilot could direct jet aircraft with bombs in response.

Fields and Lentz were each carrying twelve Mark 82s, a 500-pound general purpose bomb; two air-to-air Sidewinders; and six hundred rounds of 20-mm ammunition. Navy tactics called for making just one weapons pass if ground fire was received from the target area. FAC McMurtry reported to Fields that he had worked the area near the river for three days without anyone shooting at him. McMurtry observed a barge on the Xe Banghiang River, three miles southwest of Tchepone, and directed Fields to take it out. The river was about five hundred feet wide, and barges were used to transport large military supplies. Navy procedures called for Fields to roll into a 45-degree dive at 12,000 feet, release two bombs at 6,000 feet at 450 knots, and pull out no lower than 3,000 feet above the target.

On his first pass he saw several sparkles of light like strobe lights from a couple of 23-mm guns, but he still made a bull's-eye (direct hit) on the barge. After Fred Lentz struck the target, Fields planned to make only one more pass because of the ground fire to drop all ten of his remaining bombs.

This time Nail 66 designated an underwater bridge for Fields to strike. As he established his 45-degree dive, Fields saw red balls (enemy tracer ammunition) coming near him on the left. So he maneuvered to the right, only to see more 37-mm tracers on that side also. He thought to himself, "These are bigger and more accurate guns than on the first pass. I'm not going to make it through this ground fire." He started his pull-up when he got hit and the aircraft began tumbling with the control stick shaking in his hand. He was fighting to regain control of the A-7 when he heard Nail 66 scream, "Eject, eject, you're hit!" Fields claims to this day that John McMurtry saved his life by transmitting that urgent command. Fields did eject at an extremely low altitude and swung only twice in his chute before hitting the ground. Had he waited a second later to eject, he believes he would not have gotten a full chute and probably would have been killed. The 37-mm ground fire actually severed the A-7's right wing, which was what caused Fields's complete loss of control.

Wingman Fred Lentz saw Fields eject and decided to remain at altitude and not make another pass. Meanwhile, Sidewinder 406, lead aircraft of a flight of four A-7s, also off the carrier USS *America*, arrived over Tchepone. Sidewinder 406 declared himself on-scene commander and ordered Lentz to remain at 15,000 feet and wait overhead to be escorted back to the ship. He didn't want a junior pilot like Lentz to return alone for fear he would develop a problem and have no one to help him.

Kenny Fields landed in a ten-foot-tall bamboo thicket. Immediately, he observed a North Vietnamese soldier in a black pajama-like uniform trying to take aim at him with a rifle. Fields removed his pistol from its holster and started to run. While running he pulled the survival radio from his vest and turned on the beeper. He hid in the brush and listened for enemy activity. The stress of the ejection and near capture caused his teeth to start chattering. Afraid that the enemy would hear him, he put both hands on his jaw. Even then he feared the soldiers would hear him, so he took out a can of Red Man chewing tobacco from his vest. The tobacco calmed him down even though the enemy was only a few feet away. They called out, "Hey, GI Joe, we see you. Give yourself up, we won't hurt you!" Over and over they chanted, hoping he would come out from his hiding place. It was a trick that might have worked for them in the past, but not this time.

While Fields was evading the enemy, Fred Lentz remained at 15,000 feet with his ten bombs. Because he felt danger from the accurate 37-mm guns located at Tchepone, he kept his airspeed up and banked back and forth. The drag from the bombs required him to maintain a high-power setting on his engine, resulting in heavy use of his remaining fuel. Having a low amount of fuel was becoming a critical factor for him. Still, Sidewinder 406 did not want Lentz to return to the USS *America* without an escort.

Once Bill Palank arrived at Tchepone, he took over as on-scene commander. He and Gene McCormack descended and attempted to determine Kenny Fields's exact location either by electronic or visual means. At 5:52 p.m. Bill Palank was making a second pass over Fields when his Skyraider took a hit in the engine and the left wing. He pulled off to the west and started climbing for NKP. McCormack escorted him, and I spotted the two-ship formation departing Tchepone. By this time, the sun had been over the horizon for several minutes. The sky was absolutely clear, with a sparkling golden glow in the western sky. To this day, some thirty-three years later, I can vividly remember the silhouette of the two A-1s framed in that beautiful golden sunset, flying toward NKP. Smoke was trailing from Palank's Skyraider, and I wondered if he could nurse the battered aircraft for the ninety-plus miles remaining before he was home. Later I heard that his engine seized up just as he landed. Bill Palank only had a close call that late afternoon over Tchepone. As Ed Leonard had predicted, Palank's "real bad day" was still to come.

With Palank and McCormack gone, the leadership of the rescue of Streetcar 304 fell into the hands of Ed Leonard. Leonard and I left the two Jollys in their orbit and flew toward Tchepone. At that time it was dark on the jungle floor and the burning wreck of Fields's A-7 could clearly be seen. It was located in the northern portion of an oval clearing about a half a mile north of a section of the river that made a 150-degree loop. Leonard asked me to stay above him, watch for ground fire, and maintain radio contact with Crown. Crown was the call sign for the four-engine turboprop C-130 that acted as a rescue airborne command and control post. Leonard continued to descend and started making a figure-eight pattern over the A-7 wreckage. Kenny Fields did not realize that Bill Palank was returning to NKP. When Ed Leonard called on the UHF radio that he wanted to make an identification pass, Fields thought it was strange since a Skyraider had already flown directly over his position only minutes before and received heavy ground fire. Fields said to himself, "Why would a pilot fly over me twice in such a hot area? This guy has balls of steel!" In fact, the first Skyraider pilot was desperately trying to get back to NKP. Leonard needed to pinpoint Fields's exact position for a first-light effort the next day.

As I orbited overhead I realized that two American aircraft had already been shot up over Tchepone. The enemy gunners were good and surely were waiting for Leonard. I watched him circling below and received a call from Crown on my UHF radio. Flights of jets were being diverted from their pre-briefed strike targets and sent to us to help in the rescue effort. On my five-by-seven-inch mission card I wrote the names of a Gunfighter flight of four F-105s that would be with us in five minutes, with Scuba, Spitfire, and Hot Rod flights to follow. I hurriedly copied the information about radio frequencies and ordnance load while banking back and forth, keeping Leonard's Skyraider in sight.

Now the sun had set, leaving only a ghost-like aura of trees blending into the dark abyss. As I looked at the burning wreckage of Streetcar 304's A-7, an explosion nearby caught my attention. Then I saw the white canopy of a parachute drift into the darkness of the jungle.

"Sandy 7, this is 8," I called.

"Sandy 7, this is 8," I repeated.

Only silence and darkness followed.

At 6:10 p.m. a third American aircraft had been hit by ground fire over Tchepone. Now two pilots were in the jungle and only I and two Jolly rescue helicopters remained. I was stunned to watch the events of this rescue unfold so quickly. This was a situation Leonard had not briefed me on. What was I supposed to do? What action should I take? In a quavering voice I called Crown and reported that Sandy 7 was down. Crown responded, "All SAR [search-and-rescue] forces are to be pulled up high and wait for further instruction!"

Lieutenant Lentz, Streetcar 307, had his own problems, being dangerously low on fuel as he flew eastbound toward the carrier USS *America*. Another A-7, Sidewinder 412, escorted him and asked for a fuel tanker to meet them over the Gulf of Tonkin. Several miles over the water they made visual contact with a twin-engine A-3 Skywarrior tanker. Lentz was not carrying an external fuel tank; all his gas was stored in the A-7's wings. Close to flameout, Lentz connected to the A-3 tanker, and fuel started to flow into his starved Corsair. Then the A-7's engine flamed out! Because of an aircraft malfunction fuel was flowing into the internal wing tank and not the fuselage feed tank, so the engine quit. After the engine's rpm dropped to zero, the A-7's generator went off the line, preventing Lentz from obtaining electrical power to transfer fuel to the feed tank. He glided his lifeless Corsair toward the carrier and prepared for ejection. Twenty-five miles from the North Vietnamese shoreline he punched out. Jolly Green 7 followed him over the Gulf of Tonkin and prepared for his rescue. Floating in the water Lentz saw the Jolly fly near his position without spotting him. He was afraid to fire his pen gun flare for fear the Jolly would think it was enemy ground fire. Finally Jolly Green 7 spotted him and came in for the rescue. Lentz was surprised to see the Jolly land on the water. Initially he thought the Jolly also had an engine problem but it was actually their planned procedure at sea. A PJ (pararescue jumper) swam over to him and helped get him in the helicopter. The Jolly took Lentz to Da Nang.

Later, I asked Fred Lentz if his first combat mission was a harrowing experience. He said it was not that bad. Two weeks later he experienced complete engine failure just as he was catapulted off the carrier, and he ejected for his second time—that was a "real bad day," he said.

Kenny Fields had a grandstand seat for Ed Leonard's ejection. With a clear sky of dusk as a background, he watched the Skyraider fly directly over his position. He actually heard a *thud* when the A-1 was hit by 37-mm ground fire. Fields saw the Skyraider's propeller seize and then heard Leonard's extraction rockets fire.

Ed Leonard said later that as he flew in a left-hand bank he saw 37-mm guns firing at him, so he reversed to the right only to find more guns firing at him on that side. He felt his Skyraider shudder and saw his right wing fold up above him. He immediately pulled the extraction handle and departed his stricken A-1. He was so low to the ground that he went through the fireball of his Skyraider during descent in his chute.

Leonard tried to remember to bend his knees and relax before making contact with the ground. However, he said he was as tight as a spring coiled up and broke a foot when he hit. Because of the stress of the moment, he didn't realize that he had broken it. Later, though, he felt severe pain and could hardly walk.

Since enemy troops were in the immediate vicinity, Leonard removed his harness and started moving west toward high ground. Over the UHF emergency frequency, both Fields and I heard Leonard say he was resting before crossing a trail and planned to head northwest. That was the last we heard from Ed Leonard.

As Leonard got halfway across the trail he was spotted by three North Vietnamese soldiers carrying Russian AK-47 rifles. One of the soldiers yelled at Leonard and waved his hand. Since it was dark, Leonard thought the soldier probably assumed he was also North Vietnamese. Leonard fired a shot at the soldier and took off running again.

While being chased, Leonard fired many rounds from his .38 pistol. He had difficulty reloading the gun while being pursued and dropped more ammunition than he inserted into the pistol's chamber. Finally he was down to his last shells, only to find out they were tracer loads. He now was reluctant to fire for fear the enemy could easily determine his position.

Leonard ran most of the night and thought he had outdistanced the pursuing troops. As daybreak arrived he felt it would be safer in a tree than on the ground. Being raised in the state of Washington Leonard always hid in trees as a youngster. He found that other children looking for him usually spent most of their time head down watching where they stepped. Safety could be found hidden in a tree.

This time he climbed about seventy feet into a tree and tied himself to a branch. He saw small beams of light moving through the jungle. When morning arrived he saw soldiers carrying flashlights with cardboard placed over the lens, a pinhole allowing a small beam of light. Approximately two hundred North Vietnamese soldiers formed a base camp around him, with five soldiers directly under his tree. Leonard was safe for the moment but how was he ever going to come up on his survival radio to be rescued? The enemy would be able to hear him talk any time he tried to contact the Sandys he knew would be looking for him.

Meanwhile, Kenny Fields knew the approximate location of Ed Leonard's crash. Although he assumed they were probably only half a mile apart, there was no chance they could join forces in the night. Fields struggled just to move at all during the first night as he was surrounded with thick brush. He heard a gunfight in the direction of Leonard's crash site. He said it sounded like a pistol firing against machine guns. Fields surmised that Leonard had shot it out with the North Vietnamese and lost since Leonard did not come up on the radio again.

Overhead, a Spectre AC-130 gunship kept in touch with Fields every hour by radio. He was told that a first-light effort was planned, to get some rest, and to be ready for a pickup the next morning. That was the good news; the bad news was that Fields only had one radio and two batteries. He was slowly depleting the energy in his first battery. Battery life would later become a determining factor in his rescue.

The next morning, a new group of Sandy pilots was assembled to rescue Streetcar 304. They were: Sandy 1—Maj. William Palank in an A-1E; Sandy 2—Capt. George Marrett in an A-1E; Sandy 3—Maj. Glede Vaughn in an A-1E; Sandy 4—Maj. Charles Kuhlmann in A-1E. Held in reserve were Sandy 5, Maj. Eustace "Mel" Bunn Jr., and Sandy 6, Maj. Charles Flynn. All five of the other Sandy pilots were majors and had been in the squadron much longer than I and flown more combat missions. I thought the operations officer would probably replace me with someone with more experience. Instead, he said since I had flown over Tchepone I now knew it as well as anyone. He told me to get some sleep in the Jolly Green squadron building and be ready for a 3:30 a.m. brief. At daybreak we would make a "first light" effort to rescue Fields.

Thirty-two F-4s and F-105s were scheduled to strike around Streetcar 304's position early the next morning. Nothing was heard from Ed Leonard, so his potential rescue was on hold until radio contact could be made.

Although the previous day had been sparkling clear with no clouds, the weather on this June 1 morning was extremely poor. At 4:45 a.m. our flight of four Sandys got airborne from NKP and immediately encountered weather. There were multiple layers of clouds and turbulence as we tried to stay close together without colliding. When we arrived over the rescue area, Nail 66, Capt. John McMurtry, was already FACing in jet aircraft. I saw flight after flight make one pass each and drop tons of bombs. I even saw ordnance go off northwest of where I had seen Ed Leonard's parachute in the trees the night before. I wondered how far Leonard could have moved in the jungle in the eleven hours he had been on the ground. The fact that he did not come up again on the radio was discouraging. Nail 66 was in voice contact with Streetcar 304; he reported that he had survived the night on the ground. McMurtry asked Fields to authenticate his identity with a personal code. Fields gave him the name of his dog, which correlated with information on file.

Over the course of the next two hours, the bombing continued. As we orbited, Crown reported that four A-1s from Pleiku Air Base in South Vietnam were on ground alert. Each of them carried riot control gas (CBU-19, code named Juicy Fruit) and could get airborne in ten to fifteen minutes after being scrambled. It would then take them an hour and fifteen minutes to travel to Streetcar's location. Other Jolly Green, Nail, and Sandy aircraft were being prepped, awaiting the call to attempt a rescue.

A massive armada of aircraft was being assembled for use over Tchepone. At 7:35 a.m. two of the Spad aircraft with riot control gas were scrambled. It sounded to me like gas would be used in this rescue. I had a gas mask in a bag by my right knee but hoped I would not need it. The mask was difficult to put on while flying and severely restricted outside vision. Most of the experienced Skyraider pilots said they wouldn't wear the contraption, they would just try to do their best without it.

Gradually, the weather deteriorated even more. Soon low scud was flowing off the hills to the west and covering Streetcar 304's position. With cloud tops of 10,000 feet and multiple layers of clouds underneath, the jets couldn't maneuver safely in this heavily defended area. To make matters worse, light rain started to fall, reducing the visibility between layers. Crown directed Nail 66 to pull all aircraft out of the area and orbit them a few miles away. If a break in the weather occurred, they wanted everyone close by so a quick pick up could be accomplished.

Right after we moved west a few miles Fields called, saying that the enemy was closing in on him. He asked Nail 66 to get some air cover or he would be captured soon. The only aircraft that could maneuver under the less than five hundred-foot cloud cover was a Skyraider. Bill Palank, as Sandy low lead, said he and I would go down. We dove for the ground, banking back and forth to find open holes in the clouds. I followed in trail position, not sure what we could do to prevent Fields from being captured. After only a few moments, we started taking heavy ground fire. At 8:48 a.m., four hours and four minutes after we took off from NKP, Palank got hit in the fuselage. He called on the UHF radio that he was on fire and heading west. I got him in sight immediately and started to join up in formation. As I got in close I could see that Palank had jettisoned his fuel tanks and ordnance. From a position of about fifteen feet directly below him, I could see either fuel or oil streaming from his fuselage. Initially, he climbed to about 1,000 feet and held around 160 knots. We were about five miles west of Streetcar's position when Palank reported that his engine was starting to miss and hot oil was coming into the cockpit. I pulled up on his left wing, only twenty feet away. I had an extra seat in my A-1E but no way to get him into it. Then he said hot oil was covering his flight control stick and he was having a hard time holding on to it. By then he was starting to lose both altitude and airspeed. The previous day he had nursed a Skyraider about ninety-five miles back to NKP and got it on the runway before the engine seized. He wasn't going to make it back this time; ejecting was his only hope.

I maintained my position on his left wing, unable to think of anything he could do. I hoped we were heading for a safe, unoccupied area, but I had no idea where we were flying. My eyes were fixed on Palank and his Skyraider; I didn't look inside my cockpit or straight ahead out of the windscreen. Palank then called in a calm voice, "I'm getting out." In a fraction of a second the A-1 canopy flew off and I had a perfect view of Palank departing his Skyraider. Unlike a jet aircraft ejection, where the pilot rockets out sitting in a seat, in the Skyraider the Yankee escape system pulled the pilot out. Two rockets located behind Palank's head fired. They started spinning around each other and propelled vertically. As the twin rockets blasted up, a nylon line trailed behind and eventually pulled Palank out of the cockpit. It appeared to me that he literally stood up in the cockpit and was yanked out, looking like a puppet supported by strings. His arms and legs extended straight out, and his parachute deployed fully about fifty feet above me. I saw him swing one time and knew he was safely out of his Skyraider.

His A-1 started to nose over and pick up speed. I followed it, feeling foolish flying formation on an unoccupied plane. Palank had trimmed the wings level; the aircraft's nose aimed for the jungle below. During my years in military service I had heard pilots describe what it was like to see an aircraft "go in." I had never witnessed that event before, but on June 1, 1968, at 8:54 a.m. I saw a Skyraider "go in." It was sad to lose another A-1, but I was happy Bill Palank got out.

After the impact, I started a right-hand turn and circled Palank as he descended in his parachute. I called Crown to report that Sandy 1 was safely out of his plane and that I needed a rescue helicopter. Jolly Green 16 jettisoned his external fuel tanks and asked for a vector to my position. I told him to give me a ten-second transmission on his radio and that I would use my UHF homer to give him directions. The UHF/ADF homer was a device within the Skyraider's UHF radio where a needle in a flight instrument would point to the aircraft transmitting. Within a few minutes Jolly Green 16 came into a hover over Palank. It appeared that he landed in the top of a seventy-five-foot dead tree.

Major Palank was a memorable character. At forty-two Bill Palank was a terrific A-1 pilot who could do any maneuver with a Skyraider. Regardless of whatever heroics we heard about a jet pilot flying combat in Southeast Asia, Palank would ask us while seated at the Sandy Box, "But could he land a Skyraider at night on wet PSP [pierced-steel planking] in a crosswind?" Palank could; many pilots couldn't. Bill Palank was born and raised in Chicago and wanted to join the Army Air Corps during World War II. Because he was only fifteen years old when Pearl Harbor was bombed he had to wait until 1944, when he was eighteen, to join. By then all the pilot slots were taken so he became a B-29 flight engineer. After the war he stayed in military service and graduated from flying school in 1948 and was commissioned as a second lieutenant in the reserves. In Korea he finally got combat time flying A-26s on night attack. In the early 1960s he became an advisor to the South Vietnamese, flying both the A-1H and A-1J models out of Bien Hoa, South Vietnam. In 1967 he volunteered to become a Sandy rescue pilot in the 602nd. But now he was suspended in a parachute over a dead tree.

The aircraft commander for Jolly Green 16 was thirty-year-old Capt. David Richardson from Glendale, California. Richardson was six-feet-two-inches tall, a no-nonsense, conservative, straight-arrow type of person and a born-again Christian. Richardson wore a crew cut and looked like the teacher he would become years later after he retired from the Air Force. He had only a week remaining in his year tour and was scheduled for a choice helicopter assignment at Ramstein Air Base in Germany. Flying as Richardson's copilot was Maj. Paul Reagon, with S. Sgt. Coy Calhoun as the flight engineer and Sgt. Peter Harding as the PJ. As Jolly Green 16 hovered over the tree, the downwash from the whirling blades broke some of the branches and sent Palank crashing to the ground. The Jolly reported that Palank wasn't moving and might be unconscious. If needed, a PJ would go down the hoist on a penetrator (a metal device like an anchor with three arms to sit on) to recover him.

Palank told me later that while he was hanging in the tree he saw an enemy soldier holding a weapon go by directly below him. He assumed the soldier was running toward the location of Palank's crashed aircraft and didn't look up to see him in the tree. As Palank came up the hoist on the penetrator, he saw an Air Force photographer filming him with a movie camera. Palank explained to me that he was an older major, hadn't received a regular commission and had been passed over for colonel. With over twenty years of military service the Air Force wanted to retire him. He liked to fly and resisted retirement until he spotted the camera. At that moment he thought to himself, "I could get a disability retirement." When he was brought aboard the helicopter he started to limp and then held his right leg in his arms even though his real injury consisted of a cut lip and broken tooth. Palank even acted like he was injured as he came off the Jolly at NKP to a hero's welcome.

After Palank was picked up by Jolly Green 16, I escorted them back to NKP. In the previous thirteen hours I had lost two Sandy leads but somehow managed to escape getting hit myself. After this harrowing flight, I landed at NKP, completely exhausted, after five hours and ten minutes of flight time. It was my longest flight yet; the word *Tchepone* now caused the hair on my neck to rise.

Back at NKP another group of Sandy pilots was being assembled for an afternoon rescue attempt. My A-1E was performing poorly, so I wrote in the maintenance records that the plane was out of commission. All of the 20-mm guns were jammed and the engine was running rough on the right magneto. In addition, the AC generator failure light had flashed a couple of times and the fuel boost pump circuit breaker popped and wouldn't reset. It didn't seem wise to takeoff for another rescue attempt over Tchepone with a malfunctioning aircraft. Also, I wasn't sure any of the other experienced Sandy pilots wanted to be my lead after I lost two so fast.

By 4 p.m. a Nail FAC had returned to the scene and asked Kenny Fields to authenticate. Fields answered the question correctly and was told to prepare for another rescue attempt. While on the ground Fields's mental outlook soared when he thought his rescue was near, only to sink when it was called off. His rescue had been called off because of darkness on the first attempt and because of a Skyraider loss on the second. By now the first battery on his survival radio was exhausted and he was using his second and last one. He told the FAC he was not hungry but was very thirsty.

Some officers in the command structure suspected the North Vietnamese could capture Fields at their leisure and that the enemy was using him as bait to lure additional search-and-rescue aircraft into a deadly trap. The commander of the 7th Air Force in Saigon, Gen. William Momyer, consulted with his Navy counterpart, Rear Adm. Ralph Cousines, commander of Task Force 77, and directed that a maximum effort be made to recover Fields. The general said, "Group all forces, run everything in at once, knock out the enemy, and put the search-and-rescue forces in behind. Effect rescue immediately, regardless of cost." Senior pilots in the 602nd scoffed at this audacious plan. Even if Streetcar 304 was picked up using this throw-everything-at-it method, without beating up the guns in advance, we would probably lose another aircraft and be right back where we started with another pilot on the ground.

Nevertheless, that was the approved Air Force plan and rescue aircraft departed for Tchepone. This time there would be four Sandy aircraft, three Jolly Green helicopters, four Spads with disabling gas, and twelve jet aircraft all maneuvering in a small space and no one directing traffic. By 5:35 p.m. the forces were assembled; all that was needed was to refuel all three Jollys in flight. At 6:14 p.m. it was reported over the radio that the forces were underway. Those of us left in the Jolly Green squadron building listened to the radio transmissions as if it were the last out of the last inning of the last game of the World Series. It was tense in the room; everyone stared at the floor. No one spoke; there was only the crackling of excited voices over the UHF radio. If the search-and-rescue forces made the pickup, the rest of us would not be needed for the next effort. If not, we all were candidates for flying over Tchepone the following day.

At 6:19 p.m. we heard that Jolly Green 20 had an overheated transmission and was looking for a field in which to set down. Jolly Green 37 would accompany the disabled Jolly and pick up the crew. The one remaining helicopter, Jolly Green 16, would make the pickup of Streetcar 304 but without a backup. The plan was starting to fall apart just as predicted. The whole effort was hanging by a thread. Next we heard that Jolly Green 20 was safely on the ground on the 76-degree radial, forty-eight miles from the NKP TACAN. We were running to look at a map to check out the area when we heard someone on the radio transmit, "The area is hostile." Crown directed all search-and-rescue aircraft to divert to support the rescue of the Jolly Green 20 crew.

The third attempt to get Kenny Fields out of the jungle had just failed. Now the score was two A-7s lost, two Skyraiders destroyed and one heavily damaged, and a Jolly Green sitting in a hostile field in Laos. With all the rescue aircraft gone, Crown told Fields that the rescue attempt was officially terminated for the day and that we'd be back tomorrow. Unlike the previous rescue attempts where a Nail or Sandy pilot would calmly ask him to take care of himself and encourage him to be positive and hopeful, the words from Crown were very short and curt. The tone of the transmission from Crown made a big impression on Fields; he thought he would not get rescued unless he moved from his extremely dangerous position.

After the three failed attempts to get Streetcar 304, I realized I would probably be on another first-light effort the following day. I started to prepare myself for getting shot down and either captured or killed. While flying combat, Air Force regulations stated that we would sanitize ourselves. This meant that we should not carry anything on our body that identified us as a specific person. We should not carry photographs of our family, no letters from home, no billfold with ID, nothing that could be used against us if we were captured. We did carry an Air Force-issued photo ID card with name, rank, and serial number. We also carried our military dog tags on a chain around our neck. I hadn't been following the directive completely. I did carry some American currency in a clear plastic bag, which I used to pay for meals at the Officers Club. I now took the bag out of my flying suit, placed my wedding ring in it and stored it in a metal locker. My wife had given the ring to me four months earlier for our tenth wedding anniversary. Now I was completely sanitized. After flying two days of rescue for Streetcar 304, I knew American dollars had no value in downtown Tchepone.

Another first-light effort was scheduled for Sunday, June 2, 1968. Flying would be: Sandy 1—Maj. Glede Vaughn in an A-1G; Sandy 2—Maj. Charles Kuhlmann in an A-1E; Sandy 3—Maj. Eustace "Mel" Bunn Jr. in an A-1E; Sandy 4—Capt. George Marrett in an A-1E.

Vaughn had flown in the right seat as an instructor pilot for me on my first combat flight three weeks earlier. He seemed nervous then; now he was beside himself. Vaughn sent a message to higher Air Force headquarters that said, "Unless area [Streetcar 304's position] is completely sanitized [destroyed] one hundredfold greater than today, any Jolly Green sent into the area will be shot down! I estimate many guns have yet to be seen. The enemy is waiting for slow movers [Sandys and Jolly Greens] to show their hand. I estimate extremely heavy gun positions within ten to twenty meters of survivor. Survivor in open area fifty-to-seventy-five-meters long, running north and south. Defenses along entire western edge. I feel it is a trap; enemy could take survivor at will!" Glede Vaughn was reluctant to lead the rescue.

My Sandy lead, Mel Bunn, was well over six feet tall and as skinny as any man I have ever met. Guys in the squadron said Mel ate a normal amount of food, he just didn't gain any weight. Over the past two days of flying rescue I had barely eaten anything myself and probably lost a few pounds. The situation was very tense; eating was not a high priority.

Because Ed Leonard was still missing, his call sign, Sandy 7, would not be used. It would be very confusing to have two Sandy 7s talking on the radio at the same time. We reserved the Sandy 7 call sign for Leonard to use when he would finally make contact with us.

Although we did not know it then, Leonard spent the entire second day of the rescue seventy feet high in the same tree. The enemy soldiers were still below him, and he was reluctant to come up on his survival radio for fear of being heard. None of the bombs dropped by the jets hit close to him, but he could hear them in the distance. He was happy to know that we were still attempting to rescue Streetcar 304.

Leonard had a plan for his rescue. By being patient he could come up on his radio when the North Vietnamese troops departed; then he knew we would come for him. Leonard carried three radios and five batteries, a virtual walking Radio Shack.

Strapped in the tree, Leonard's biggest fear was that he would drop part of his survival equipment. If he fumbled around at night and let go of a whistle, a mirror, a Mark 13 flare, or other survival equipment, it would fall to the ground and he would be discovered. He was so tense he didn't have to urinate the entire time he was in the tree. But he had a plan for that also; he would make sure he hit the trunk of the tree in short bursts so that it didn't run too far down. Leonard had a plan for everything.

Even though Leonard had been missing for many hours, I felt in my heart that he was alive somewhere in the jungle. For some unknown reason he was not talking to us, but soon we would hear from him.

While Ed Leonard was trapped in a tree, Kenny Fields was wandering all over the jungle. The first night he did not sleep at all. As he hid in a thicket, mosquitoes drove him crazy. During his second night he smeared mud in his ears to keep them away. Since he did not sleep the first night, on the second he leaned against a tree and dozed off. Moments later he was startled when he felt a hand on his shoulder. When he woke he saw a white face about two feet in front of him. On each side and just beyond the face were two more glowing faces. At first he thought he was dreaming and having a nightmare, but then he knew for sure that he was awake and not imaging this weird situation directly in front of him. Fields said, "It scared the livin' crap out of me!" As he moved, the mysterious creatures scrambled away. He guessed the round faces were monkeys, which climbed in the trees when he moved.

With his eyes adapted to the dark he saw that both his hands and boots were also glowing white in the darkness. Some type of phosphorus chemical must have been in the soil and attached itself to anything that touched it.

Fields had been on the ground now for thirty-six hours with nothing to eat or drink. He wasn't hungry, but he was very thirsty. As he crawled through the thicket he managed to drink dew that had settled on some plant leaves. He crawled and climbed through the brush until he came to the edge of the woods. In a clearing he saw a single lone tree in the center of a field. His plan was to hide at the base of the tree, a location that could easily be seen from the air by pilots looking for him. His thought was to put himself in a spot where the rescue force couldn't refuse to pick him up. His second and last battery powering the survival radio was getting low and he was getting desperate.

On the morning of the third day, another character would play a meaningful part in this grueling rescue. Twenty-eight-year-old Capt. Peter Lappin would be Nail 69, the primary O-2 FAC for the next rescue attempt. Lappin had flown two combat tours in F-4s before he volunteered for a tour in the O-2. He punched out of two F-4s, so he knew rescue tactics from both a FAC and a survivor point of view. Lappin was a smooth-talking young aviator who felt as invincible as Ed Leonard. It was reported that he probably had the best eyesight of any American pilot flying combat. If anyone could spot Fields from the air it would be Pete Lappin.

Lappin had not been involved in the first two days of the rescue of Kenny Fields. As a matter of fact, he was vacationing in Bangkok when called back to NKP. He hurried back and was given a briefing on the now grave situation. Intelligence officers told Lappin that Fields was a guinea pig or decoy and could be captured any time the North Vietnamese wanted to scarf him up. They were using him as bait to lure the rescue forces into a deadly trap, hoping to down more aircraft. The thousands of North Vietnamese soldiers who had fought three months earlier at Khe Sanh in South Vietnam had been pulled back to Tchepone to regroup and rearm for another attack. The Air Force master strategy was to bring in a massive B-52 Arc Light strike as soon as Fields and Leonard were rescued. It was imperative to get both of them out as soon as possible, even if riot gas was needed to do it.

Pete Lappin had his marching orders. He would be the first pilot on the scene next morning to make radio contact with Fields and make a positive determination of his exact position. Two other Nail pilots would fly at a higher altitude a couple of miles from the rescue area and feed fast-mover jets to Lappin. Lappin's goal was to place ordnance on the outside perimeter of Fields's position and then gradually move in closer. Up until this time no Sandy rescue pilot had determined Fields's position accurately enough to make certain he would not be hit by ordnance from friendly American aircraft.

By this time Ed Leonard had also spent about thirty-six hours in the Laotian jungle, most of it hiding in a tree. As daylight arrived on the third day,

Leonard could see smoke from a campfire as the North Vietnamese prepared to cook rice for breakfast. Soldiers were eating and starting to pack up their gear; Leonard was hopeful they would move out of the camp soon. He planned to wait about two hours after they departed and then come up on his survival radio and ask to be rescued. Unlike Fields, Leonard still had plenty of battery power; he just needed the enemy troops to move away.

The soldiers directly under his tree ate their rice and started packing. One soldier finished his meal, rolled a cigarette and lit it. He sat on his pack and leaned against a tree. As Leonard said, "We made eye contact." Leonard humorously described his action as pretending to be an "olive-drab banana." The soldier grabbed an AK-47 and shot at Leonard who was now trapped in the tree like a squirrel. One bullet grazed his face, causing a razor-like burn, and then the enemy's gun jammed. Leonard said he was found fair and square; he dropped his pistol to the ground and became a POW. Ed Leonard had a bad day when he crashed a Skyraider two and a half months earlier; he had his real bad day when he was captured on June 2, 1968.

The weather was poor over Tchepone on the third day, just like it had been on day two. Low stratus clouds and fog covered the valley where Kenny Fields was hiding. He was still surrounded by hostile troops carrying AK-47s, and there were up to ten 37-mm gun positions near him. As the weather started to clear, he spotted several North Vietnamese soldiers strapped to the top of trees, armed with automatic weapons. Not only would the rescue force be confronted with extremely dangerous antiaircraft guns but also with a determined enemy, who even placed their soldiers in the tops of trees, where they would not be able to cover themselves from American bomb attacks. On the previous two days, Fields had seen many, many guns fire at every American aircraft that expended ordnance. He was amazed that any aircraft could survive such a massive assault. With his battery getting low and the large number of enemy positions that would need to be suppressed for a rescue, his spirit was dropping. He realized for the first time that he might never be rescued.

At 4:55 a.m. Jolly Greens 9, 19, and 37 got airborne from NKP and aimed for Tchepone. Jolly Green 19 would be the prime helicopter for the rescue, with Jolly Greens 37 and 9 held in reserve. It would take them about an hour to fly to the target and prepare for the rescue. Thirty minutes later, Jolly

Green 19 reported he had hydraulic fluctuations and had begun having control difficulties. He would return to NKP, and Jolly Green 37 would escort him home.

The aircraft commander for Jolly Green 9 was Captain Richardson, the same helicopter pilot that picked up Bill Palank the previous day. Flying as Richardson's copilot was Maj. Louis Yuhas. The other crew members were flight engineer S. Sgt. Coy Calhoun and PJ Sgt. Peter Harding—both had been with Richardson for Palank's rescue. Richardson thought, "In the blink of an eye, my status changed from backup to the prime helicopter—but [there was] no backup for our crew if we went down." Richardson's roommate followed the events of the three-day rescue effort. He thought Richardson's chances of survival were slim and bet him a nickel he wouldn't come back alive.

Pete Lappin used holes in the clouds to mark targets for both the F-4s and F-105s, which were deployed from bases in both South Vietnam and Thailand. Flight after flight dropped bombs and cluster bomb units. Cluster bomb units (CBUs) were containers that held hundreds of small baseball-sized bombs filled with thousands of BBs. After contact with the trees, they would explode, injuring anyone in their path.

As the weather started to clear, Lappin talked to Fields and began to get an understanding of where he might be hiding. Fields spotted Lappin circling above in his O-2 and flashed a reflection of the sun from his survival mirror directly at him. Suddenly, the two pilots found a low-tech method to pinpoint Fields's position very accurately. Few pilots would be so resourceful as to communicate with such a basic survival tool. Knowing Fields's precise position, Lappin was able to place each succeeding flight in a gradually tightening circle around him.

Meanwhile, our Sandy and Jolly forces were orbiting nearby, awaiting the destruction of opposing forces. We listened to the radio communications, trying to get a sense of what we would be faced with when called in for the final rescue. By this time another Sandy pilot had replaced Vaughn. Thirty-six-year-old Maj. Thomas Campbell from Farmington, Illinois was the new Sandy low lead. His call sign was Sandy 9, and Maj. D. Brock Foster, his wingman, was Sandy 10.

Tom Campbell was one of the best gunners in the squadron and had flown F-86s in the 12th Fighter-Bomber Squadron at the end of the Korean War.

He had been an instructor pilot in both the T-33 and T-37 for seven years prior to arrival in Southeast Asia. Two weeks earlier I had flown on his wing when I got my final strike wingman flight check. I didn't know it then but Campbell was a great aerial tactician, and he had a special knack for unraveling a multitude of facts to come up with a plan to lead the vulnerable Jolly Green helicopter through enemy fire. Campbell had been on the afternoon rescue attempt the previous day and had had a chance to view the terrain. Since Fields had moved overnight, Campbell listened intently to the conversation between him and Lappin. At that time Campbell started to plan a possible route for leading the helicopter in and avoiding the massive array of guns.

Over the radio I heard an F-105 pilot report that he had been hit by ground fire and was heading home. He said he was changing his radio to another frequency. I could only speculate what happened to him after he left. Crown might cancel the rescue attempt for Kenny Fields for the fourth time if we were diverted to rescue the F-105 pilot. I thought, "If a fast-moving F-105 couldn't make it in and out of Tchepone, what hope do I have in my slow-moving Skyraider?" Unconsciously, I tightened my lap belt another notch.

Pete Lappin was slowly tightening the noose around Fields's position in the clearing. Because of the weather, the jet strike aircraft would burst out of the bottom of the clouds and have little time to take final aim before releasing their weapons. Bombs were flying everywhere. Finally, an F-4, flown by a pilot who was on his 100th combat mission, came in directly at Fields. Suspecting he would be hit by the falling ordnance, Fields urgently called on his radio, "Abort, abort, you are heading right for me!" As the F-4 started its pull-up, Fields saw a cluster bomb pod open and the sky fill with hundreds of bomblets spinning down on him. He turned around and dove into an old bomb crater as he heard the first munitions strike the tree above him. The ordnance exploded everywhere; he was surprised that he wasn't hit.

But when he rolled over he saw blood on his waist and legs, and one foot was numb. In actuality he had taken eight or nine hits to the body and was afraid his foot had been blown off. For the first time, Fields lost his cool and thought, "That's it; I have had enough." His second thought was, "They just bombed me. The god-dammed Air Force just bombed *me!*" Trying to be as cool as possible he transmitted on his radio, "I've been hit. If you're ever going to get me, do it now!" By then his radio was very weak as his last battery was running down. I didn't hear Fields's call but did hear Pete Lappin say, "We're on our way." Lappin added, "Get your smoke ready, we might use the agent and put you to sleep." Lappin was referring to CBU-19, the riot-control agent that resembled tear gas. It had been approved for use by General Momyer just moments before.

Sandy lead Tom Campbell was now faced with one of the worst possible circumstances any rescue leader could ever imagine. His survivor was surrounded by enemy guns, his last battery powering the radio was weak, and he was injured and might not be able to come up on the hoist without the assistance of a PJ. Tom Campbell had no choice. He said, "Okay, Sandys and Jolly Green 9, let's go."

What took place then was later described by Fields as the most outstanding air show he ever witnessed. A-1s were crisscrossing down the tree line, spraying 20-mm ammunition and rockets at the troops strapped in the trees. The Skyraiders were flying so low the 37-mm guns couldn't be depressed at low enough angle to get a shot off. The A-1s were flying so close to each other that Fields worried they might have a midair collision. Tom Campbell got hit on one pass and pulled off. His wingman joined up and told Campbell he had several holes in his Skyraider but no fluids leaking. In a gutsy maneuver, Campbell flew back into the battle.

There was a high degree of anxiety among Captain Richardson's Jolly crew. They thought Kenny Fields's position was still full of guns, and there was no backup for them if they were shot down. To them it looked like a trap, and they expected to be shot out of the sky when hovering over the survivor.

It was time for the Jolly Green crew to jettison their external fuel tanks. In an attempt to calm his crew, Richardson authorized his copilot to drop the tanks and bet him and the crew a steak dinner he could not hit a small sandbar in the river directly ahead of them. The bet focused the crew's attention on something other than their predicament. Against all odds, the copilot hit the sandbar squarely with both tanks. Richardson caused laughter among the crew when he grumbled that he was now out four steak dinners.

Kenny Fields later said, "Just like in a movie, suddenly the Jolly Green popped up over the horizon, veering away from my position." He yelled on the radio, "Turn port, turn port!" The helicopter didn't change course. Then he realized he was using Navy talk. So he called again, "Hard left, hard left!" Finally the Jolly came into a hover just about directly over his position. Because he was hidden in thick brush the Jolly crew could not see him. "Drop the hoist!" he screamed, and soon it came down.

Dave Richardson came into a hover directly over Fields. He could see orange smoke from Fields's flare blowing parallel to the ground. If Richardson moved the helicopter even as much as a foot, the hoist could tangle in the dense undergrowth. He concentrated on holding the chopper in the exact spot, expecting the gunners to open up on him any moment. Unable to visually acquire Fields, Richardson hovered and waited . . . and waited . . . and waited.

On each of Richardson's previous rescues, he noticed, out of the corner of his eyes, a brilliant white light. The light lasted only until the survivor got on board and then extinguished. As a Christian he believed this shiny light represented the glory of God protecting him. On the day of Fields's rescue, the light was exceptionally strong. Kenny Fields grabbed the penetrator and was soon aboard the helicopter, with branches still clinging to him. The helicopter threaded its way out, following the same route it had used to come in. Richardson wanted to get his helicopter out of the valley as quickly as possible and aimed for a nearby ridge. With his chopper straining to get enough altitude to clear the ridge, an antiaircraft gun began firing at him. He rolled sharply to the right but then immediately back to the left, almost colliding with a Sandy just off his wing. As Richardson rolled level, the Sandy pilot fired two rockets, which blew the gun position away. Richardson was so close he flew through the debris cloud.

Once onboard, the PJ gave Fields a drink of bourbon. Still concerned that he had lost a foot from the cluster bomb hits, Fields asked the PJ to remove his boot. The PJ verified that his foot was uninjured. Later, he learned that the cluster bomb pellets hit his sciatic nerve, causing him to lose feeling in his foot. From the stress of the rescue, lack of sleep, and a couple of shots of bourbon, Fields fell asleep in the helicopter and didn't wake up until medics were unloading him on a stretcher at NKP. Quickly, he was carried through a crowd of well-wishers and whisked to the Air Force dispensary. To this day, Fields says the Air Force owes him one boot, one .38 pistol, and his trusty survival radio, all left on board the Jolly Green helicopter when he was carried off.

As the welcoming crowd back at NKP was backslapping and congratulating Richardson, Sandy lead Tom Campbell arrived. Campbell shook Richardson's hand and said he was the pilot who fired the rockets into the gun position. Campbell was out of 20-mm ammunition—the rockets were the last two he had. Then Richardson shook Campbell's hand—if he hadn't been such a good shot, they would both be dead. Unlike Campbell's aircraft, which was riddled with bullet holes, Richardson's Jolly was undamaged. Campbell couldn't believe the Jolly came through unscathed. He started his clock when Richardson went into a hover, and it showed he was absolutely stationary for seven minutes. Richardson silently thanked God. He stills carries the nickel from winning the bet with his roommate.

I was elated that our Sandy and Jolly Green team was able to finally rescue Streetcar 304. Fields was on the ground for thirty-nine hours while 189 combat sorties were flown to rescue him. It was a record for the war at that time. We had pulled off the proverbial "stagecoach robbery" by holding Tchepone just long enough to get Fields out.

Somehow, some way, no more aircraft were shot down; it was absolutely a miracle come true for me. For three days I had flown over one of the most dangerous enemy locations in all of the Vietnam War without getting hit. I had cheated death! It certainly wasn't skill on my part; I just chalked it up to being supremely lucky. With eleven months and a week still remaining in my year tour, I wondered, would my luck last?

Because I had completed my three-day Sandy alert cycle, the command post ordered me to fly back to Udorn rather than land at NKP. After all we had sacrificed to get Kenny Fields out of the jungle, I was anxious to meet him and hear his description of the rescue. Because he was injured, he landed at NKP. So I was sad that I would not get the opportunity to meet him face to face. When I landed at Udorn, the squadron leaders were more interested in determining the fate of Ed Leonard than discussing Kenny Fields's adventures.

The next day Colonel Jones flew from Udorn to NKP to start a new three-day Sandy alert. After landing, he went to the dispensary late that morning. He told me the dispensary was a very small hospital built from prefabricated parts. Jones contacted the sergeant at the front desk and was surprised to hear that he had not heard of a Navy Lieutenant Fields. Jones later said, "That's a hell of a note, to go to all the trouble to find this guy, only to have the hospital lose him!" The sergeant finally found Fields's room number and ushered Colonel Jones to his ward. Colonel Jones said he found a small, enigmatic, sandy-haired Navy lieutenant with a little mustache, lying in bed reading a magazine. He had a bandaged hand but otherwise appeared okay for having undergone such a harrowing experience. Fields said he saw two A-1s shot up, both right over him. The tracers first went past Leonard's Skyraider, he reported, then into it where he saw it catch fire and Leonard eject. All he could add to the mysterious disappearance of Leonard was the short garbled radio transmission he made before crossing the road. It was a transmission we all heard and it didn't give us any more information about Leonard's situation.

Colonel Jones told me that Kenny Fields was a very cool head and that he was convinced the North Vietnamese were trying to capture him, not kill him, unlike the U.S. Air Force, which had (inadvertently) dropped cluster bombs on him. Fields said the cluster bomblets came down all around him and must have finished off the gunners strapped in the trees. He explained to Jones that he saw the bomblet that struck him. He dived to the ground and pellets hit all around his waist and groin. The doctor at NKP removed some of the pellets, but one remained floating in his body. He still has scars on his penis where one hot, searing pellet stopped too close for comfort.

When Colonel Jones returned to Udorn, he regaled us in the Sandy Box with what he called the Saga of Streetcar 304. It was an amazing story that was published in the *Air Force Times* and an AP story that my wife read about back home in the *Omaha World Herald*. Back in the States, Walter Cronkite announced on the *CBS Evening News*, "Today in Vietnam the Air Force rescued Navy pilot Lieutenant Kenny W. Fields after thirty-nine hours and 189 sorties, in the largest rescue effort of the war thus far. And that's the way it was on June 2, 1968."

Jones saved the most interesting part of his conversation with Fields to the last. Fields's wife, Shirley, was expecting a baby at the time he was shot down. She was understandably very worried about him during his three days in the jungle. They decided to name their child—no matter whether it was a boy or girl—Sandy as a tribute to the pilots who saved Kenny's life.

5 TORTURE GARDEN

Just as I experienced in the Philippines while attending the Jungle Survival School, the rain at Udorn was coming down in bucket loads. We were well into the monsoon season, and it would rain for most of the next six months. During the month of June, sixty-two inches of rain fell, a little over two inches a day. One evening, I was sitting outdoors on a metal bleacher watching a movie. The wind blew fiercely; rain hit the screen so hard it caused the image to blur. The sound of the rain hitting the bleachers blanked out the voices in the movie. One of the squadron pilots, Captain Furtak, and I were watching a movie called *Torture Garden*.

Torture Garden had been released earlier in 1968. It was directed by Freddie Francis and starred Burgess Meredith and Jack Palance. The story was about a group of patrons at a carnival sideshow who have their possible futures revealed to them by a screwball barker (Meredith) who exclaims, "I've promised you horror . . . and I intend to keep that promise." From my perspective he did more than that in this frightening film, which was laced with plenty of shock, plot twists, and intense situations. In a similar manner, combat was also laced with plenty of shock, plot twists, and intense situations. We

Skyraider pilots wished we could have our fortunes told, wished we could learn what our fate in this war would be. As the wind and rain continued, we could only hear part of the dialog, while we sipped the beers we kept safely hidden under our green military ponchos that covered our bodies. Reading between the lines of the film we could see that the patrons got what they asked for— but at a price that compromised their futures. It was a thrilling movie that I clearly remember to this day; but I'm still afraid to have my fortune told.

As I completed more missions, I was beginning to feel more comfortable. On each succeeding flight, I put my bombs and rockets closer to the target, and I now recognized all the way points we used to navigate by as we flew in and out of the clouds. We had about twenty of these points and named them by their appearance from the air. One was called the "fish's mouth," another the "parrot's beak"; there was the "Donald Duck bridge" and the "whale." We could speak about these sites over our UHF and VHF radios without concern about whether the enemy was intercepting our transmissions, as they wouldn't understand the locations we were talking about.

I tried to fly a perfect flight every time I went on a combat mission. It was both a challenge and technique I had developed as a test pilot back at Edwards. There, I had limited fuel, instrumentation recording tape, and range time to accomplish all the test points needed to accomplish the flight test objective. The challenge in combat was to find the target no matter what the weather was like, spot potential gun sites, perform a stabilized and accurate weapon drop, and finally pull off the target without getting hit by ground fire or hitting the ground. It was very easy to screw up. Now, thirty years later, I can remember more about some of my mistakes than about the totally successful missions.

One time, after returning from a mission, I needed to taxi directly in front of the squadron building to get to the parking area. Unlike, conventional aircraft with a nose gear, the Skyraider was directionally unstable on the ground because its center of gravity was behind the main landing gear. It required the pilot to apply a small amount of rudder to turn but then opposite rudder to keep from ground looping (causing the aircraft to do a 360-degree circle on the ground). When taxiing a straight line, the pilot would lock the tail wheel and could relax a little. This particular time I needed to unlock the tail wheel for a small turn at slow speed. Unfortunately, the A-1 got away from me and I did a complete 360-degree turn directly in front of the squadron building. I felt certain that one of the Skyraider pilots was looking out the window, seeing me mess up. Reluctantly, I returned to the squadron building after my debriefing. I expected to get ragged on for my poor taxiing techniques. No one made a comment about it; either none of the other pilots saw it happen or they had done the same thing themselves. Writing now, I confess to the incident for the first time.

On another occasion, I completed a bombing pass and pulled up and did a vigorous bank to the left and then back to the right. We always jinked to prevent the enemy gunners from getting an easy shot at us. Because I am left-handed, I always strapped my clipboard on my left thigh and inserted my five-by-seven-inch mission briefing card in it. The clipboard sat on my knee about level with the flight control stick on which was located the aileron and elevator trim, gun trigger, and bomb and rocket release buttons. This time, while pulling up from a dive-bombing pass, I pushed the stick hard over to the left a little more vigorously than usual. Looking back over my left shoulder to see where my bombs landed, I suddenly saw out the corner of my eye a projectile with a white exhaust trail streaming out ahead of me. I also heard a *swish* sound. My first thought was that someone had fired at me and barely missed, going slightly under my Skyraider. I banked hard to the right, expecting to see a MiG firing another projectile at me from my six o'clock position. Seeing nothing, I whipped the A-1 back to the left again while looking for the elusive MiG. Another *swish* and for a second time what appeared to be a rocket passed under me and streamed out in front. It was then that I realized what happened. When I pressed the flight control stick hard over to the left, the corner of my clipboard accidentally pressed the rocket release button. Both of the rockets I had seen out in front of me were mine! Fortunately, I had not called out a MiG encounter on the radio. I was embarrassed and never said anything to my lead.

On another mission, I was flying as wingman with Tom Campbell. We dropped our bombs and fired rockets on an enemy position in Barrel Roll. Then we started strafing the target with our 20-mm guns. We were banking back and forth, zooming the Skyraider back up into the sky and crisscrossing each other's tracks. Suddenly, Campbell called out that he heard a noise and suspected he had been hit by ground fire. We pulled off target and I joined up in close formation so I could look him over. I couldn't see any damage, and Campbell reported that his Skyraider and engine instruments were all normal. He said he heard the noise behind him, possibly on the backside of the A-1's sliding canopy. I could not find any damage in that area either. Finally, we came to the conclusion that he had probably been hit by one of the expelled 20-mm shell casings from my own firing. After the wing-mounted 20-mm guns were fired, the empty casings would automatically eject from the bottom of the Skyraider's wing and slowly fall through the air, landing in the jungle. Because we were crisscrossing in track and getting lower on each pass, it was possible he flew under me just as I fired at the target. Another lesson learned flying the A-1.

On one flight I gave the aircraft mechanics a good laugh. Since it took an hour for the heavily loaded Skyraider to climb to 10,000 feet, sometimes I carried food with me for a snack during long missions. This particular time I had an overripe banana. I trimmed the Skyraider so that it continued to fly, making small adjustments with the flight control stick using my knees, while I peeled away the skin of the banana. The first three inches of the banana were very soft and dark in color from oxidation. I didn't want to eat that section but had no method of disposing of it. I thought I could bite it off and spit it in my glove, helmet bag, or the leather folder that carried my maps and photos. That didn't seem like a very good idea. Then I realized that, unlike a jet aircraft, I could open the canopy and spit part of the banana into the airstream. At 140 knots indicated airspeed, 165 knots true airspeed, and about 190 miles per hour, I opened the canopy and placed my left hand out of the cockpit a few inches. The air felt solid at that speed; it would take a monster spit to keep the banana residue off the tail of the aircraft, I thought. I bit off about three inches, turned my head to the left and leaned over just to the edge of the hot rushing air. With a mighty heave, I spit the banana into the blast of jungle air. The oozy banana stopped in midair for a fraction of a second and then sprayed back onto my face, helmet, harness, and flight suit. I used my gloves to wipe off my face and eyes; the rest would get cleaned up after landing. The ground crew got a big laugh when they saw banana all over my flight suit. I made a full confession; the guys could use a little humor during their twelve-hour work shift. One mechanic reminded me that the Skyraider prop rotated clockwise from the cockpit and the resulting airflow would make it better to spit out the right side of the cockpit. He suggested we put a placard on the instrument panel that read: "Attention jet pilots! Recommend spitting right side only."

MiGs

An Air Force plane equipped with long-range radar kept continuous watch for MiGs (code named Bandits) flying in the Hanoi area. Also, a Navy destroyer with the call sign Red Crown sat out in the Gulf of Tonkin and tracked the MiGs. If a Bandit was detected, the controller would transmit a warning to all strike aircraft on UHF emergency frequency. Hanoi was code named Bullseye, so the warning we would hear might be, for example: "Bandits southwest of Bullseye seventy-five miles."

I heard the call one time and quickly checked my map to determine the location of the Bandit. On the map the MiG looked like it was very close to me. I was in the extreme northeast corner of Laos near the town Sam Neua, only a hundred miles from Hanoi. At the same time, I was two hundred miles from my home base at Udorn. Making a run for Udorn at 140 knots against a jet that could fly 500 knots faster than I could didn't seem like a very good strategy. Flying at 8,000 feet, I looked up and saw a contrail directly above me going the opposite direction.

The lack of speed, altitude, and zoom capability severely limited the Skyraider from assuming an offensive role against a jet-powered MiG aircraft in air-to-air combat. But with respectable firepower and a short turning radius, the A-1 was a formidable adversary in a defensive role. Pilot proficiency was often the determining factor in air-to-air engagements with jets. In this case, the Skyraider pilot needed to know the A-1's maximum G loading, stall and spin characteristics, and the effective range of the weapons it carried. Pulling maximum G would create the shortest turning distance. Knowing the stall and spin characteristics would help the pilot keep from losing control of the Spad. And knowing the maximum lethal range of the guns and rockets would prevent the wasting of ordnance by firing too far out. We practiced defensive maneuvering against a T-33 at Hurlburt Field during our initial training in the Skyraider. Would I remember my training if I really needed it against a MiG?

The single-seat A-1H and A-1J models had great visibility both left and right and in the vertical plane. That could not be said for the side-by-side–seated A-1E and A-1Gs we were flying. An E/G Skyraider pilot was essentially blind out the right side, and the most critical part of air-to-air combat was keeping the enemy in sight. I was instructed at Hurlburt to keep the plane moving in altitude and heading and to check each other's six o'clock position. If I spotted a MiG soon enough, I could turn into him and keep his plane in sight. If he chose to attack, he must accept a head-on pass. In that case I could arm my 20-mm guns and rockets and take a shot at him on each encounter.

The Skyraider had an advantage in both turn radius and rate of turn. At any speed we could turn tight enough to prevent a jet from getting on our tail. We also had greater endurance than a jet if we descended to a couple hundred feet above the jungle and set up a cruise mixture setting where we could continue to fly for four or more hours. The MiG would burn a lot more fuel at low altitude and eventually need to break off the engagement and fly home. We also had armor plating on each side of the cockpit and directly under the center section of the wing. Although an A-1 presented a large profile, only a bullet in the engine, canopy glass, or one that damaged a flight control surface could cripple you.

On the other hand, the Skyraider was at a disadvantage because of its slow speed. While slow speed was an advantage in turning, it restricted the A-1 from initiating an attack. If the MiG pilot was smart, he would keep his speed up, make a head-on pass, and zoom back up to altitude. The Skyraider didn't have any zoom capability, and airspeed lost in high–G maneuvering was hard to get back again. While keeping my eye on the contrail of the suspected MiG, I armed my four 20-mm guns and started to descend. I watched him carefully for several minutes. For a moment or so I secretly wished he would make a pass on me. It would be fantastic to hassle with a MiG in any aircraft. It was the only time in my year tour I wished I was back in a jet fighter again. However, the contrail made a slow 180-degree turn and returned toward Hanoi.

SURFACE-TO-AIR MISSILE

MiGs weren't the only danger Skyraider pilots experienced while flying in the northeast corner of Laos. Surface-to-air missiles (SAMs) were known to exist in this area and would be deadly to a slow-moving Skyraider. In addition, we did not have any electronic warning devices to alert us to a missile launch. While I was working with a flight of F-105 Thunderchiefs, one of the pilots radioed that he observed a SAM missile launch on his electronic display. All four F-105s dove for the trees and accelerated to high speed out of the target area. I was a sitting duck at 8,000 feet, flying at a relatively slow 140 knots. Rolling the Skyraider into a 135-degree bank, I pulled it into a vertical dive and headed for the trees too. As soon as I leveled off, fifty feet above the jungle, my speed returned to 140 knots. At that speed it was difficult to get a lot of distance from the location where the SAM warning occurred. I didn't see any SAMs in the sky but kept up my speed, heading south back to Udorn. The Thunderchief pilots sped out of the area, tanked on the way home, debriefed, and were probably in the Officers Club bar having a beer before I got home. I didn't get a chance to thank them for the warning.

Maj. Robert Kraus was my flight commander. Bob Kraus was a bit overweight and had a husky voice. He wanted to fly every day and made sure we got our share of the combat sorties. He had flown fighters for nearly twenty years, starting in the early 1950s as an instrument instructor in the F-86 Sabre jet, and later flying the F-100 Super Sabre for a year in Germany. He even had over a hundred hours in the tail-wheel P-51 Mustang. Bob Kraus loved to mix it up with the enemy and enjoyed flying one particular aircraft that he had named. (When a pilot finished his tour and returned to the States his plane became—unofficially—available for another pilot to name.) His aircraft was an A-1H, which he named *Nick the Tiger*. We flew a lot together, he as lead with me as his wingman.

Before long we were notified by the Intelligence Office that we had some good bomb damage assessments. One time we destroyed two trucks and killed twelve North Vietnamese Army soldiers. Another time we destroyed five trucks and killed eight Pathet Lao soldiers. Five days later it was reported we had killed four Pathet Lao and wounded eight by aircraft.

By the end of June, I was scheduled to be upgraded to a Firefly lead. Tom Campbell followed me on the first of four evaluation flights. Campbell taught me how to do what was called stand-off marking. If a Skyraider pilot was on a standard Barrel Roll strike mission and encountered multiple 37-mm guns, he would be outgunned and likely to get shot down. So the squadron came up with a safer plan on how to place white phosphorus rockets near the area where the Skyraider pilot was acting as a FAC for the jets. The plan called for climbing to 3,000 feet above the target altitude and placing the target on the Skyraider's wingtip. This would put you two to three miles away. Then the pilot would make a 90-degree turn, putting the target on the Skyraider's nose, pull the nose up to 10 degrees above the horizon, and fire a rocket. Then he would continue up to 20 degrees above the horizon and fire another rocket. Now two rockets would be burning on the ground near the scheduled strike area and the exact position could be described over the radio in relation to the rockets. This technique was not written in any of the official tactics manuals.

My second and third upgrade flights were flown with Major Bunn. Like Tom Campbell, Mel Bunn was part of the flight that successfully rescued Streetcar 304 just a month earlier. He was very near the end of his year tour and would return to Hurlburt Field in Florida to become a Skyraider instructor. On July 3, I flew my fourth and last Firefly upgrade mission with Major Flynn. Like Mel Bunn, Charlie Flynn was finishing his year tour, one of the old guys going home soon. Now I was qualified as a Firefly lead with forty-one combat missions and 128 flying hours under my belt. I was finally not a new guy anymore.

After my lead upgrade flights, I started to carry my American-made Argus C-3 camera loaded with color slide film on every flight. I took shots of my wingman and some of the target areas. I was starting to feel comfortable flying combat, a feeling I never would have thought possible a few months earlier.

There was one flight maneuver I accomplished several days later that I was actually proud of. Returning from a mission, I trimmed the aircraft for level flight, took out my smoking pipe and lit up. When flying jets, I could never smoke in the plane. With the need to breathe pure oxygen through the face mask, it would be extremely dangerous to have an open flame, even if it were physically possible. On the other hand, the Skyraider was not pressurized, and we only wore a mask so the sound of our radio communications would be better. There was even an ashtray in the cockpit. With my mask hanging to the side, I was puffing away and felt the urge to take a pee. Holding the pipe in my mouth, I pulled out the pilot relief tube, which had a funnel attached to the end. Just as I was relieving myself, the external fuel tank I was running on went dry. The engine started to cough and sputter. Talk about fast hands—I managed to switch fuel tanks while not dropping my relief tube, peeing on my boots, or even losing my pipe. Certainly this procedure was not in the A-1 checklist. Only an experienced Skyraider pilot could do what I did that day. It would take a very proficient aviator to juggle all those requirements at one time. However, this highly unusual maneuver did nothing to help win the war, and I didn't dare talk about it in the Sandy Box.

ROMAN 2 A AND B

Maj. D. Brock Foster was about to finish his combat tour flying the Skyraider. He was one of the oldest pilots in the squadron and had flown fighters in World War II. Brock Foster had pure white hair and acted as the squadron duty officer for the last weeks of his tour. I flew on his wing for my second, third, and fourth combat missions going north to Barrel Roll. Ed Leonard acted as an instructor pilot for me on all three of those flights sitting in the right seat of an A-1E. As Foster completed his tour, Leonard had been missing in action for just over a month. I went over to the Intelligence Office every couple of days to check on him; no new information had surfaced. No contact had been made on our emergency radio frequency, no sightings by FACs, nothing. However, I was positive that Ed Leonard was still alive. Like Alfred E. Newman from *Mad* magazine, Ed Leonard was grinning up at us from somewhere in the jungle, still waiting to be picked up or to escape.

Foster was looking forward to the end of his year tour and retirement from the Air Force. A going-away party was set up in the Udorn Officers' Club. He had a personal "calling card" that was unique in our squadron. Proud to be a Skyraider pilot, he played a joke on the F-4 Phantom pilots stationed at

Udorn. Because we were in the six-month-long monsoon season, the Udorn runway was usually wet with strong crosswinds. Under those circumstances it was vitally important for F-4 pilots to use their drag chutes for landing. After touchdown, often they would call the control tower and ask, "Did I get a good chute?" Sometimes the drag chute deployed but didn't open properly. If the F-4 pilot didn't get a good chute, he could either abort the landing or lower the tail hook and make a cable arrestment.

Foster acquired one of the F-4 pilot's chutes, a small, spring-loaded three feet in diameter chute that opened first and pulled out the main eighteen feet in diameter drag chute. He attached this pilot chute to a fifteen-foot shroud line, rolled it up, and carried it with him in the Skyraider cockpit. Before landing at Udorn, Foster would open the Skyraider's sliding canopy and tie the end of the shroud line to the canopy frame. After touchdown, he would throw the pilot chute out into the airstream. The chute would blossom and whip around in the air just aft of the A-1's cockpit. To add a flare to this very unique display of airmanship, Foster would cleverly ask the control tower, "Skyraider on landing roll out. Did I get a good chute?"

During Foster's going-away party, he passed the small pilot chute to me because I was a former F-4 pilot and still had ten more months to go to complete my tour. I promised to keep up the tradition.

I continued to be less than impressed with the accuracy of the F-4s. On the other hand, it seemed to me that the F-105 attack missions were near perfection. A four-ship formation flight would arrive in the strike area on their scheduled time. As Firefly FACs, my wingman and I would already have expended our bombs, rockets, and napalm. With only 20-mm ammunition and two pods of white phosphorus marking rockets remaining, the Skyraider would be very light and maneuverable. Sometimes in high-threat areas, we would be at 12,000 feet, often 1,000 feet or more above the jets streaming into the combat zone at 450 knots. Many times we told the jets to look up for us instead of looking down.

On our prearranged strike UHF frequency, I would hear the F-105 lead pilot call, "Firefly, Robin flight of four Thuds approaching strike area." I would confirm his call and say, "Firefly rolling in to mark target." After firing a rocket, I would call the F-105 flight, "Firefly off target, holding south, hit my mark." The lead F-105 pilot would transmit, "Robin flight, do you have the smoke?" In rapid succession would be the answer, "Robin 2, Robin 3, Robin 4." Next I would hear, "Robin lead in from the north," and "Twos in from the west," then " Threes in from the south," and "Fours in from the east." In a very organized and efficient manner, the flight would continue, "Ones off," followed by, "Twos off," then, "Threes off," and "Fours off." Practically every time I would observe their string of bombs all hit the target. The lead F-105 pilot would call out the ordnance they had dropped and ask for bomb damage assessment. In a few moments they would be off target and heading for the tanker on their way back to their base at either Korat or Takhli. The F-105 flights were always very professional, accurate, and easy to control.

I couldn't say the same for the F-4 flights. They would usually arrive in the target area late. The lead F-4 would call, saying that because of an aircraft malfunction, one of the four F-4s had not been able to get a full load of fuel off the tanker and would need to drop ordnance first. Another of the F-4s would have radio failure requiring the leader to use hand signals for communication with him. I would again mark the target with a rocket and clear them in for the attack. Usually one of the F-4 pilots couldn't find the smoke, one would drop ordnance several valleys removed from the mark, and another would pull off with a hung bomb. The leader would then try to reform his flight on their way back to the tanker. They had great difficulty even finding one another. Giving them bomb damage assessment was a joke. Normally I just said, "Why don't you guys go home, regroup, and come back tomorrow."

Only six months earlier, I had been a test pilot at Edwards AFB flying evaluation missions on the F-4. When I was on my grand tour I briefed F-4 pilots at the Wheelus AB Officers' Club in North Africa on some of the poor handling qualities of the Phantom, I got a lot of opposition. Most of the pilots thought the F-4 was a fine aircraft with no flaws. It was ham-handed pilots who were the cause of mishaps. The F-4 pilots at Wheelus told me they could hit within twenty feet of any target. Such was not the case with F-4s flying real combat missions in Barrel Roll. Either the pilots were very inexperienced, the aircraft was in poor maintenance shape, the aircraft was being flown out of balance, or some combination of those factors. If I ever needed support for a hotly contested rescue mission, I'd have picked F-105s.

As time went by, many Air Force and Navy jets were shot down along the

Ho Chi Minh Trail and rescued by the Sandys and Jolly Green helicopters. We always had a rescue party at the Officers Club to celebrate the survivor's return to civilization. The survivor would buy a round of drinks for all the Sandys and Jollys who rescued him. As a copious quantity of beer was consumed, we heard the survivor's personal story of doubt, fear, and finally thrill in being rescued and living to fight again.

One Navy pilot complained, in jest, that surviving his rescue party was more difficult than being down in the jungle surrounded by enemy forces. He celebrated too much; the last time I saw him, he was lying fully dressed in a flight suit on the floor of the shower with cold water spraying on him. He was rolling back and forth, moaning, groaning, and calling out, "Throw me back, throw me back!" He may have looked and acted like a fish, but he was a free man.

Another time, an Air Force pilot parachuted into the jungle, hid among the trees, and watched enemy soldiers only a few yards away. He was safely hidden and had no immediate expectation of being seen or captured. Unfortunately, he felt his heart beating very rapidly and had a tremendous sense of fear. Unable to stand it any longer, he pulled his loaded .38 pistol from its holster and started running through the jungle. While firing into the air, he was just running, not in any particular direction or toward any destination. He didn't aim the pistol at anyone or anything. He just ran and shot his gun. He told me he just felt better running and shooting. Evidently, he scared some of the enemy soldiers because several of them started running also. Sometimes he would be running toward them, sometimes right next to them. It reminded him of the old Keystone Cops movies—everyone running in a different direction and nothing accomplished. Every story about being on the ground in enemy country was different. I was glad I didn't have one to tell.

By July 7, two months into my year tour, I had flown forty-five combat missions and was scheduled for another Sandy alert. I looked at the assignment board: Sandy 1—Maj. Peter Brown Jr. in an A-1H; Sandy 2—Major Raymond Shumock in an A-1H; Sandy 3—Lt. Col. John Carlson in an A-1H; Sandy 4—Capt. George Marrett in an A-1E.

Like Ed Leonard, John Carlson completed his year tour but extended six months. He did this so that he could rotate back to the States with his wife, Lt. Col. Mary Carlson, who was an Air Force nurse, working in Okinawa.

Both Pete Brown and John Carlson were experienced combat pilots and had been on many rescues.

Just as had been the case in the Streetcar 304 rescue, I would be Sandy 4 flying a side-by-side–seated A-1E. Sitting in the left seat, a Skyraider pilot could not see out of the right side of an E model. This forced him to make only left-handed firing runs, an extremely dangerous technique on a hostile rescue. The gunners knew where to aim at you if you always turned to the left.

While we were eating dinner at the Officers Club that evening, Colonel Carlson told me that an F-4 crew, Roman 2A and Roman 2B, successfully ejected that afternoon in North Vietnam. We had a rescue briefing scheduled for 3:30 a.m. the next morning and an early takeoff planned. The similarities between this upcoming mission and the Streetcar 304 rescue debacle were quite obvious to me. I would be the new guy again, flying an E model again, and tail-end-Charlie. I remembered Ed Leonard telling me that every Sandy pilot could count on having a real bad day at least once during his year tour. Leonard had two bad days. Would this be my real bad day? I wrote a good-bye letter to my wife. In it I said I would be flying another rescue in a very dangerous area—just like the Streetcar 304 mission a month earlier. There was a good chance I would either be shot down and captured or killed outright. If I didn't make it back I wanted her to know I loved her and to take care of our two sons. Then I went to bed; I didn't sleep at all that night.

The next morning the Sandys and Jollys met in the Intelligence Office and briefed our mission and tactics. Roman 2A and Roman 2B were known to be alive on the ground the night before. They were about fifteen miles west of the Gulf of Tonkin, near Highway 101 and several small trails. From a small town nearby, Lang Gieo, we could expect small-arms fire, multiple anti-aircraft guns and possible SAM missiles. The weather was crappy—there were multiple layers of overcast clouds and low visibility with fog near the mountains. This area of North Vietnam and the existing weather sounded bad to me, but as long as American airmen were on the ground in enemy territory we would attempt to rescue them.

Takeoff time was set at 4:45 a.m.; this was called a first-light effort by the old-timers. I wasn't sure I would live long enough to become an old-timer. Pete Brown and Ray Shumock would go directly to the crash site and try to get visual and radio contact with both pilots. John Carlson and I would escort Jolly Greens 19 and 37 to a safe area, expected to be about five nautical miles southwest of the crash site. Misty 11, a two-seated F-100F high-speed jet FAC, was in radio contact with both Roman 2A and Roman 2B and had authenticated them when we arrived. Carlson and I left Jolly Green 37 in a safe orbit and looked for a clear area to descend. We banked back and forth and dove through several layers of clouds. When we broke out it was still quite dark in the jungle, and I couldn't make out anything. I didn't know what direction we were flying, only that I didn't want to get lost over North Vietnam flying at 180 knots. I had a hard time keeping up with Carlson, cussing at the slow Skyraider I was flying. Once we were under the clouds, I started looking for enemy gunfire. I continued to fall behind the other Sandys and added full engine power. After a couple of turns I noticed my airspeed was slow and that the rest of the flight was above me in altitude. One of the Sandys called for me to climb back up; I was getting too low. I quickly checked the engine gauges—everything was okay. My flaps were up and so was the landing gear. Still I was getting lower and slower—something was terribly wrong. I thought about jettisoning my ordnance, but I needed it for the rescue. The fear factor started to increase in me. Frantically, I checked everything in the aircraft. Had I been hit already? Was one landing gear down? Was a bomb loose? Then I realized what I had done. I had done something a pilot *never* does in a Skyraider. It was something I had never done before, something that accounted for my loss of airspeed and altitude. When I realized what it was, I gave myself the "dumb s—" award on the spot.

In our attempt to get through small openings in the clouds, Carlson and I rolled into several steep dives. To keep from going too fast and overrunning him, I opened my speed brakes. Speed brakes were hardly ever used in the Skyraider; for a jet pilot the plane was too damn slow anyway. After we broke through the clouds, I forgot to close them. That accounted for my loss of speed and altitude.

As I recovered from my misadventure, I heard on the radio that we were going in for the rescue. All four Sandys escorted Jolly Green 19 from the safe area to the site of the downed airmen. Roman 2A had removed his parachute and was now northeast of it. Roman 2B said he was two to three hundred meters north of the crashed F-4. As we approached the first pilot, antiaircraft guns opened up at us from Highway 101 just north of Lang Gieo, and small arms fired from the trail east of it. I made seven passes on Highway 101, putting in 1,500 rounds of 7.62-mm shells from the minigun on my left stub position. Also, I fired three pods of rockets and about three hundred rounds from my four 20-mm internal guns.

During one pass I saw tracers from enemy guns make an *X* directly in front of my propeller. It was a pink *X*, framed against a background of gray clouds— I couldn't miss it. The gunners had led me a little too much; they couldn't believe I was flying so slowly. They must have been used to aiming at jet aircraft.

After both pilots were picked up, the rescue armada headed east for a couple of miles so the Jolly Green could climb to altitude before recrossing Highway 101. We then turned south and crossed Highway 101 near the town of Cha Cung. Carlson and I each made four firing runs on the highway as the Jolly Green crossed. I fired 300 more rounds of 20-mm, a pod of rockets, and another pod of rockets. We joined up with the second Jolly Green, who was still in a safe orbit, and headed home. The Jollys were stationed at NKP and would return the two survivors there. The Sandys would return to our home base at Udorn. I never got to meet Roman 2A and Roman 2B. We landed at 7:10 a.m. The day was still young, but I was dead tired.

After shutdown, the crew chief called attention to my Skyraider. During one pass, I was hit in the right wing near the knee of the landing gear. It was the first time I had been hit flying a combat mission. I had been very, very lucky. Had I been in a right bank that single bullet would probably have come into the cockpit. Or, if the bullet had penetrated ammunition in the right 20-mm gun, it could have caused a wing fire and probably an explosion. Had it hit the engine I might have gone down in enemy territory. Getting hit served as a reminder to me from then on how thin and fragile is the thread of luck, and just how close I came to using my entire allotment on a cloudy morning in North Vietnam.

While the day was over for me, other critical events happened to pilots in the 602nd. Lt. Col. William Buice was shot down later in the day. Maj. Howard Jennings went down the next day.

Several days later I got a copy of the official military newspaper *Stars and Stripes*. The article with the headline "North Viet Down Phantom" read:

SAIGON—An Air Force F-4 Phantom was shot down Monday evening northwest of Dong Hoi in North Vietnam, U.S. spokesmen said Tuesday.

The two crew members were picked up at 6 a.m. Tuesday by Jolly Green Giant helicopters. The crewmen were identified as 1st Lt. Charles W. Mosley, 26, and 1st Lt. Don M. Hallenbeck, 24, AP reported. The 7th Air Force said both pilots were uninjured.

The Phantom brought the unofficial total of U.S. aircraft losses over North Vietnam to 864.

American planes flew 140 missions over North Vietnam's southern panhandle Monday, meeting moderate antiaircraft fire. Air Force crews damaged or destroyed 26 gun sites.

Air Force Phantoms and F-105 Thunderchiefs also caused more than 90 sustained fires, eight secondary explosions and 20 petroleum, oil and lubricant fires.

The writer for the *Stars and Stripes* called it "moderate antiaircraft fire." How did he know it was moderate? At my altitude, airspeed, and with my stupidity of leaving the speed brakes extended, it became heavy for me. And if the two F-4 lieutenants ever read this book, I want them to know they still owe me a rescue celebration drink.

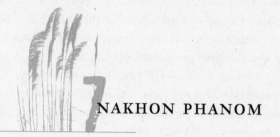

7

NAKHON PHANOM

Big changes were in store for the 602nd Fighter Squadron starting July 1, 1968. We would get a new commander, change our squadron designation, and move about a hundred miles east to Nakhon Phanom RTAFB. Our present commander, Lieutenant Colonel Bechtold, was finishing his year of combat and returning to the States. My classmate from training at Hurlburt Field, Lt. Col. William A. Jones III, would take over as the new commander.

Our official squadron designation had been the 602nd Fighter Squadron (C). We took pride in being the only propeller fighter squadron left in the Air Force, and the name Commando added a touch of mystery or mystique to our image. As Skyraider pilots we had a little of the spirit of the distinguished Flying Tigers of World War II celebrity. Like Phil Cochran of *Terry and the Pirates* comic strip fame, we were brash young Americans fighting a dirty war in an exotic setting.

Our new designation was the 602nd Special Operations Squadron (SOS). Special Operations as a name was stupid—it could stand for anything. SOS was even the international aviation code for an emergency. We A-1 pilots continued to call ourselves a fighter squadron. After all, we were still flying strike and rescue missions in the Skyraider; that had not changed.

In addition, our squadron still reported to the 56th Air Commando Wing, also located at Nakhon Phanom. It would now become the 56th Special Operations Wing (SOW). The new name sounded like a pig.

The Thai base at Nakhon Phanom, shortened to NKP, was sometimes referred to as "Naked Fanny," or even "the end of the world." This field was more of an outpost than a base and situated smack on the border with Laos, less than sixty air miles from parts of the Ho Chi Minh Trail. About two thousand people lived in the town located next to the Mekong River, the dividing line between Thailand and Laos. From the river you could see the karst mountains in Laos, the beginning of enemy territory, or, as we called it, like the pioneers of the alien West, "Indian country."

Air Commando veteran Tom Wickstrom later recalled for Col. Michael E. Haas, who included it in his book *Apollo's Warriors*, "NKP was far enough in the jungle to make it an undesirable point for visiting brass . . . a short enough pierced-steel-planking runway to discourage anything that consumed kerosene [that is, jets] from landing except in extreme emergencies . . . uncomfortable enough that the crews were happy to fly combat missions in return for an occasional motivational trip to Bangkok . . . and, finally, big enough to hide men and equipment purloined from other unsuspecting organizations throughout the world."

Other combat units were already at NKP when we arrived. The 1st Special Operations Squadron, nicknamed "the Hobos," also flew the A-1 Skyraider. Their A-1s could be identified by a white "TC" on the tail, as opposed to our aircraft, which had a white "TT." The 1st had been transferred to NKP from its previous base at Pleiku, in South Vietnam's central highlands. The Hobos specialized in seeding the Ho Chi Minh Trail with "gravel"—thousands of small firecracker-like explosives that detonated when stepped on or driven over by a vehicle. Gravel was placed directly on the trail and designed to blend in with the existing rocks and debris on the road. When detonated, the gravel would not kill, but rather severely injured people who were either repairing the trail or carrying supplies. The Hobos also planted acoustical sensors in the jungle trees. These sensors could detect enemy voices and truck engines. They were monitored by technicians located in a blockhouse at NKP as part of a classified program called Igloo White.

Another A-1 squadron was scheduled to join us at NKP later in the year.

The 22nd Special Operations Squadron, called Zorros, were assigned the night interdiction role. Their Skyraiders would have a white "TS" on the tail. One of our pilots remarked that there would then be "three little pigs" (or SOSs) working for the SOW.

One squadron had been located at NKP for a couple of years. The Nimrods flew twin-engine A-26K attack bombers. Their call sign became synonymous with the aircraft itself during their multiple years of trial through fire in Southeast Asia. The Nimrods specialized in night attack on trucks driving southbound on the Ho Chi Minh Trail.

Another unconventional mission was flown out of NKP. Twin-engine C-123 Provider transports, using the call sign Candlestick, provided aerial flare capability. The aircraft were painted black, and, with their exterior lights off, they would fly at night over the trail, waiting for the movement of trucks. With strike aircraft at the ready, the C-123 pilot dropped six-million-candlepower flares over the trucks. Before the Vietnamese truck drivers could find a place to hide, Skyraiders or A-26s would strike them.

Most of the pilots in the 602nd didn't look forward to our move to NKP. We had many creature comforts at Udorn. Our hooches were very near the Officers Club, within easy walking distance. The base had a large BX (Base Exchange) and a gym with handball courts. The trip to downtown Udorn was a five-minute cab ride for 5 *baht* (U.S.25¢). Several of the major hotels served steak dinners on fresh linen for a couple of dollars and included a bottle of Thai beer. Custom-made suits, and boots made from elephant skin, were very inexpensive. Children's toys were plentiful, as were a large variety of items made of monkeypod wood. Even jewelry made of opal and set in silver was easy to find and cost very little. In our spare time, shopping for our family and friends was a good pastime. For being in a war zone, Udorn was a good life.

Now the 555th Tactical Fighter Squadron (called the Triple Nickel) would be moving their F-4s from Ubon and taking our hangar space and living quarters. Their commander drove an olive-drab World War II jeep with twenty red stars painted on its side. The red stars signified the number of MiGs shot down by Triple Nickel pilots. While at Udorn their pilots would shoot down another seven MiGs, the greatest number of kills by a fighter squadron in the entire war. Some of us thought our commander's jeep should have stylized F-4s painted on the side of his jeep to represent the number of Phantom aircrew we rescued. The F-4 aircrews were our best rescue customers.

As pilots, we would be giving up Udorn's 10,000-foot concrete runway for a 7,000-foot pierced-steel planking strip at NKP. However, we would be closer to the Jolly Green squadron and the Ho Chi Minh Trail, which would be a tactical advantage from a rescue perspective.

On the positive side, I had flown long enough in Southeast Asia to get an A-1 designated as my personal aircraft. This meant I could give it a nickname and have my name painted on the plane. My Skyraider would be A-1J, serial number 142029. The plane had just arrived from Cam Ranh Bay after being refurbished at McClelland AFB in California. I decided to call it *Sock It To 'Em* after the popular 1960s TV show *Rowan and Martin's Laugh-In*. My crew chief, A/2C Joseph Toback, liked the idea and painted my name on the left side of the fuselage, just below the canopy. He placed his name below mine; we were both very proud to have our own aircraft.

But all these factors didn't matter to our move; military orders said our squadron would move from Udorn to NKP. So we moved.

STRIKE LEAD CHECKOUT

Lt. Col. William Buice arrived at the 602nd in early June 1968, just as I was flying as part of the rescue of Streetcar 304. Bill Buice listened to the rescue on a UHF radio in the squadron building. He was astonished at how great was the threat of getting shot down and captured.

Buice had the distinction of waiting the longest time to become a Sandy rescue pilot and serving one of the shortest combat tours on record. In his mid-forties, he had a small mustache that was starting to gray; he was of medium build and height and was a southern boy from Mississippi. He spent two and a half years in World War II on an antisubmarine ship but missed the Korean War because of duty in the research and development field. Before coming to Thailand, Buice was assigned to the Defense Atomic Support Agency at Kirtland AFB in Albuquerque, New Mexico. He was attached to the Navy Weapons Evaluation Squadron, humorously called the Rio Grande Navy. Even though his job was in R and D, he got to fly all the Navy aircraft stationed on the base. Among the planes he flew were the F-9 jet fighter and

S-2F antisubmarine bomber. His greatest thrill was flying two of the Navy Skyraiders located at Kirtland. These two aircraft were the last A-1s in the Navy inventory. Buice flew about three hundred hours in the Navy version, called the AD, before he decided to volunteer for combat in the Air Force Skyraider. Since he was working with classified nuclear information, he was restricted for a year before serving in an area where there was a risk of his being kidnapped or captured. Buice laughed, "I had to cool my heels for a year."

He became combat ready in the Skyraider and on July 2nd flew into North Vietnam for the successful rescue of Lt. Col. Jack Modica, an F-105 pilot. Buice flew on the wing of Lieutenant Colonel Carlson. As a matter of fact, he was scheduled to be John Carlson's replacement as deputy commander of the 602nd.

On July 9, 1968, exactly a week after Bill Buice helped rescue the F-105 pilot, he was scheduled for a lead checkout flight in an A-1 as Firefly 16. He would be evaluated by Maj. "Smilin'" Jack Watts using call sign Firefly 17. Their mission was to support General Vang Pao's troops as they attempted to secure another Laotian hilltop as a replacement for Lima Site 85, which had fallen to the North Vietnamese six months earlier.

When they arrived in the target area, Jack Watts said, "Bill, you take the lead." Buice checked in with the Raven FAC and was given a target near a tree line. After dropping some of his bombs on the first pass, he set up for a 20-mm strafing run. Just as he fired his guns, he took hits in the left wing. Buice said, "A big orange ball of flame erupted, looking like an arc welder torching my wing." He turned his Skyraider 180 degrees to a bailout heading and jettisoned his remaining ordnance. Afterward he thought, "My only regret was that I didn't jettison my bombs over the gunner who hit me." But it was too hazardous to turn back one more time. Buice saw the magnesium bell crank of his left aileron slowly burn away, requiring full aileron and rudder to keep the Skyraider upright. The wing fire shorted out the gun system—now the right gun was firing on its own. Finally, he felt he was going to lose all control of the plane, so at about five hundred feet above the ground and around three hundred knots airspeed he ejected.

Meanwhile, Jack Watts watched Buice's plane go down. It looked to him like he didn't eject in time, and Watts thought, "He didn't get out." Then when he saw Buice's chute blossom, he thought he was descending into the fireball of the Skyraider crash. It was close—Buice landed about fifty yards from the A-1 impact point on a steep hillside. He made a one-point landing, his shoulder smashing into a tree.

Fortunately, Watts was able to direct an Air America UH-1 Huey helicopter, call sign Durex 401, in for the pick up. Buice was taken to Lima Site 36 and then transferred to a U-10 Courier. The Courier was a single-engine short-takeoff-and-land aircraft also flown by Air America pilots. They took Buice to a second dirt field. Finally, a Jolly Green helicopter transported him to the hospital at Udorn.

In the hospital Buice ran into another patient, Lt. Col. William Griffith, who had worked for him in R and D at Albuquerque. Bill Griffith, also a Skyraider pilot from the 602nd, had been shot down eight months earlier and rescued. About seven days before Bill Buice got shot down, Bill Griffith suffered a heart attack. He was now in the hospital and scheduled to be evacuated back to the States later in the day.

The following day Maj. Howard Jennings, also a Skyraider pilot from NKP, was shot down and rescued. He, too, was transported to the hospital at Udorn. Jennings was shot down on his first combat mission. He was attacking bunkers when he was hit coming off a pass. His aircraft also caught fire; he lost control and ejected. Like Buice, he was rescued by an Air America helicopter. Jennings wasn't hurt that bad, but Skyraider pilots were filling up the hospital at Udorn.

Bill Buice spent several days in the hospital finding out that he had a broken collarbone and a crack in the socket of his shoulder. Hoping to return to the 602nd in a month or so, he got Colonel Jones to sign him out on convalescence leave so he could be transported back to the United States on an Air Force tanker. Lt. Col. Mary Carlson, Lt. Col. John Carlson's wife, changed his bandage in Okinawa. Back in the States surgeons evaluated Buice's shoulder and found nerve damage. This severe injury would prevent him from returning to NKP to fly more combat. He was medically grounded.

After an extensive evaluation, Bill Buice retired from the Air Force with a medical disability. He said he was only a combat lead for about four minutes, probably the shortest time on record. For Buice's six weeks in combat, he was awarded the Air Medal, the Distinguished Flying Cross for the rescue of the F-105 pilot, and the Purple Heart. Buice remarked, "That's about as good as you could do in forty-two days."

FUNCTIONAL CHECK FLIGHT

On the day after I participated in the rescue of Roman 2A and Roman 2B in North Vietnam, the squadron operations officer asked me to fly a functional check flight (FCF) on an A-1E. Military regulations called for an FCF to be performed on every Air Force aircraft after an engine change, flight control repair, or other major maintenance. The FCF pilot would take the aircraft up and wring it out to certify that the repair was properly completed and the plane safe for squadron pilots to fly. Because of the extra hazard, flying an FCF was restricted to daylight hours, clear sky, with no ordnance onboard, and only a partial fuel load to keep the aircraft light.

I had flown many FCFs in my Air Force career, starting with the T-33 and F-101B at Hamilton AFB. I also flew FCFs in the T-38, F-104, and F-4 at Edwards AFB. I saw flying an FCF as an opportunity to work more closely with the maintenance troops and also as a way to learn more about the inner mechanical workings of A-1s. But the benefit in flying an FCF in the Skyraider in Southeast Asia was pure and simple comfort. I would fly wearing only my military web belt holding one survival radio and my pistol. I could take off with the canopy open, climb to 10,000 feet over friendly Thailand in just under ten minutes, relax, and cool down from the jungle heat. In comparison, a combat mission required sitting through an exhaustive briefing, preflighting five tons of ordnance, and flying a hot three-and-a-half-hour flight dressed in a mesh survival vest and gloves. I also relished the opportunity to use my test pilot skills to maneuver the Skyraider near its flight limits.

By July 10, I had flown about fifty combat missions and around two hundred flight hours in the A-1, counting the training time at Hurlburt Field. During that time I had grown to enjoy flying a tail-wheeled propeller aircraft.

The Skyraider had many good features. The cockpit seat was designed in such a way that the pilot sat abeam of the leading edge of the wing. A tall pilot could see over the nose while taxiing. In World War II fighters, like the P-47 and P-51, the pilot sat abeam the trailing edge of the wing and could not see straight ahead. This design required him to make *S*-turns to see in front of him.

Sitting in the A-1 cockpit I could see the front portion of all my bombs, rockets, cluster bombs, and napalm extending a few inches in front of the leading edge of the wing. With fifteen weapons stations it was easy to get confused as to what ordnance was on each station and what I had already dropped or was still carrying. If I was in doubt flying the Skyraider, I could simply look out at the leading edge of the wing.

There were six weapon stations on each wing. The innermost station, called the "stub," could carry up to a 750-pound weapon. The stub station and dual 20-mm guns could be used to set up dive angles. If I flew so that my target passed under the left stub my dive angle would be 40 degrees. If the target passed under the inboard gun the angle was 30 degrees and the outboard gun 20 degrees. This procedure worked like a charm; there was nothing fancy about the Skyraider.

It was great to have three radios (UHF, VHF, and FM), although sometimes they were weak and drowned out by the noise of the engine. All Skyraider pilots wore a jet helmet and oxygen mask to help us communicate better with one another and the survivor in the jungle.

The Yankee escape system was a blessing compared to the old manual bailout method used by the Navy. Since rescue missions required us to fly at a very low altitude above the jungle, many pilots were able to eject after they were hit by ground fire only seconds before their A-1 hit the ground.

During an FCF, while flying without any ordnance and a partial fuel load, I could pull two and a half Gs at 140 knots and four Gs at 190 knots. The Skyraider was very maneuverable, although the stick forces were high (eight pounds per G at 250 knots going up to twenty pounds per G at 300 knots).

On the other hand, the Skyraider had some bad characteristics. Both the 300-gallon centerline fuel tank and the 150-gallon stub tank lacked quantity gauges. On a rescue mission, it was important to use the external fuel first and then jettison the tank to reduce drag and increase speed. But if you were flying at low altitude when the tank went empty, the engine would sputter, and it required fast hands to turn the boost pump on and select another tank. In jets, external fuel was always automatically transferred directly to an internal feed tank and then to the engine.

The four 20-mm internal, wing-mounted guns were a continual problem. The wing-mounted guns were always fired as pairs, either the two internal together or the two outboard. Unfortunately, before many of the rounds were fired (200 rounds per gun), one gun would usually jam. Besides losing half your firepower, you would need to use the rudder to counteract the force of just one gun firing. Accuracy was lost with only one gun firing. But the most serious aspect of gun jamming had to do with the ammunition we used. We carried armor-piercing incendiary rounds that had an explosive head. If a shell jammed in the barrel and another round was forced in behind it, the shell would explode. The resulting wing fire was catastrophic—you could literally shoot yourself down!

At Hurlburt we learned how to prevent a torque-roll. If a Skyraider pilot came in to land and suddenly decided to use full engine power to go-around, the torque from the engine would overcome any amount of aileron and rudder deflection a pilot could apply, and the A-1 would roll inverted and crash. Only seventeen days before I flew my first FCF, one of my classmates from Hurlburt, thirty-one-year-old Capt. Richard Russell, returned to land at Pleiku, South Vietnam. He was coming back to base with much of his ordnance still on board and, for some unknown reason, decided to go-around at the last moment. The Skyraider torque-rolled, and Russell was instantly killed.

Although the Skyraider was not difficult to fly, it was difficult to fly well. Unlike a jet with only one throttle, the A-1 had a throttle, prop lever, and mixture control. Care was required to make sure the settings were proper. With fifteen weapon stations and four 20-mm guns, the armament panel and gun sight mil settings needed to be memorized. You flew the Skyraider like you would play a musical instrument in front of an audience, with no sheets of music in front of you. Accomplished musicians don't need to read their music—they know it by heart. The same was true for Skyraider pilots. Between looking outside for ground fire and other aircraft, and physically flying the plane, no time was left to read a checklist.

It was easy to make a mistake flying the A-1. Some pilots bombed off their rocket pods and cluster bomb containers because they forgot to make the proper switch settings. Some went through "dry" (that is, with no weapon release) because they forgot to turn the master arm switch to "On." If they forgot to release a bomb from each wing, some pilots experienced wing drop on pull-up from a bombing pass. Every pilot made mistakes; you hoped to keep from making one at a critical time.

I flew many FCFs in both the side-by-side–seated A-1Es and A-1Gs and the single-seated A-1Hs and A-1Js. Each flight was a pleasure, reminding me of flight test back at Edwards AFB. The most remarkable discovery I made was that at 140 knots I could get one-half more G out of the A-1H and A-1J models by trimming the horizontal tail full nose down and one more G at 300 knots. More G meant a shorter turning distance, something nice to have on a rescue mission. I tucked that information away in my mind for future use.

Also, I found that when there was no ordnance being carried, the H and J models' high-G stall warning was simply mild airframe buffet. This buffet might be overlooked by the pilot in the heat of battle. In a maximum G stalled turn to the left, the A-1 would roll over the top to the right. In a maximum G stalled turn to the right, the A-1 would pitch down and roll to the right to an inverted attitude. These maneuvers could be deadly when flying a rescue mission at low altitude.

Super FAC

After the 602nd moved from Udorn to NKP, we continued to stand Sandy alert and perform Firefly strike missions in Barrel Roll. On July 14, I led a two-ship formation mission flying as Firefly 17 in an A-1H. My wingman was Capt. Donald Dunaway, who had been give the nickname "Christmas Help," a humorous designation indicating he was a part-time warrior. Dunaway was Firefly 18 in a slower A-1E. He was a good old boy from Oklahoma and attended Skyraider training at Hurlburt Field two classes behind me.

Our mission was to fly to the extreme northeast corner of Laos and work with a single-engine Porter aircraft. The Porter, a lightweight spotter plane, was flown by a Thai pilot with a friendly Laotian soldier sitting in the back seat. The plan called for the Laotian soldier to make FM radio contact with soldiers on the ground and then contact us on VHF (very high frequency) to direct us in for an air strike. Once the soldier identified where the Pathet Lao enemy troops were located, he would drop a smoke bomb out the window of the Porter, marking a target for us.

After we expended our bombs and rockets, Dunaway and I planned to fly about fifteen miles northeast and FAC in three flights of F-105s into a *Y* in the road. The CIA intelligence briefer gave me an eight-by-ten-inch black and white photograph showing the *Y* marked in red grease pencil.

Dunaway and I got airborne mid-afternoon and flew for about fifty minutes to our strike area. We had difficulty making VHF radio contact with the Porter pilot. Finally, we spotted him and asked for strike instructions. The

Laotian soldier in the back seat was having a hard time finding the exact target. We were always very careful in defending the Royal Laotian Army when they were battling in close quarters with the Pathet Lao. The last thing we wanted was to get wrong instructions and drop ordnance on friendly troops. This mistake was called a "short-round" by the Air Force and considered a very serious offense. However, we heard the Laotians were reluctant to report when they had been hit, for fear the U.S. government would make an investigation and stop supporting them. Finally, the target was designated, and we dropped our bombs and fired our rockets.

Meanwhile, it was near the time when the first flight of F-105s was scheduled to arrive. The F-105 flights were never late. I was briefed that the first flight of two would be Seabird; each flight was carrying six 750-pound general purpose bombs and two pods of anti-personnel bomblets. Before we finished our last pass with the Porter, Seabird flight called on the UHF radio and asked for information on the strike area. I was listening to both VHF and UHF radios and anxious to complete our weapon drop and head for the new target area. My A-1H could outrun Dunaway's A-1E, so I pulled the power back and took another look at the black and white photo with the *Y* marked on it. Time was running short; I wanted to spot the target before the F-105 flight arrived.

Usually the F-105s were fuel limited when they arrived in the strike area with a heavy load of high-drag bombs. They wanted to get in and out fast and return to the tanker. I divided my attention between the photo, the road we were flying over that led to the *Y*, and looking up and to the right, hoping to get a visual sighting of the F-105s. My Skyraider was humming along about 180 knots true airspeed—about three miles a minute—five minutes to the new strike area.

Seabird flight lead asked me my position just as I spotted the *Y* in the road. Without hesitating I rolled in, fired a white phosphorus marking rocket, and pulled off to the south. I cleared the flight in, telling them there were no friendlies in the area and to expect guns as large as 37-mm to fire on them. My warning was standard military strike information—I had not seen 37-mm ground fire in this area before.

Seabird flight put their ordnance right on the target, and to my surprise enemy 37-mm guns blazed away. Grayish-white puffs of smoke filled the air as each F-105 beat up the target. We had quite a battle going on. Seabird expended all their ordnance in just nine minutes and headed back to the tanker. Then, Ozark flight of two F-105s came in with the same ordnance and in eight minutes got 50 percent of their weapons on target. The gunners were firing at each aircraft on every pass. We had a real fight going on. Fortunately, I didn't have to mark the target again; I must have caught them by surprise the first time. The Skyraider was no match for a 37-mm gun.

I told Dunaway that we must have found a large truck park or supply area the Pathet Lao felt they must defend. Finally, the CIA briefers found a lucrative target. The Marlin flight came in and, just like Seabird and Ozark, really smashed the target. On their last pass they received less ground fire. We had really beat up on the enemy this time, and no one got hit—a real successful mission.

After the three flights of F-105s departed back to the tanker, Dunaway and I climbed to 9,000 feet and turned back south to NKP. I contacted Cricket, an EC-130 Airborne Command and Control aircraft, to report the location and results of the jet strikes.

Our squadron commander, Colonel Jones, was flying on a Sandy orbit monitoring the progress of our strikes. When he heard me give the location of the strikes and bomb damage assessment, he questioned me. He believed I had given the wrong coordinates. I rechecked the Y on the photograph and the target coordinates also written in red grease pencil. I thought the information I gave to Cricket was correct and confirmed my report to Cricket and Colonel Jones. Colonel Jones asked me to check in with him after I landed and debriefed.

About two hours later, after giving the strike information to our intelligence section at NKP, I met Colonel Jones in the squadron flight planning room. We looked at a wall map of northern Laos and at my photograph. Colonel Jones was absolutely correct—I had put the jets in on different coordinates than I reported. As a matter of fact, in my rush to find the Y in the road and make visual contact with the first flight of F-105s, I had flown over the first Y and struck the second Y. This second Y in the road was a couple of miles inside the ten-mile buffer zone in Laos next to North Vietnam. At the time, all American attack aircraft were restricted from bombing North Vietnam because of a formal bombing halt agreed to between the two governments. So a ten-mile buffer zone was created over Laos to prevent accidental overflight of North Vietnam. By mistake I had put three flights of jets carrying eighteen of the huge 750-pound bombs and six pods of cluster bombs in the buffer zone. The Pathet Lao knew of the bombing halt and that strikes in the buffer zone were off limits. They were probably surprised we struck them. Colonel Jones said, "What the hell, they deserved it for being in a neutral country!" We both laughed and walked off. As far as the official Air Force records were concerned, the F-105s struck the original pre-briefed targets.

Three days later, the CIA reported to me that the F-105s destroyed 300 Chinese Communists soldiers, three AAA guns, twenty gun crews, and all the Pathet Lao officers in the area. It was the most successful strike ever conducted in Barrel Roll.

Colonel Jones and Don Dunaway always called me Super FAC after that mission.

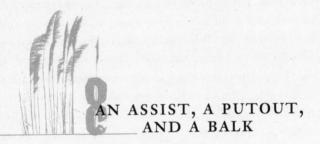

AN ASSIST, A PUTOUT, AND A BALK

In mid-July I was flying as lead on a morning two-ship Firefly strike mission over the central part of the PDJ in northern Laos. After flying combat missions for two months, it seemed to me that the war was going nowhere. Our Skyraiders would destroy and silence a few gun positions one day only to have one of our aircraft hit in the same area a few days later. I thought it was a war without purpose and direction.

Just as I released ordnance over the target in a steep dive-bombing pass and started my pull-up, the engine began to run rough. Leveling off, I attempted to add power, but the engine backfired badly. My best guess at the time was that I had probably taken a hit in the engine from ground fire. The cylinder head temperature went to full hot. I knew I was at least a hundred miles from my home base at NKP. With only partial power available, I could not maintain level flight. The aircraft was slowly dropping. I couldn't make it home.

Approximately twenty miles west of my position was a field called Lima Site 2, located on the western corner of the PDJ. Lima Site 2 had a narrow east-west dirt landing strip used by the CIA and Laotian military. It was surrounded by enemy territory. I headed west.

Recently, one of my squadron mates, Smilin' Jack Watts, experienced engine failure and attempted an emergency landing on that dirt strip. It was late in the afternoon, and the sun was just above the horizon. Watts had never landed on the strip before and set up a dead-stick landing pattern (a landing without power) so as to land heading to the west. Engine oil was leaking over the front windscreen, causing him to have great difficulty seeing the landing field. On final approach the sun was directly in his face. It was only because of his expert skill in handling the Skyraider that was he able to successfully land on the near end of the strip. Unfortunately, the strip had a big hump in the middle, and with the sun in his eyes and the engine oil blocking his view, Watts thought he was going to run off the end of the strip. If he went off, the Skyraider would probably nose over, turn upside down, and he would be trapped in the cockpit. No fire or rescue units were stationed at Lima sites; he would have to take care of himself. Trying to avoid this danger, he retracted the landing gear, and the aircraft skidded to a stop with dust flying behind him. He opened the canopy and stood on his seat cushion. To his great surprise, when the dust cleared he found out that about half of the strip was still in front of him.

Capt. Ronald Furtak had a somewhat similar experience. Furtak was flying a strike mission near Lima Site 2 when a red chip light came on. A chip light indicated that small metal parts of the engine could be coming loose and attaching themselves to a magnetic plug in the base of the engine block. This light was usually the first sign of impending engine failure. Furtak pulled the power back and headed for Lima Site 2. He did not jettison his ordnance, but set up for a dead-stick landing. Furtak came in hot (high speed), passed up the first third of the dirt strip in a full skid, and finally set the Skyraider down. He got on the brakes and just barely stopped. Two Raven FACs landed just after Furtak. They were so short of rockets that they removed them from Furtak's aircraft and kept them. He didn't care; his A-1 might never fly again anyhow. He got a ride in an Army C-7 Caribou back to Udorn. An Air Force maintenance crew arrived to fix the Skyraider engine. After repair, one of the airmen, who was doing an engine run up, got a stuck throttle, and the plane jumped the chocks. The airman jumped over the side; the A-1 ran off the side of the strip and burned.

Having heard the details of Jack Watts's and Ron Furtak's close calls, I very carefully looked over the dirt strip from the air. I had the advantage of the sun over my left shoulder and a clear windscreen. My wingman contacted Crown, the C-130 Hercules airborne command and control ship, reported my airborne emergency, and asked them to initiate a rescue effort. He joined in formation and helped me set up a partial-power, dead-stick landing pattern.

As I touched down on the end of the dirt strip, the field did indeed look short and narrow, but I applied brakes and easily slowed down. I looked for a place to park the Skyraider. I found a flat spot off to the side, taxied over, and shut down the engine. My wingman radioed he was heading back home to NKP, and I saw him fly away. I stood up in the cockpit, took off my helmet, and watched him fly off to the southeast. I thought to myself, "This is going to be a long day."

Within a few moments, a man in a jeep drove up to the side of my aircraft and parked. A white-skinned, grizzled-looking male in his late fifties, dressed in dirty rumpled clothes, got out of the jeep. I was quite apprehensive knowing I was in territory surrounded by the enemy and on my own. The man spoke English and indicated he was with the CIA. Even though it was only late morning, he seemed to be a little incoherent and maybe even intoxicated. My first thought was that living in a remote area like this, behind enemy lines, it might be smart to get paid every day. You wouldn't know if you would live through the day. Maybe he converted his pay to alcohol every day, or maybe he was, in fact, "paid in drink," meaning he received payment in alcohol rather than cash.

He asked me if I wanted to take a tour of the airfield. I was reluctant to leave my Skyraider, but, on the other hand, I felt I might be safer some distance away from the plane. Certainly the Jolly Green rescue helicopter wouldn't be able to pick me up for at least ten or fifteen minutes, if then. As we drove around the dirt strip, I saw aircraft that had crashed and been pushed off to the side. Laotian men and women in bright red and black clothing were squatting some distance away; all were watching me. They were not in any type of military uniform, at least nothing that I could recognize. On the other hand, I would easily be identified as an American pilot by my flying suit and equipment. How would I recognize the enemy? My jeep driver's clothing began to take on a more favorable appearance.

But before long I heard that wonderful sound of helicopter blades spinning in the air, *wop-wop-wop*. A Jolly Green landed on the dirt strip. I gathered my helmet, maps, strike photos, checklist, survival vest, and gas mask, and jumped aboard. Soon we were airborne and flying south to the nearest base: Udorn. I lay on a bunk bed in the back of the chopper, put on my flight helmet, and plugged into the intercom. The chopper pilots wanted to know what had happened, and I explained my engine problem. They contacted Crown and reported to them that the Skyraider pilot was safely aboard with no injuries.

Finally, I began to relax. The day might actually be short and maybe even enjoyable. I imagined myself at the Udorn Officers' Club having a late lunch, stopping in at the Base Exchange for some shopping, then catching a flight home on the C-130 Hercules, which circled all five Thailand bases. No sweat, I thought, another combat mission in my logbook. One more day closer to going home. "Only 159 days left, but who's counting?" was the phrase in vogue at the time. Don't kid yourself, we all counted the days remaining to rotation back to the good old U.S.

As the chopper crossed the Mekong River, separating Laos from Thailand, the NKP command post called the Jolly Green crew on their UHF radio. The wing headquarters had scheduled a C-123 aircraft to fly a group of Skyraider mechanics and tools to Lima Site 2 to attempt to repair my broken aircraft. If the Skyraider couldn't be repaired by sunset, the crew would be prepared to blow up the plane to prevent it from falling into the hands of the enemy. It would take several hours to round up the resources, so they didn't know when the plane would actually arrive. The command post ordered the Jolly Green to reverse course and fly back to Lima Site 2. A pilot would be needed to fly the Skyraider back to Thailand if it could be repaired. I was the pilot.

The Jolly Green helicopter landed back at Lima Site 2. I assumed the crew would shut down their engines and stand rescue alert there. They informed me that it was too dangerous to leave the chopper on the ground, and they needed to be airborne in case another rescue was required. They took off, heading southeast as my wingman had done several hours before. This was going to be a long day after all.

Hours passed. I waited for the C-123 to arrive. The sun moved west across the sky, and I was still far from my home base. I got out my .38 caliber revolver and rechecked the six shells in the chambers. Sitting under the wing of my aircraft, I wondered if the CIA-looking guy might have been a Skyraider pilot who had also made an emergency landing there some time ago and never got back home.

The C-123 finally arrived with five mechanics and a mixture of tools. The repair was actually quite simple. Evidently, a couple of magneto leads had come loose in the ignition system. Within a few minutes, I started the engine and the sound of the huge Wright Cyclone was as sweet as I had ever heard it. Just as the sun set, I got airborne. It was easy to find my way home, just head the same direction that my wingman and the Jolly Green had gone many, many hours before.

That evening, back at NKP, I was apprised that my Jolly Green rescue crew was expecting me at the Officers' Club for the standard rescue party, as it was the custom for every person rescued by the Jolly Green and Sandy force to buy a round of drinks for all involved in their rescue. Tradition called for the survivor to be lifted in the air by the rescue crew and thrown over the bar. A three-foot-tall Jolly Green Giant cloth doll stood on the counter behind the bar. Its hands held an eight-inch-square white-plastic board on which the total number of aircrew rescued by the Jolly Greens was written in black grease pencil. The survivor would erase the old number and print the new to the applause and celebration of all in attendance.

I found my Jolly Green rescue crew at the bar. They were having a good time and talking about my rescue. I bought a round of drinks for them and explained, as Paul Harvey would say, "the rest of the story." We finished several rounds, and they were ready to throw me over the bar. But I wasn't planning to go over the bar. It was my view that the Jolly Greens should not get credit for a rescue, since I was returned to the same place I was originally rescued. They explained that they had picked me up in enemy country and transported me over the Mekong River to friendly country. That was all that was required for an official Air Force rescue. It wasn't their fault that the command post ordered them to return me to Laos. To make my point, I said if we were playing baseball they would be lucky to get an assist; it was definitely not a putout.

Nevertheless, I was lifted in the air. Unlike previous survivors who gladly went along with this tradition, I resisted. We struggled for some time. I was finally thrown over the bar, but two of the Jolly Greens who I held tightly in my arms also crashed over the bar with me. In the process, I struck my forehead on the corner of the wooden bar and ended up with a deep gash that started to bleed. It was unlike any rescue celebration conducted at NKP at that time. Maybe ever.

The injury to my forehead left a scar that remains to this day. Years later my two young sons asked me about the scar. I simply said I got hurt in the war. I never explained to them what actually happened to me. Vietnam was the kind of war you couldn't explain to anyone.

HELLBORN 20

On July 24, 1968, I flew an FCF on a single-seat A-1J, serial number 142033. Getting to fly a single-seat model on a noncombat flight was a real joy and a break from my daily routine. The A-1J model was the last of the 3,180 Skyraiders built at the Douglas Aircraft Company plant in Long Beach, California. Only seventy-one copies of the J model were manufactured; they were streamlined and fast—I liked that model the best. My personal aircraft, the one nicknamed *Sock It To 'Em*, was also a J model (serial number 142029) and flew like a dream.

When I returned to the hooch, my roommate, Maj. Alan Hale, was unhappy. He was stocky with a blond crew cut and hardly had a neck, so the squadron pilots nicknamed him "the Brick." We both arrived at the 602nd in May when the squadron was stationed at Udorn. Each of us had flown about fifty combat missions in the time we had been in Southeast Asia and thought we were starting to pull our weight in the squadron.

Hale was disappointed that he had not had a chance to be on a rescue yet. He said that I was lucky to have flown on both the Streetcar 304 and Roman 2 A and B rescues. Hale thought he might not get the opportunity to rescue anyone during his twelve-month tour. I knew that with the number of Air Force and Navy aircraft being shot down on a daily basis, Hale would get his turn sooner or later. I explained to him that I found the rescue missions to be very hazardous compared to our Firefly strike missions and didn't think a pilot would survive many of them. Hale was scheduled for Sandy alert the next day.

Late that afternoon a Marine Corps A-6 Intruder from Marine Air Group 12 at Chu Lai in South Vietnam was flying an armed reconnaissance mission in Route Pack 1 (North Vietnam was divided into six route packs, starting with number 1 in the south, with number 6 by Hanoi). The aircraft, Hellborn 20, was hit by 37-mm antiaircraft guns, and the crew were forced to eject. Both crew members successfully ejected, and pilot Maj. Curtis Lawson, Hellborn 20A, noted a good chute on his observer, Capt. Paul Brown, Hellborn 20B. As they both descended, Major Lawson observed Captain Brown land in a populated area and assumed he was immediately captured, as they never established voice contact on their UHF survival radios. Major Lawson landed in the Dai River, approximately three miles east of the intersection of Routes 101 and 103. This position was thirty-two miles north of the DMZ (demilitarized zone) that separated North Vietnam from South Vietnam. The river was about 150 feet wide and ran in an east-west direction with a village on both the north and south sides of it.

Major Lawson swam fifty feet to the east, pushed his parachute below the water, and concealed himself under the trees on the north bank of the river. Misty 41, an F-100 FAC, was first on the scene and established radio contact with him. Because of darkness, Major Lawson was told to bed down for the night; a first-light effort was planned for the next day.

The next morning my roommate Al Hale took off before sunrise as Sandy 1. His wingman was Charlie Flynn, flying as Sandy 2. Because the survivor's position was closer to Da Nang than NKP, two Jolly Green helicopters from the 37th Aerospace Rescue and Recovery Squadron were scrambled that morning from Da Nang. To support the Sandy rescue aircraft, three A-1s from Da Nang, using the call sign Spad, were launched about 10 a.m. Flying the A-1s were Majors Donald Dineen, Gene McGinnis, and John Hayes. Al Hale asked the three Spad pilots to orbit with the two Jollys and hold about five miles west of the survivor's position. Flying the low helicopter with the call sign of Jolly Green 31 was aircraft commander Maj. Charles Wicker with copilot Maj. Robert Booth, flight engineer S. Sgt. John Enriquez, and PJ Sgt. Steven Northern.

While Hale was communicating with Major Lawson and trying to determine his location on the river, two Misty FACs were putting jet strikes on enemy gun positions every five minutes. One Misty flew over the Gulf of

Tonkin and refueled three times on a tanker before he ran out of ordnance and returned home.

Hale and Flynn found Major Lawson's position in the river and started shooting at enemy automatic weapons and small-arms fire coming from the nearby village. During this time, Hale's Skyraider was hit badly by ground fire. He pulled out of the area and attempted to make it to Da Nang, since it was closer than NKP. Charlie Flynn followed Hale southbound and joined up in case he had to extract from his stricken A-1. Hale nursed the heavily damaged Skyraider, barely able to keep it airborne. He turned over the on-scene commander responsibility to other Sandys that had recently taken off from NKP. Hale instructed the Spads and Jolly Greens, "Go home and have lunch." Major Dineen remarked to himself, "What a war, you can go home, have lunch, and return!" Hale thought there were too many enemy guns in the survivor's position to attempt a rescue very soon; more strike aircraft were needed to soften up the area.

Al Hale made a crash landing at Da Nang and was lucky to survive uninjured; his A-1 was severely damaged. Hale had wanted to get some action on a hostile rescue and got more than he asked for. Fortunately, Flynn was flying a side-by-side A-1E, so Hale came back to NKP sitting in the right-hand seat.

The next Sandy to assume command of the rescue was Maj. Edwin Conley Jr., and his wingman was Ron Furtak. Conley was from Boston and served part of his tour in Southeast Asia flying F-102A Deuce interceptors from Don Muang Airport in Bangkok. He had flown in the F-102A only a few months before becoming a Sandy at NKP.

Ed Conley hardly ate anything; he was thin as a rail. No one ever saw him eat breakfast, lunch, or dinner. Conley coined a phrase, "There's a loaf in every can." What he meant was that there was the nutritional value of a loaf of bread in every can of beer. Most likely Conley survived on just beer.

For several hours the fast movers worked on the large 37-mm guns, and Conley and Furtak tried to suppress the smaller guns in the village on the north side of the Dai River.

Ron Furtak, nicknamed the "Polish Air Pirate" because of his Polish heritage, was from New Jersey. He had flown the drone version of the F-104 Starfighter at Eglin AFB, Florida prior to his checkout in the A-1 at Hurlburt. Furtak was in the class before me. He was tall and slight of build, well over six feet, and one of the best pilots in the squadron.

On account of darkness approaching, Conley decided to attempt a rescue. By then about 120 strike sorties had been put in around Major Lawson's position. Ed Conley, Ron Furtak, and two other Sandys met the Jolly Green 31 over the Rockpile, a cone-shaped hill made up of huge rocks that could easily be seen from the air. The Jolly Green crew removed their chest parachutes and put on flak jackets. Major Wicker asked for heavy fire suppression by the escort aircraft and planned to use his chopper's M-60 guns. As Jolly Green 31 descended to less than 1,000 feet above the ground, both the flight engineer and PJ started firing from the side of the chopper. The rescue copilot observed heavy automatic weapons fire coming from the village. One of the Sandys immediately suppressed that enemy fire. Major Wicker called for the survivor to pop his smoke when the chopper was approximately one and a half miles out. The PJ observed a large number of enemy troops in ditches as they passed over the village south of the river.

During one extremely low firing pass, Ron Furtak's engine quit. At the time he was using fuel from his 300-gallon centerline tank. He thought he had run out of fuel, so he pulled up, switched to an internal tank, and put the fuel boost pump on. The engine caught on; if it hadn't, Furtak would have been down in the jungle too.

The Jolly Green copilot observed smoke on the north bank of the river and proceeded toward it. Just then a Sandy pilot called, "You're going the wrong way, he is in the river behind you!" The Jolly crew made a steep 180-degree turn and spotted the survivor's smoke. The PJ and flight engineer fired their M-60s just above the riverbanks to keep the enemies' heads down. With the survivor still in the river after almost a day, the Jolly crew dragged the penetrator over to him, and he grabbed it. As soon as Major Lawson was on board, the Jolly took off, staying just above the water.

Meanwhile Captain Furtak's radio, which was working intermittently, finally quit completely. Without voice communication with Conley, his Sandy lead, Furtak assumed the Sandys would escort the Jollys back to Da Nang. When he finally found Conley, he was heading west, aimed at NKP. Furtak joined in close formation and with hand signals requested Conley to look over his plane for damage. Conley reported that Furtak's centerline fuel tank had been blown apart by an enemy shell. All the fuel had drained out—no wonder his engine quit. Conley and Furtak safely landed at NKP with very little fuel remaining. Conley was awarded a Silver Star for the mission and Furtak the Distinguished Flying Cross.

The Jolly Green helicopter flew back to Da Nang with Don Dineen's flight escorting them. Dineen met Major Lawson when he got off the helicopter and said that after twenty hours in the water, he was wrinkled like a prune— but a very happy prune. Lawson's backseater, Captain Brown, Hellborn 20B, was captured by the North Vietnamese and repatriated on March 14, 1973, as part of Operation Homecoming.

Boa Constrictor

As it got to the middle of August, I was due a couple of days off from flying combat missions. This was called combat time off, or CTO. Every six weeks a pilot was given about three days of rest. I had been gone from the United States for about four months and had flown sixty combat missions and just over two hundred flying hours.

In early June, when I got my first break from combat, I flew as copilot in an O-2 FAC aircraft looking for Ed Leonard, who I had seen get shot down over Tchepone. Although I spent hours looking for a parachute or other survival signs, nothing could be seen of Leonard. Seventy-five days had passed now and no information surfaced on Leonard. It didn't look good.

Some of the Skyraider pilots in the squadron suggested that I fly space-available to Bangkok in one of the C-130 cargo aircraft that circled the five Royal Thai Air Force Bases each day. Shopping was much better in Bangkok than the small town of Nakhon Phanom. The trip to NKP was a dusty 30-minute ride in a school bus. Only 10 percent of the squadron members could be off base at the same time, and a 10 p.m. curfew was in effect. There was not much to see in NKP. In many respects the airfield there looked like a prison from the air. A tall metal fence surrounded the perimeter of the field and Air Force military police patrolled the area to prevent infiltration by the enemy. Spotlights were mounted on tall poles. I felt like I was trapped in a cage, unable to get away from NKP even for a few hours. I only went into town a couple of times, and it wasn't worth the time and effort. I looked forward to escaping both the mental and physical rigors of the war.

In downtown Bangkok there was an American officers club called the Chao Pia Hotel. There I could bed down for only a couple of bucks, watch TV, and enjoy a hot steak. When I got to the hotel and unloaded my gear from a zippered military B-4 bag, I found that my Argus C-3 camera was missing. Some place along my travels it had been stolen.

I was told that a major attraction in Bangkok was the zoo. Guys in the squadron said I should go to the zoo and see the boa constrictor. It had become a custom for Skyraider pilots to visit the zoo and get a photograph of themselves with a boa constrictor wrapped around their body. The boa was a special attraction located outside the entrance to the zoo, run by an entrepreneur not associated with the official zoo.

In mid-afternoon as the hot Asian sun beat down, I found myself standing about ten feet in front of the infamous boa held by his caretaker. A large sign nearby described the Southeast Asian version of the boa. The boa was a nonpoisonous tropical snake that lived completely independent of water. Its brown and tan color provided excellent camouflage, allowing it to wait in concealment until prey approached. "Or an American pilot crawling through the jungle," I thought. In Asia the boa could reach lengths up to eighteen feet and live twenty-five to thirty years. Some lived in underground holes while others lived in trees. Boas were nocturnal hunters of mammals, birds, waterfowl, frogs, fish, as well as lizards and other reptiles. Nothing about hunting downed airmen, but the sign looked old.

The boa killed by constriction. The snake closed in on its prey and struck suddenly with a wide, gaping mouth, seizing the prey in its jaw. At the same instant, the boa coiled its body around the victim and immobilized it. The boa's tightening coils prevented the animal from breathing, and it soon died.

Though it was fascinating to view the snake from a distance, I found it difficult to move in closer. While not frightened of snakes, I was certainly uncomfortable around them. Years earlier, during Air Force flight school in Texas, my class spent a couple of days at a survival camp. A student pilot killed a rattlesnake, skinned it, and placed it in boiling water. After it had been processed for about four hours, I ate a small portion of white meat. At that point it didn't look like a snake. It was cut up into small pieces, was kind of flaky, and tasted like chicken to me.

After watching the boa for a few more minutes, I decided it would be easier to get my photo after I consumed a beer. Thai men are big beer drinkers by Asian standards, and their favorite is Singha beer. The beer was produced locally and packed one hell of a punch.

A popular place in Bangkok was the Thai beer garden. Thais enjoyed drinking beer outdoors any time of the year and an outdoor bar was across the street from the zoo. I sat in a wicker chair, relaxed, and thought about the eight months remaining in my year tour. What thrills and spills lay ahead of me? The first Singha beer went down easy; I ordered another. In many respects wrapping a boa around myself would be like experiencing another danger, another flight over the Ho Chi Minh Trail, another chance to get hacked in this crazy year of war. It would be like flying over known gun locations at low altitude and speed and daring the gunners to shoot, like throwing all caution to the wind. I had been lucky so far, hit only once in my sixty missions. Maybe I was living on borrowed time; maybe my luck would soon run out.

I paid my bill and was ready to face this unknown danger. In a few moments I found that two Singha beers were not enough for me to get a photo taken. The boa appeared larger than it had been a few minutes earlier and looked even hungrier.

I returned to the beer garden for another Singha beer, another reason to be wild and reckless, another way to talk myself into being foolish and stupid. As I sat there and thought, I realized I had to fly combat missions because I was a trained military pilot serving the Air Force and my country. Years before I had held up my right hand as an officer and promised to defend and protect our nation. I knew I needed to support my Skyraider squadron and all the pilots who flew with me. I still wanted to rescue every pilot shot down in the snake-infested and enemy-controlled jungle; it was the only mission that made any sense in this screwed-up war.

I didn't really need a photo with a boa constrictor wrapped around my body. And to this day I still don't have one.

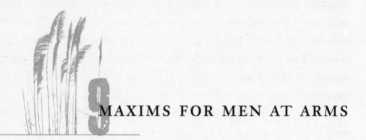

MAXIMS FOR MEN AT ARMS

Winston Churchill once said, "Nothing in life is so exhilarating as to be shot at and missed." Churchill was rarely wrong, but he was in this case. To be shot at and to get hit is more exhilarating.

It was another supremely hot evening in the middle of August. Several of the other squadron pilots and I were drinking a few beers in the Sandy Box. We were sitting on bar stools and, as usual, discussing rescue tactics and exchanging both facts and rumors about the state of the war. This wasn't unusual; we did the same every evening. We never talked about politics, women, or automobiles. All we ever talked about was the Skyraider and the pilots who flew it.

Our squadron commander, Lt. Col. William A. Jones, was sleeping in an overstuffed chair in the corner of the room. Bill Jones had taken over as commanding officer on the first of July when we moved from Udorn to NKP. Forty-six-year-old Jones was originally from Warsaw, Virginia, and was a 1945 graduate of the U.S. Military Academy at West Point. Jones had logged over 7,000 hours of flying time in bombers, fighters, and transport aircraft during tours in England, Spain, Germany, and now Asia. Prior to the Skyraider he flew the six-engine Boeing B-47 in Strategic Air Command.

When we were stationed at Udorn, we played handball together. He was a good player and very competitive. It was so hot on the court at Udorn that the facilities office installed an overhead fan to keep the air moving. Unfortunately, the blades moved so slowly you could see each one circling above us. It wasn't very effective but it was the best we could get, considering we were in a war zone. The floorboards were very uneven; as a player you didn't know which way the ball would bounce. But this unevenness didn't really make any difference; we played for the exercise and a chance to forget about combat for a few moments.

There was no handball court at NKP for the colonel to play on. As a matter of fact, he didn't have time to the exercise anymore. He now spent many hours in the squadron building working on administrative duties, hours more inspecting the maintenance activities down on the flight line, and he also flew combat missions most days. He usually attended our parties, although frequently he showed up late. With his busy daily schedule, I was sure he was dead tired. Sleeping in the chair that night at the Sandy Box was rest well deserved.

The door to the Sandy Box was left open so a large floor fan could circulate as much of the humid night air as possible. Bugs and insects were out in full force every evening in Thailand and were flying freely in and out of the Sandy Box. Out of the corner of my eye, I thought I saw a bug go through the large fan we placed near the door. The bug was about three inches long and was crawling around on the floor in front of the fan. I didn't think a bug could go through a fan without injury and brought this to the attention of the other pilots. They concurred, so I got up and took a closer look. The bug appeared normal—the wings were intact, and its six legs were moving it across the floor.

Since I thought the bug went through the fan, the other pilots suggested I release the bug behind the fan and let it make another trip through the whirling blades. As I released the bug, it got sucked into the rushing air and made a *thunk* as it came out the other side. This time it was missing one complete wing and was fluttering in a circle on the floor. Evidence seemed to indicate that a bug could not go through a fan uninjured.

Some of the Skyraider pilots were convinced a bug could go through a fan uninjured and bet a beer on it. We would bet a beer on anything. So each of us went back to our room, got a flashlight, and started looking in the weeds next to the hooches for likely candidates. Some selected small fighter-type bugs, and others selected husky bomber-type bugs. A line formed behind the fan and each pilot had a chance to launch his bug.

After we had consumed a few more beers, the scoring system seemed to break down. Few bugs escaped the trip through the fan uninjured, but a couple did. One of the more sober Skyraider pilots took a psychological approach to our fun and games and suggested that we A-1 pilots were similar to the bugs. In a sense we, too, flew through a fan of ground fire each day and sometimes through the luck of the draw came out the other side unscathed—but sometimes we also lost a wing and crashed. Colonel Jones slept through the bug trials.

Several days later he asked me to come over to his room in the hooch. That night I took a shower, put on a clean shirt and slacks, and walked to his room. Some squadron commanders had a room to themselves and lived quite comfortably. Jones turned down a private room and split quarters with Tom Campbell so that his room could be used as the Sandy Box. I knocked on his door; it opened and there stood Colonel Jones with a pitcher of martinis and a devilish grin. I sat down and Jones filled two glasses.

"Would you like to try the world's greatest martini?" he asked. Actually, I didn't really care for the taste of a martini. Years before, when I was in college, I believe I drank three on a Saturday afternoon while watching a football game on an old black and white TV. I still felt dizzy the following Monday. Martinis were not my drink of choice.

But when the squadron commander of our distinguished 602nd Sandy outfit offered me a drink, I planned to drink it. We toasted our squadron and then sat down to talk. It felt totally incongruous to be sipping a martini in a nice room, sitting in relative comfort, only an hour or so flight away from the Ho Chi Minh Trail. Unlike Army soldiers who spent their year walking through the jungle, sleeping and eating in the open, vulnerable to enemy action at any moment, Skyraider pilots were like a special team in football. One moment we were safe on the sideline and the next moment we could be flying low and slow over the jungle on a rescue mission.

Colonel Jones got to the point. He said, "I read your request for resignation from the Air Force today." While I was thinking of a proper response, he added, "You're not mad about losing at handball, are you?" We both laughed and I explained that it was now the time in my tour to work with the Air Force personnel office and put in my forecast for assignment after my year at NKP. The Air Force suggested I return to Hurlburt as a Skyraider instructor. While flying rescue missions in the Skyraider were exciting and rewarding when we pulled another guy out of the jungle, I wasn't interested in flying the A-1 in a peacetime training organization. My wife Jan suggested that I ask for an assignment in Europe; she had never been overseas like most of the other Air Force wives she knew. But, in fact, the only duty I wanted was to return to flight test either at Edwards or Eglin. Since I had not made arrangements in advance for either of these locations, I was told by military personnel that the odds of getting either assignment were slim.

Finally, I came to the conclusion that I might have more opportunities as a civilian test pilot than I would staying in the military. I always considered myself more of an aviator than a military officer anyway. I joined the Air Force to fly, not to go through all the devious steps it took to continually get promoted.

I told Colonel Jones I had thought long and hard about getting out of the Air Force after ten years of military service. I explained to him that I had previously gotten a copy of the official military form to resign, filled it in, and walked down the hall to his office. He was not in at the time so I placed the form in his "In" basket and walked out. Back in the hallway I had second thoughts, went back in and retrieved the form. For several minutes I reevaluated my thinking, realizing I would be returning to the States married, with two small children, and unemployed. That thought seemed as risky as flying combat over Laos. But I really thought becoming a civilian was the right choice and the best decision for me. So I returned to Colonel Jones's office once again and replaced the form in his "In" box. This time I walked out and never looked back.

Jones had served twenty-five years of active duty—he loved and respected the Air Force. He tried to talk me out of my decision, but I had already made up my mind.

He poured another drink. We started talking about the Skyraider and went to dinner at the Officers Club. He approved my resignation from the Air Force; I would leave military service after I completed my combat tour and returned to the States in April of 1969, seven months in the future.

It was a true pleasure for me to join Colonel Jones that evening. Even though I was just a captain and he a colonel, he was a good friend and a gutsy, determined combat pilot. We had flown nine missions together in the last four months, beat up some enemy targets, and I looked forward to flying with him again. Back in July we had flown an attack on a Lima site dirt runway that had been overrun by the enemy. Because it was a hazardous target, our squadron tactic called for us to drop napalm in a dive rather than a low-level delivery. I put my napalm smack dab on the center of the strip, and the Raven FAC gave me bomb damage assessment as a runway-burn. Colonel Jones laughed over the air and got quite a kick out of the FAC's comment. He couldn't wait to debrief our flight with the intelligence officers back at NKP; he was certain no one had ever claimed a runway-burn in this screwy war.

On the early morning of September 1, 1968, just a couple of days after our conversation about my retirement, Colonel Jones got a scramble order to fly A-1H, serial number 139738, on his 98th combat mission. The aircraft was named *Miss Illini* (the nickname for Illinois, pronounced "A-line-I") by Colonel Jones's roommate, Tom Campbell. Campbell's brother was a flyer in World War II and had used the name on his aircraft. Tom wanted to keep up the family tradition.

Colonel Jones and his wingman, Capt. Paul Meeks, were off to find and try to rescue an F-4C Phantom crew. The Phantom was down about twenty-two miles west-northwest of Dong Hoi, North Vietnam. Flying as Sandy 3 was Maj. Eugene McCormack Jr., and his wingman, Sandy 4, was Lt. Col. John Carlson. Sandy 3 and 4 would escort the two Jolly Greens to a safe area where they would orbit, waiting for Colonel Jones to call them in for the rescue.

As on-scene commander, Colonel Jones's first duty was to establish radio contact with the crew of the F-4 that was assigned to the 555th Tactical Fighter Squadron Triple Nickel at Udorn. Shortly after Colonel Jones and Sandy 2 entered North Vietnam, they established radio contact with another flight of Phantoms, code named Liner. Liner flight was in voice contact with Carter 2A, a Captain Wilson, the pilot of the downed aircraft. The second crewman had already been captured. Carter 2A had not been spotted yet, and his exact location needed to be determined.

Skyraider pilot Major Jimmy W. Kilbourne later interviewed Jones and published an account of this mission in a book called *Escape and Evasion.* He wrote:

"LINER was able to talk to the survivor," Jones later recalled. "I heard him a little bit on my way in and he thought he knew where the survivor was. LINER flew over, wiggling his wings [meaning, "Can you see me?"], but it turned out this was off about eight miles, and we got no more contact for almost an hour. We wasted a considerable amount of time—almost an hour—searching in the wrong area." Jones finally did spot two parachutes, which turned out to be flare chutes.

Later, an F-100 "super FAC" located a survivor about eight miles further to the east, and vectored the two [Sandys] into the area. They searched the site, getting a few brief contacts with him.

The contact on the UHF radio did not come through very strong to Colonel Jones, either because the survivor's emergency radio battery was weak, or because of the Skyraider's engine noise in his helmet, or because Jones had difficulty hearing on the radio. All of us who flew with him knew he had a hard time hearing radio communication, either because of his age or as a result of the years he was exposed to the sound of jet engines. Jones tried to hone in on this survivor but had no success. Kilbourne described it:

It was on one of these passes that he came within range of the well-concealed antiaircraft artillery position that gave him his first blast of fire for the day.

Jones began his search again, after deciding the first encounter had done no serious damage to his A-1H. The weather, terrain, and hostile fire were all bad, almost impossible. Abrupt karst formations rose from 600 to 2,000 feet above the valley floor. The higher peaks jutted up into the scattered-to-broken cloud deck. Jones was forced to operate his heavily laden, slow, propeller-driven A-1H in the narrow valleys and around the peaks—always subject to the dozens of hostile gun positions ringing the survivor's position.

Jones remained in the area, making pass after pass, realizing that he must find Carter 2A's precise location if he was to be rescued. He also knew his Skyraider had been hit, though he could not determine where it was damaged. As he continued to search, the other Sandys and jets began calling out enemy positions in his vicinity.

Suddenly, Captain Wilson radioed that there was an A-1 directly overhead. Jones was elated, knowing it was his Skyraider the survivor had seen. At this very moment, however, antiaircraft artillery opened fire. According to Kilbourne:

Although Jones noted the gun's position, he could not return the fire on that pass for fear of endangering the survivor. Instead, he left himself completely exposed to the enemy gunners, who were now firing almost directly down on him from their position on the side of a peak. Calmly, Jones pulled his aircraft back around, raised the nose, and laced the gun position with 20-mm cannon fire and rockets. It was impossible to call in a bombing run by the high-speed jets. The gun was just too close to the survivor. . . .

As he bored in time and time again, his A-1H was hit with multiple rounds of 14.5-mm automatic weapons fire. One of the exploding shells ignited the rocket motor to the seat's extraction system, which was mounted directly behind his headrest. The explosion was large, and it was loud. Jones described the scene:

> I looked over my shoulder and saw fire coming out of the back end of the airplane. The instrument panel was clouded with smoke. Fire seemed to be everywhere. I knew there wasn't anything for me to do but get out.
>
> I pulled for altitude and headed for a clear area. Then I reached down and grabbed the extraction handle with my right hand and pulled. The canopy went off immediately, and I waited for the ejection for what seemed like an eternity. But nothing else happened! Here I sat in this thing, with fire all around and I said to myself, "This just can't happen to me. This is not the way it's supposed to be. I've got to get back and see my family. This simply can't happen!" I reached down and grabbed the secondary escape handle, which releases the extraction mechanism, so I could climb over the side.

The absence of the canopy and the influx of fresh air caused the fire to burn with greater intensity for the next several minutes. Jones was being roasted alive. [There was] a barbecue odor in the cockpit. The realization gnawed its way into his brain that it was he who was on the grill. So intense was the heat that the strap that fastened his oxygen mask to his face burned through, letting the mask, which had provided some protection in the first seconds of the flash fire, drop to one side. More of Jones's face was exposed to the searing flames. With shock he saw the damage done to his hands. "They looked," he said, "like mozzarella cheese!"

Now the cockpit deteriorated rapidly. The windshield and left panel of the windscreen were blackened. The right windscreen panel was completely burned out. The upper half of the entire cockpit area was burned, and half of the instrument panel was unreadable.

Despite excruciating pain from his severe burns and a tremendous windblast in his face, Jones flew the aircraft and attempted again to transmit the location of the survivor and gun positions to the other aircraft. However, all radio channels were blocked with frantic calls: "*Sandy One*, you're on fire. Bail out! Bail out!" It was hardly news to Bill Jones. He figured he was about to die.

But now the fire began to subside and the smoke cleared. Jones decided that he would not bail out. It would, after all, only subject the SAR force to the added hazards of another pickup in this hostile area. Besides, [he thought] he was the only person who knew exactly where the survivor and guns were located.

However, this was not the case; both Gene McCormack and John Carlson were watching and listening to the events as they unfolded and knew exactly where both the survivor and the guns were located. But Colonel Jones had no way of knowing this fact.

Jones's A-1H was now totally out of action. All he could do was try to get the Skyraider home and brief the search-and-rescue force. By now, only his radio receiver was working; he could no longer transmit. In order to brief anyone, he would have to get back to home base.

Colonel Jones got on Sandy 2's wing and was escorted toward home base. It was at least a forty-minute flight. En route, Jones found that the windblast was affecting him in two ways. His badly burned face was causing severe pain . . . and his eyes seemed just about to swell shut. He thought he could possibly endure the pain. But the loss of his vision would be disastrous.

Drawing on years of flying experience, he trimmed the Skyraider for uncoordinated flight—a skid to the right, thus moving the opaque left windscreen directly in front of his face. This helped block the windblast and provided him some relief.

As Kilbourne reported:

As if by some gruesome design of fate, the weather was deteriorating at [NKP]. The field was overcast. Jones would have to make a ground-controlled approach. But, once again, experience and skill pulled him through. He followed [Sandy 2] . . . down through the overcast, lowered his landing gear by the emergency system, and made a no-flap landing.

"The mission was not over as far as Colonel Jones was concerned," said Colonel Leonard Volet, vice-commander of the [56th] Special Operations

Wing. "Bill Jones insisted on briefing intelligence on the location of the survivor and guns." Colonel Volet was the first person to reach the cockpit after Jones shut down his engine.

"I couldn't believe what I saw," Volet said. "Everything was burned to a crisp, including Colonel Jones's helmet, oxygen mask, survival vest, neck, and arms. Yet, he kept flailing about the cockpit, reaching for his maps, as we struggled to lift his nearly 200-pound frame plus equipment out of the aircraft. We got him out, but he refused medical attention until he was satisfied that we knew where [Captain Wilson], the survivor, and guns were located."

When Colonel Jones landed, I was in the 602nd squadron building preparing to go out on a mission. By the time I got to the colonel's aircraft, he had been transported to the dispensary. His A-1H aircraft was a total shambles. The inside of the cockpit reminded me of the interior of a fifty-five gallon drum that had been used as a burn-barrel. (A burn-barrel was used to destroy classified paperwork.) All the plastic knobs and controls in Jones's cockpit were melted. Burned skin from his hands was still on the throttle, the flight control stick, and canopy sill. The plane looked like a complete loss to me.

Meanwhile, Gene McCormack, Sandy 3, and John Carlson, Sandy 4, took over the rescue effort, and Sandys 5 and 6 were scrambled to escort the Jolly Green waiting in orbit. Carlson, vice-commander of the 602nd, was giving McCormack a Sandy-lead upgrade. Both McCormack and Carlson saw the enemy gun that had hit Colonel Jones. They easily took out the gun and called Jolly Green 36 in for the rescue. Capt. Edward Heft, my helicopter test pilot friend from Edwards, was aircraft commander of Jolly Green 36. His copilot was Maj. Stuart Silver. Sergeants Gallager and Beasley were flight engineer and PJ, respectively. Before Colonel Jones landed at NKP Captain Wilson, the survivor, was safely onboard the helicopter and en route home.

I rushed over to the dispensary to see Colonel Jones. He was propped up in bed and fully conscious. By this time burns caused his head to enlarge to the size and shape of a basketball. He could barely see because his eyelids were swollen. I could only spend a few moments with him, as medical personnel were preparing him to be air evacuated from NKP. His spirits were good; it was the last time I ever saw him.

The awards and decorations officer in the squadron was asked to write a description of the Carter 2A rescue and request that a Distinguished Flying Cross be awarded to Colonel Jones. Usually when an award request was submitted to higher headquarters it was downgraded one rank before it was approved. When this request was received by wing headquarters, it was returned to the squadron with orders to refine the story and upgrade the request to a Silver Star. This process of refining the story continued for some time; there was a possibility Colonel Jones might be recommended for the Air Force Cross, an even higher award. Some pilots in our squadron believed that the wing commander wanted a Sandy rescue pilot to win the Medal of Honor. If a pilot was awarded the Medal of Honor it would enhance the wing commander's chance of being promoted to general. Jones's action seemed to fit the qualification. Some Sandy pilots on the rescue did not agree. The political component of awards and decoration was at play again.

MYSTERIOUS DIVE

Exactly three weeks after Colonel Jones was hit by ground fire, we lost Maj. Charles Kuhlmann. Charles Kuhlmann, age thirty-eight, was from New Britain, Connecticut. He was six-feet-four-inches tall and as skinny as a rail. Kuhlmann had no hair: he was as bald as a billiard ball. He had been a bomber pilot for most of his sixteen years in the Air Force and a B-25 flight instructor at Vance AFB in Oklahoma. A student remembered Kuhlmann when he was flying another B-25 and got into a rat race with him. He said Kuhlmann put the B-25 through maneuvers it was never designed to do. Some pilots in the 602nd thought Kuhlmann was more of a bomber pilot than an attack pilot; they said he just didn't have the right mental attitude.

Kuhlmann came from a family of wealth. For his R and R, he met his wife in Madrid for two weeks in September. Shortly after he returned, on September 22, 1968, Kuhlmann led a two-ship Sandy flight flying an A-1H. He was Sandy 3 and Maj. Thomas O'Connor, his wingman, was Sandy 4. On that afternoon Kuhlmann and O'Connor flew to an area in the northeast corner of Laos. They were flying over a dirt road designated as Route 6, a winding north-south trail used by the enemy to transport weapons and supplies to the PDJ. They were a few miles east of Lima Site 36 in a position close to where other American aircraft were making air strikes. In that position they would be available to quickly rescue anyone shot down in their vicinity. They were flying what we called "Sandy orbit"—they were airborne and near the action but without an active rescue.

While flying over this dirt road in high terrain of about 4,500 feet but only 1,000 feet above the ground, Kuhlmann called to O'Connor on the UHF radio, "I see something on the road; cover me." O'Connor had an unobstructed view and watched as Kuhlmann rolled his fully fueled and armed Skyraider past 90 degrees of bank and into a steep dive. At the time O'Connor thought to himself, "Kuhlmann, you're a dead man, unless you roll out and pull up now." O'Connor thought that Kuhlmann was at too low of an altitude for that steep of a dive angle. His judgment was that Kuhlmann would hit the ground unless he immediately pulled up. O'Connor followed the Skyraider with its nose pointed straight down. Then, as if Kuhlmann himself realized he was in mortal danger, O'Connor said he reefed it in, meaning he vigorously pulled maximum G to recover. The A-1 snap-rolled and hit the trees. These events happened so fast that O'Connor did not have time to make a warning call to Kuhlmann. At the moment of impact, O'Connor saw a flash of light. He thought to himself, "Was the flash from Kuhlmann ejecting from the Skyraider? Was it his ordnance exploding? What was it?"

O'Connor descended and flew multiple circles around the crash site looking for any sign of life. He didn't see any. He also didn't think there was enemy in the area, although he saw a person standing on the road. Was it a good guy or a bad guy? O'Connor flew over him several times and nothing happened. The next time O'Connor flew over him the person shot at him with an automatic weapon, hitting the Skyraider about ten times. He said the hits "bounced my feet off the floor." Although he didn't see anyone else, he figured if he saw one person there were probably more.

O'Connor called Crown and told them Sandy 3 was down. He also asked them to send a Jolly Green helicopter up to his position. He thought there would not be any way to absolutely determine Kuhlmann's fate unless someone was on the ground at the crash site. Unfortunately, Crown thought O'Connor wanted the Jolly to put a PJ on the ground. O'Connor told Crown that he didn't want a PJ on the ground, someone was shooting at him; he simply wanted to inform Crown that a positive determination of Kuhlmann's condition could not be made from the air, only from the ground.

After taking a couple of hits in his Skyraider, O'Connor thought there might be damage that could eventually cause him problems. He figured he should probably head back to NKP.

When he landed, a crowd met him at the plane. "What did you see?" they asked. "What happened to Kuhlmann?" O'Connor stated firmly, "Kuhlmann didn't get out; he went in with the aircraft!" A colonel took O'Connor aside and said, "You know if we declare him dead, his wife gets no more Air Force pay." O'Connor responded, " I didn't know that. Why didn't someone let me know before I shot my mouth off?" Charles Kuhlmann was officially reported as missing in action.

On October 14, twenty-two days after Kuhlmann crashed, the Air Force reported that unspecified "evidence of death" was received, which indicated that Kuhlmann died at the time his aircraft crashed. His status was changed at that time to killed in action. This report did not filter down to the pilots in the 602nd. However, O'Connor's visual sighting of Kuhlmann's crash did not give us reason to be optimistic about his fate.

A few months later, O'Connor received a letter from Kuhlmann's wife. She said she wanted to know the truth about what happened to Charles. We had been ordered to never make contact with the next-of-kin. The official Air Force position was that if a pilot was airborne in a flight where another plane and pilot were lost, they were to prepare a written statement giving all the facts and opinions they held on the incident. This report would be passed up the chain of command, and the proper officials would contact the family. At the time, this seemed like a logical procedure. Additionally, I did not know any of the wives and children of the pilots in the squadron and would not contact someone I had not previously met. We did not have access to a phone for a long-distance call back to the States. All communication I had with my wife was by airmail, which took five days to travel back to the States. O'Connor wrote to Kuhlmann's wife and told her exactly what he had observed. He never heard from her again.

10 NIGHT FIGHTING

Capt. Michael "Bat" Masterson loved to make people laugh. His wife Fran recalled, "He was one of those happy persons who could make a joke out of anything; nothing was sacred." Just a month before Christmas in 1967, Fran and Bat were married in the Eglin AFB chapel at Fort Walton Beach, Florida. Toward the end of their wedding ceremony, as Fran and Bat knelt together at the front the chapel, she became aware that the congregation was trying to suppress chuckles and laughter. Ron Furtak and his wife Eleanor attended and were sitting a couple of rows behind Bat and Fran. Ron heard laughter and, though he could not see what it was about, suspected that Bat might have split the pants of his tuxedo when he knelt down. Instead, he found Bat had printed, in bold white letters, *HE* on the black sole of his left shoe and *LP* on his right shoe. Everyone in the church broke up with the exception of two people—Fran and, of course, the minister, the only two who couldn't see Bat's shoes. Ron's wife realized the shoes spelled *HELP* and looked at Ron disapprovingly. She asked him, "Did you do that?"

"No," he replied.

"Bat did it himself as a joke." It was truly a Kodak moment.

The wedding reception was even more irreverent. While most people would serve glasses of champagne, Bat served magnums. Waitresses walked around the Eglin Officers' Club with magnums of champagne on their trays sans glasses. My test pilot friend Capt. Donald Madonna, his wife, and others at the reception tried to shoot out the overhead lights by popping corks from the bottles. It was obviously a wedding reception people remembered forever.

Thirty-one-year-old Bat Masterson was always the life of the party. His roommate at NKP, Gene McCormack, remembered him as being a joy to be around; he had a great sense of humor and brought a lot of cheer to those near him. Ron Furtak said Masterson was the pilot reincarnation of comedian Bob Newhart. Masterson would sit on a bar stool in front of a group of pilots, acting as a master of ceremonies and telling stories. He had a way to get people to laugh, to cheer up his flying mates and have a good time himself. Comedy may have been Masterson's method to dance his demons away.

Masterson and McCormack wrote a song dedicated to Sandy and Jolly Green rescue pilots. The song used the lyrics of "Wabash Cannon Ball" and was sung by Capt. Samuel Wheate, a Jolly Green pilot, and recorded on audiotape.

Sandy Cannon Ball

Listen to the hotline, the jingle and the roar
   It's Compress on the telephone says, "Sandy go to war"
We've got a pilot out there that needs some help today
   So wake up from nap alpha and get upon your way
We dashed out to our aircraft, the weather it was bad
   We'll take on any mission in our mighty Super Spad
We roll on down the runway with a rattle and a roar
   Pass across the threshold, saying, "Climb you frickin' whore!"
Headed for Mu Gia with a full head of steam
   Trying hard to overtake those frickin' Jolly Greens
Put them in an orbit and then on into fight
   It lasted throughout the day and on toward the night
The sun is sinking lower in the western sky

"Send the Jolly in there," we hear old Blue Chip cry
    Listen to the rumble the rattle and the roar
There's 37-millimeter and small arms by the score
    The Sandys roll on in there; survivor if you please
Dig yourself a big hole and hide among the trees
    We'll plan a first-light effort and be back in the morn
We'll get you out of this here fix as sure as you are born
    The sun comes up next morning: Misty says its right
The Sandys roll on in there looking for a fight
    The low lead looks it over and finds some ground fire there
They daisy chain around it and blow it in the air
    We put in 20 mike mike and a willy pete smoke screen
To clean up the area for the big Jolly Green
    Listen to the rattle the rumble and the roar
CBU and minigun and Charlie is no more
    Jolly come on in here, the area is clean
From here on this pickup is going to be routine
    The Jollys come on in there thinking things are great
And go into a hover when things begin to break
    Jolly we're here with you so you don't have to fear
Get on back to the Sandy Box and have a glass of cheer
    Headed back to NKP Compress is on the air
JSARC, King, and Blue Chip too are singing praises there
    Sandys set the whole thing up to answer a pilot's prayer
Jollys had their photog out to keep their record clear
    The success of the mission was Sandy all the way
Their fighting bombing and strafing saved the day
    Sandys were the heroes, but the Jollys got the cheer
Hell it doesn't matter, so hang it in your ear

Bat Masterson, Ron Furtak, and Gene McCormack were all members of the same class at Hurlburt, the class in front of mine. They completed their training about three weeks before me and shipped out immediately for Udorn. While at Hurlburt, I got a chance to fly in the right seat of an A-1E acting as an observer while Masterson was making bomb, rocket, and strafing passes in the weapons range. Masterson was short, probably only around five-feet-four-inches tall. His previous assignment in the Air Force, before the Skyraiders, was flying the F-104A Starfighter in the drone squadron at Eglin. The F-104A had a small cockpit with a tricycle landing gear. It would have been easy for someone as short as Masterson to adjust his seat height and rudder pedals on the F-104 so that he could both see out the front windscreen and still have full throw on the rudders. The Skyraider, on the other hand, was designed for a much taller person. Either Masterson could run the electric-powered seat to its full "up" position and see over the nose of the A-1 or he could run the seat down and obtain full rudder pedal movement—but not both. Masterson handled the Skyraider well on his weapon passes in the range but was constantly readjusting his controls.

In early October of 1968, the 602nd was fragged (received written strike orders) by higher headquarters to fly more sorties per day than could be flown during daylight hours. A-1 aircraft that had been flown on combat missions earlier in the day would be rearmed, refueled, and flown again at night. The duty officer scheduled a two-ship Firefly flight for departure at 6 p.m. and another for 9 p.m. Masterson was in the first group to be scheduled for a night mission.

During our checkout in the Skyraider at Hurlburt, we got a chance to fly a couple of night flights in the Eglin bombing range. However, the A-1 was being flown with just lightweight practice smoke bombs over the low elevation Florida terrain. Our night combat missions over Laos would be flown with 500- and 750-pound bombs over jungle-covered mountains, some reaching as high as 8,000 feet. A heavily loaded Skyraider was much more difficult to fly. In addition, even on a moonless night over the Eglin range, we could still see the city lights of Fort Walton Beach and Niceville and keep a sense of orientation. There were absolutely no lights on the ground in Laos—it was pitch black.

Masterson flew his first night mission from the right seat of an A-1E. On this flight the engine cowling came loose and required him to abort the mission. On his second flight, now flying the left seat, he again experienced an aircraft emergency and was forced to return to NKP after flying only two weapons passes. Even though the mission was considered marginally complete, it was called a success, and Masterson was cleared to fly night combat solo.

Like most of us in the squadron, Masterson had his share of airborne emergencies and close calls. But his night misfortunes were different. He told Ron Furtak, "You better learn from my experiences; this night flying is very hazardous." He added, "I don't know if I'm going to make it."

Roommate McCormack considered Masterson to be a thorough and cautious person. Most Skyraider pilots carried two survival radios; Masterson carried three. He also carried a compass and three mirrors, telling McCormack, "I want to be covered." Masterson seemed to have a premonition that he would not survive his year of combat.

On October 13, 1968, Bat Masterson was the wingman on an evening flight of two, using the call sign Firefly 26 and flying A-1G. The A-1G model was similar to the A-1E. Both were side-by-side seated and had a complete set of flight instruments for both seats. The biggest difference, I recall, was that there was not a flight control stick in the right seat of an A-1G.

The flight of two got airborne at 6 p.m. led by Maj. Peter Brown Jr., using the call sign Firefly 25. They were to conduct an armed reconnaissance mission in Barrel Roll along Route 7, their primary target, and Route 6, their alternate target, in an attempt to locate and interdict enemy traffic along these well-known communist supply lines in part of Xiangkhouang Province, Laos. This area of northern Laos was considered a major Pathet Lao stronghold. Routes 7 and 6 were used by both the North Vietnamese and the Pathet Lao to move men and matériel throughout this region. Although they were frequently no more than paths cut through jungle-covered mountains, our military forces were ordered to use all assets available to us to stop the flow of men and supplies over these roads.

After takeoff, Brown and Masterson climbed to 10,000 feet, then continued in a loose visual formation. Fifteen minutes after crossing into Laotian airspace, they ran into a rising layer of stratus clouds. Masterson radioed he would climb to 10,700 feet, while Major Brown stayed at 10,000 feet. They continued to fly in and out of the stratus until roughly fifty minutes into their flight and only fifteen minutes away from their target area.

At 6:55 p.m. Masterson stated he had lost his artificial horizon or attitude indicator, forcing him to abort the mission. Major Brown asked Masterson if he was clear of the clouds, and he replied, "negative," that he was "attempting to use the artificial horizon in the right cockpit, but was experiencing vertigo." Unlike the artificial horizon that was directly in front of him on the left instrument panel, the one on the right side was about four feet away. Masterson would have to turn his head about 45 degrees to the right to see the instrument. It would be like having your speedometer installed on the front of your glove compartment—very hard to concentrate on for any length of time. Pilots were taught in flight school to disregard their feelings of vertigo when flying at night or in weather and to pay strict attention to and believe their flight instruments.

Brown directed Masterson to let him know when he rolled out on a heading back to NKP. Shortly thereafter Masterson radioed, "I'm losing it and getting out." Hearing Masterson's radio transmission, Brown began an immediate left turn, and after about 180 degrees of turn, he saw a bright orange fireball on the ground in his 10 o'clock position. The weather in the crash area was scattered clouds at about 5,000 feet, layered stratus up to 10,000 feet, with five miles visibility. Because of the clouds and darkness, Pete Brown did not observe a parachute or the aircraft until it impacted the ground. The crash site was in extremely rugged but generally unpopulated mountains. The nearest roadway was two miles to the northwest, and the nearest significant town was Phong Savan, approximately fifteen miles to the southwest.

Blindbat 2, a C-130 flareship, arrived roughly ten minutes after the crash and helped maintain contact with the crash site location. Blindbat 2 used a Starlight scope to further refine the crash site. Pete Brown conducted an electronic search for Masterson until 9:15 p.m., when he was forced to depart the area as he was low on fuel. While on station, he dropped flares from altitudes between 8,000 and 12,000 feet. During this time no emergency beeper was heard and no voice contact was established with Bat Masterson.

A formal search-and-rescue operation arrived in the area at 6 the next morning with two Skyraiders and one Air America helicopter. Tom Campbell and his wingman looked for indications of the lost plane. Twenty minutes later, the smoldering wreckage of Firefly 26 was found by SAR aircraft. The crew of the helicopter hovered about thirty feet above the wreckage. Its crew had an unobstructed view of it and reported, "Wreckage consisted of burned wings on either side of a crater in which the fuselage seemed buried, and was located about 50 meters from the crest of a ridgeline with wreckage strewn up the hill from the crater for 20 meters and down from the crater for 100 meters." The helicopter landed and four Laotian soldiers got off to search for the missing pilot. Tom Campbell, his wingman, and the rescue helicopter orbited the wreckage crater but could find no trace of an ejection seat, parachute, or Masterson. The search was suspended after about thirty minutes. When the chopper took off after retrieving the Laotian soldiers, the enemy shot at it with a recoilless rifle, barely missing it. Campbell was in a perfect position to make a strike, so he rolled in and shot some rockets.

At the time the search and rescue was terminated, Bat Masterson was immediately listed as missing in action. A ground team was scheduled to be inserted into the area a week later, but it was canceled on account of bad weather. Eleven days later a ground team did enter the area, but it was forced to withdraw before reaching the crash site because of the presence of hostile forces.

Masterson's crash not only caused those of us in the squadron to mourn his loss but also caused a fierce argument. Some pilots believed he ejected successfully but was captured or that he was severely hurt and still hung up in a tree. Others thought he simply went in with the aircraft and was killed.

Ron Furtak speculated that because of the short period of time between Masterson's frantic call and Pete Brown's observation of a bright orange fireball, Masterson did not successfully eject. Furtak said that Masterson would have to fly what pilots call cross-cockpit, essentially flying by a flight instrument that was located several feet to his right. Someone as short as Masterson would have had to lean to the right and maybe even cock his head in a horizontal plane rather than the normal vertical plane. Furtak took Masterson's loss hard because he had given him an instrument flight check in the T-33 at Eglin before they both started flying the Skyraider. Furtak gave Masterson unusual attitude recoveries while he was under a canvas hood. Masterson knew the proper procedures, flew the recoveries correctly, and passed the exam.

After investigation into the flight instruments of the A-1G model, we found out a peculiar characteristic unknown to every Skyraider pilot in the squadron. Both the left and right attitude indicators received information from a common vertical gyro. That meant if Masterson's vertical gyro failed it would provide false information to both attitude indicators. For Masterson, flying on the right attitude indicator would be as bad as flying on the left indicator. No wonder he lost control of his A-1G.

Gene McCormack had his own unique explanation for Masterson's loss. He reasoned that Masterson was leaning to the right in an attempt to recover the Skyraider using the right attitude indicator, but at the very last second decided to eject. Because there was a center structural bar between the two seats, which guided the two canopies fore and aft, if Masterson ejected while leaning to the right he would have been slammed into the metal frame. The ejection seat was designed to catapult a pilot who was sitting straight up, back against his parachute and legs on the rudder pedals. McCormack figured that Masterson was incapacitated from striking the frame and that if he did get out he would have been severely injured and bled to death. In his own heart, he didn't think Masterson survived. As his roommate, McCormack was ordered to be the summary court officer for Masterson's affairs. He packed Masterson's belongings and sent them back to the States.

After Masterson was lost, our night combat procedures were changed. While earlier it had been planned that every pilot in the squadron would fly a night mission on the average of once every two weeks or so, it was now decided that night combat was so dangerous that just a couple of pilots would be designated to fly only at night. They would therefore develop more proficiency. I was chosen to fly exclusively at night for the next month and a half.

I wasn't pleased to be selected to fly just night missions, partly because I knew it would be very hazardous—but I was also displeased because I had purchased a Japanese Pentax single-lens-reflex 35-mm camera. My roommate, Al Hale, purchased one at the NKP Base Exchange for a bargain price. He suggested I buy one since it would be a great improvement over the Argus C-3 that was stolen back in August. I planned to carry the camera on every mission and take color slides of the trusty Skyraider. My photo flights would have to wait six weeks while I flew at night.

Maj. Raymond Shumock and I started flying a lot together. Ray Shumock was a good old boy from the South with a very distinctive voice over the radio. Even though the radios in the Skyraider sounded weak and distorted from engine noise, I could always recognize Shumock's southern accent. He would lead our two-ship formation one night, and I would lead the next. We got so familiar with each other and each other's tactics that we were like a second baseman and shortstop on a baseball team. Whoever got the ball or found the target would roll in and quickly drop napalm on the target before the flare extinguished. Normally, we carried our own flares and illuminated the target. Because the flares lit up the night sky for only about twenty seconds, we needed to find the target fast and get a fire burning on the ground. Once we got a fire started we could use it for a reference point for the rest of our passes and not have to use flares anymore.

About midway into my six weeks of night combat, Shumock and I came up with a new tactic. Because we were having difficulty finding targets over the pitch-black Laotian jungle, we invited an Air Force navigator from the B-26 squadron to fly with us. Maj. Michael Morganstein would fly in the right seat of my A-1E and attempt to spot enemy targets with a Starlight scope. The Starlight scope was a battery-powered device that worked like a telescope and enhanced natural light by a factor of 10,000. Our plan was that Morganstein would open the sliding canopy from his right seat and extend the two-foot-long Starlight scope about a foot into the airstream to pick out targets in our 12 to 3 o'clock position.

Ray Shumock and I launched into the night under bright stars. Our target area was in northern Laos near Lima Site 36 about a hundred miles from NKP. Sluggishly, I climbed to 8,500 feet, and Shumock climbed to 9,000 feet; we kept a five-hundred-foot separation between us, since our navigation lights were turned off and we could not visually see each other. We kept on parallel headings and the same airspeed, which would keep us fairly close together. The tactical air navigation (TACAN) mileage from NKP rolled up in miles like on the speedometer on a car. By timing a ten-mile section we computed our ground speed and the time when we would be over our target. Usually, the TACAN would break lock around fifty to sixty miles—so an early ground speed check was important. We drove on for thirty minutes and figured we had crossed the Mekong River and were now over enemy territory with absolutely no lights on the ground. It was as dark as flying over the ocean.

As we approached our time to be on target I descended to 6,000 feet, and Morganstein opened his canopy and extended the Starlight scope into the humid air. I called Shumock on the radio and said we would take up a gentle right turn and call him if we spotted a target. Slowly, we turned in the sky like trolling for fish in a boat. Round and round we went for several minutes until I became concerned that wind might be blowing us off course. We had no way to positively determine our position.

Then Morganstein yelled out, "Oh, no!" I couldn't imagine what happened; I knew we weren't hit by ground fire. He pulled the scope back in the cockpit and started shaking his head up and down. Obviously, he was in distress and there was no place in the cockpit to perform first aid. Between his shaking and gasping I understood that he thought a bug flew up his nose. I realized he thought his injury was serious, but it seemed funny to me. I tried to keep from laughing but couldn't hold it back. He kept shaking his head and blowing his nose. I was laughing so hard I couldn't call Shumock on the radio to explain what had happened. By now we were hopelessly lost. I wondered if Morganstein's injury would qualify him for the Purple Heart. The thought made me break up even more.

Since our Starlight scope tactic had gone awry, I called the ground radar controllers and asked if any night FACs were available. They told me a twin-engine C-123 transport with flares was working near Lima Site 85 and needed help. Shumock and I turned north and soon spotted the C-123 flying at about 12,000 feet. As we arrived, the C-123 dropped a flare into the murk. The gloom gave way to the probing light, which was as bright as a welding torch at close range. As we circled, I scanned the Laotian mountains that jutted up into the dark. The jungle and mountains had a ghostlike appearance. They were two-dimensional in shape, and it was difficult to determine distance and direction. The flare flickered and drifted with the wind. Everything I saw was in shades of gray. The flare burned out and I quickly went back to flying on instruments, keeping the Skyraider's wings level.

Another flare was dropped, and this time I spotted the target. Anxious to get my dive established and hit the target I rolled into a 45-degree dive and selected several bombs on the weapon panel. As soon as I got established in the dive I realized I had forgotten something important. Immediately, the engine started running rough and then quit. Any moment the flare was going to burn out, and both the sky and the Skyraider instrument panel would go completely black. In my hurry to start the dive as soon as possible, I had forgotten to select the internal fuel tank and turn on the boost pump. I was still feeding from the external, 300-gallon centerline tank. That tank was good for cruise conditions but would not feed in a dive. My left hand came off the throttle, and I reached down on the left subpanel to the master fuel selector control. All I needed to do was rotate it to the internal position and flip the boost pump switch on with my thumb. When I reached down, the radio communications electrical cord that went from my helmet to the cockpit receptacle was lying over the fuel panel and in the way. While it would only take a second or so to move the cord, switch the fuel selector, and flip the boost pump switch on, we were hurtling at the ground with airspeed building up. I made the connections, started a pull-up without dropping my bombs, and looked up at the flare-illuminated horizon for the first time. As the engine started up again, it coughed and spit before full power came back. I anxiously looked for a low spot between mountain peaks. We still had a full load of ordnance and much of our fuel. The Skyraider staggered and bucked as I tried to nurse it through a dark mountain pass when the flare burned out. We safely passed through a low spot, but Major Morganstein was not very impressed with this captain's flying ability and told me so. He never flew with me again or with anyone in else in our squadron. I don't know if he ever put himself in for the Purple Heart. I just tried to forget about that screwy mission.

The night mission near Lima Site 85 was a close call but nothing compared to what happened to me a couple of flights later. This time I was leading a two-ship flight with our target area near the village of Ban Ban. Ban Ban was at the intersection of Route 6 and Route 7 in northern Laos where communist supplies were transported into the PDJ. It was only a few miles from where Masterson had gone down only a few weeks earlier.

On this night I quickly spotted the target illuminated by the flare. It was important to fly above the flare to spot the target and then to plan the dive-bomb delivery in such a way that you did not descend below the flare, where you could be seen by enemy gunners. It was safer to stay above the flare and force the enemy to fire at just your engine noise.

Just as I rolled in on my first pass and started to put the gun sight pipper (the pink dot used to aim) on the target, the flare floated directly between me and the target. The bright light prevented me from seeing the target, so I thought I would zig to the right and then zag back to the left. As I performed this maneuver, which I had never done before, my dive angle got steeper and steeper. Then I realized I was so steep that I could not get the pipper back on the target. I started a gradual pull-up and flew under the flare. The ground was coming up fast so I added more back stick pressure. The Skyraider started to buffet and I was still a long way from bottoming out of the dive. Finally, I pulled back on the stick with both hands and could see the trees coming up through the windscreen. As the A-1 bottomed out I barely cleared the tops of the trees when the flare extinguished. It was a stupid maneuver on my part. I nearly killed myself. I should have aborted the pass as soon as the flare got in my way. Or I should have jettisoned my ordnance when the Skyraider started to buck up and down. I had no one else to blame; I messed up. Fortunately, I survived to fly more missions. I wondered how many other A-1s just stalled out during misjudged dive recoveries and hit the ground. Whenever we lost pilots and planes at low altitude, we always suspected they were downed by ground fire. Now I was not so certain.

Several days later I got the chance to be a gunner and shoot at a flying plane. One of the enlisted airmen built a radio-controlled model plane and flew it a short distance from our living quarters. It was dusk when several of us left the Sandy Box with beers in hand to watch the plane do loops and rolls. One of the Skyraider pilots went back to his room and returned with his pen gun flare. Every pilot carried one of the eight-inch-long flares with about six cartridges in his survival vest. The pen gun flare was designed to shoot a single red ball about a hundred feet into the air to attract the attention of the rescue force searching for a survivor and to help the Jolly Green find your final position. Unfortunately, the flare also looked like a tracer from an enemy gun, and, therefore, they were only used in special situations.

After a couple of beers, the pilot shot his pen gun flare at the model plane, missing it by a large distance. All of us thought we could do better, so we retrieved our own pen guns. It was difficult to fire at the model because it was constantly banking and turning. Some pilots came close, strictly by accident, as it was impossible to aim properly. It was satisfying to realize that we, too, would be difficult to hit if we kept the Skyraider moving back and forth in the sky. As it got darker we fired at the sound of the engine but never hit the plane. Eventually, the airman also lost sight of his model plane in the darkness and it crashed. I learned a lot about aerial tactics that night from playing the part of a ground gunner.

One Skyraider pilot took the night combat missions very seriously. He flew every night just like I did but also spent his spare time in the Intelligence Office. He would sit in when my flight was briefed by an intelligence officer and be there again at our debriefing. He would argue with the officers about the best place to attack the enemy and what ordnance we should carry for maximum effectiveness. He became incensed that we weren't hurting the communists enough. His face showed extreme anger; his eyes were bloodshot with dark skin surrounding them. From my perspective he began to resemble Adolf Hitler in both appearance and mannerisms. I suspected he had lost his sense of balance in fighting the war. It was important to prepare and fly a good flight, but after that I thought it was time to let the fighting go, to relax and be ready for the next day. The war in Vietnam and Laos was a limited war, a war of attrition. Nothing happened any one day that would be pivotal to the final outcome—except for rescue missions.

We were only a few days from the presidential election of November 1968, and candidate Richard Nixon stated he had a secret plan to end the war. I was hopeful he had a better plan than the one we were presently using. By this time I had flown twenty-five night combat missions and was anxious to go back to day flights.

Actually, I was more interested in NASA's announcement that the flight of Apollo 8, with my friend Bill Anders aboard, would be launched soon. It would be the first space flight to leave earth's gravitational pull and circle the moon. The flight was scheduled for Christmas of 1968.

Col. William Jones, who was burned during his attempted rescue of Carter 2A, had been transported to a military hospital at Lackland AFB in San Antonio, Texas. I wrote to him as soon as I got an address from our squadron administration office. I sent him a copy of the Carter 2A official rescue report and news about two other Sandy pilots who were lost since he left. By late November I received a letter from him, which read in part:

Dear George,

I have about recovered now and am going home for a 30 day convalescent leave on Wednesday. My wife has been staying at the guest house here the past 3 weeks and I have been able to go out in the PM since Thursday—the [Officers'] Club for Martinis and downtown San Antone for some good Mexican food. I still haven't got full motion in my left arm and had a piece of skin from my forearm grafted to my elbow this AM—a very small painless operation to fill in one last little hole. I am still a bit stiff and sore and was burned much worse than I had thought at first—the bad burns (3rd degree) just don't hurt until they start to fix them—all nerve ends burned off. . . . I am trying to get back for my other 7 months [of combat at NKP]—got rid of an assignment they had me lined up for as instructor at the Naval War College. . . . I hope to get a medical recommendation for just a 6 months limitation away from extreme hot or cold climate [for burn recovery] possibly an interim assignment in the Washington D.C. area and then completion of my tour. I may be able to work this out if the doctors cooperate (over my family's objections) but certainly cannot get back before you, Al [Hale], Tom [O'Connor] and most of the others leave.

Best of luck.

Sincerely,

Bill

By the time I got the letter from Colonel Jones, a new commander had taken over the 602nd. Lt. Col. Walter Stueck, a veteran combat pilot of World War II, had flown P-39s, P-40s, and P-51s before becoming a twin-engine fighter pilot in the P-38 Lightning. Stueck got only two rides in a P-38 before he was sent into combat as a young lieutenant in the European theater. While there he got shot up and either jumped out or crash-landed three P-38s. Stueck said, "World War II was harder on me than Korea or Vietnam." In the Korean War Stueck flew the P-51 during an entire tour but was fortunate to not need his parachute.

When Stueck arrived at NKP, he met the commander of the 56th SOW. In Stueck's estimation the commander had stars in his eyes—he wanted to be a general. Serving as commander of a wing where a Sandy pilot was awarded the Medal of Honor would give him an excellent chance for promotion unless something went wrong. The 602nd had been at NKP for only a few months; they had been accustomed to operating on their own at Udorn and resented interference from wing officers. Stueck said he realized that most of the pilots weren't happy with the move from Udorn to NKP. A few were what he called prima donnas and let him know right away they didn't like it at NKP and being watched by what they called "Wing Weenies." One senior lieutenant colonel was the leader of this opposition faction and was joined by two lieutenants. All three were excellent combat pilots but didn't like following orders. The wing commander told Colonel Stueck in no uncertain terms that his biggest job was getting the 602nd to comply with orders from the wing.

When Stueck arrived at the squadron building he was ushered into his new office. Sitting on the commander's desk was a charred flight helmet, a helmet that showed severe fire damage. Stueck was startled to see the destroyed helmet and said, "What the hell is this?" He was told that the helmet belonged to the previous commander, Lt. Col. William Jones, who was nearly killed on a rescue mission in North Vietnam. Stueck realized he had his work cut out for him, both flying hazardous rescue missions and corralling a bunch of renegade pilots.

George J. Marrett and father, George R. Marrett,
upon return from a 1946 hunting trip in Nebraska
(Courtesy George J. Marrett)

Maj. Thomas Campbell, lead Sandy in Streetcar 304 rescue
(Courtesy Thomas Campbell)

Capt. Michael "Bat" Masterson with Skyraider A-1H at Udorn RTAFB
(Courtesy Masterson family)

Maj. Eugene McCormack Jr.
(Courtesy Eugene McCormack Jr.)

USN Lt. Kenny W. Fields,
Streetcar 304, on A-7 Corsair
(Courtesy Kenny W. Fields)

Lt. Col. Richard Walsh III as a captain on T-33 wing (Courtesy Walsh family)

Laotian Gen. Vang Pao and Maj. Edwin Conley Jr. (Courtesy George J. Marrett)

HH-3 Jolly Green on PSP at Nakhon Phanom RTAFB (Courtesy George J. Marrett)

PJ Sgt. Donald Johnson firing from rear ramp of HH-53 Super Jolly
(Courtesy Donald Johnson)

Capt. Wayne Warner in front of F-105 "Thud" (Courtesy Wayne Warner)

Capt. George J. Marrett on wing of A-1 Skyraider (Courtesy George J. Marrett)

2nd Lt. Rex Huntsman (the first second lieutenant to be combat ready in an A-1) and Maj. Albert Roberts Jr. (Courtesy George J. Marrett)

Rescue crew of Streetcar 304 in front of HH-3 Jolly Green *Front l-r:* Sandy 2, Maj. Brock Foster; Jolly Green copilot, Maj. Louis Yuhas; Jolly Green pilot, Capt. David Richardson; Sandy 1, Maj. Thomas Campbell. *Rear l-r:* Jolly Green flight engineer, S. Sgt. Coy Calhoun; Jolly Green PJ, Sgt. Peter Harding (Courtesy David Richardson)

PJ Sgt. Donald Johnson
(Courtesy Donald Johnson)

Maj. Charles Kuhlmann in cockpit of
A-1H (Courtesy George J. Marrett)

Lt. Col. John Carlson, the "Mad
Bomber," at his going-away party
(Courtesy George J. Marrett)

Capt. George J. Marrett's A-1 Skyraider class at Hurlburt Field, Florida, March 1968 *Front l-r:* Capt. Alan B. Hale (crash landed with battle damage), Capt. George J. Marrett, Lt. Col. William A. Jones III (Medal of Honor winner), Lt. Col. C. Riner Learnard. *Rear l-r:* Capt. Albert Holtz, Col. Fred Webster, Capt. Thomas O'Connor (shot down and rescued), Lt. Col. Newt Swain, Capt. Richard L. Russell (killed), Lt. Col. Charles Joseph (Courtesy George J. Marrett)

602nd Fighter Squadron (Commando) emblem
designed by Walt Disney (© Disney Enterprises, Inc.)

Sock It To 'Em, Capt. George J. Marrett's A-1J at NKP
(Courtesy George J. Marrett)

Capt. George J. Marrett awarded Distinguished Flying Cross
by Col. Edwin White (Courtesy George J. Marrett)

A-1 Skyraider flown by Lt. James Beggerly with armament load after takeoff from
NKP (Courtesy George J. Marrett)

Capt. Edward W. Leonard III in front of A-1 Skyraider (Courtesy George J. Marrett)

Captain Leonard's crashed Skyraider in Thailand (Courtesy George J. Marrett)

602nd Fighter Squadron pilots at Udorn RTAFB, Thailand, July 1968 *Front l-r:*
Capt. George J. Marrett, Lt. Col. Sam Barrett, Lt. Col. Louis Bechtold (the
squadron commander), Capt. Donald Dunaway, Capt. James Jamerson (later,
four-star Air Force general). *Rear l-r:* Maj. Charles Flynn, Maj. Peter Brown,
Maj. Eustace "Mel" Bunn Jr. (participated in Streetcar 304 rescue and raid on
Son Tay POW camp), and Capt. Ronald Furtak (Courtesy George J. Marrett)

602nd Fighter Squadron receives Presidential Unit Citation from Maj. Gen.
Louis T. Seith *L-r:* Maj. Alvin Moreland, Maj. Albert Roberts Jr., Capt. Ronald
Furtak, Capt. James Jamerson, 1st Lt. Rex Huntsman, Lt. Col. David Andrews,
and 1st Lt. James Beggerly (Courtesy George J. Marrett)

FOR OFFICAL USE ONLY   SPECIAL HANDLING REQUIRED   SEE AFR-127-4

A-1H Skyraider (no. 738), flown by Lt. Col. William A. Jones III, after being struck by ground fire in North Vietnam (Courtesy Albert J. Roberts Jr.)

PJ Sgt. Thomas Pope signaling "V" for victory to HH-53 crew. The words written on this photo read: "He lost his leg for another man—Tom Pope, 18 Jan. 69. Buff flt." (Courtesy Donald Johnson)

Capt. Richard Hall in A-1E (Courtesy George J. Marrett)

Lt. Jon Ewing (awarded Airman's Medal for saving the life of Capt. Wayne Warner)
(Courtesy George J. Marrett)

11 STATUE OF LIBERTY

By December, the four of us who had trained in the A-1 together at Hurlburt and then been assigned to the 602nd started to thin out. My roommate, Al Hale, who crash landed a Skyraider at Da Nang, South Vietnam during the rescue of Hellborn 20, now spent most of his time with the maintenance department helping them repair crash-damaged A-1s and assisting the mechanics get planes through periodic inspections faster. Colonel Jones, who had been severely burned when he was hit by ground fire back in September during the rescue of Carter 2A, wasn't expected to return to the squadron for any more combat missions. Tom O'Connor and I had managed to dodge the bullet so far. That was about to change for O'Connor.

O'Connor was redheaded, an easygoing, take-it-for-granted type of guy. He didn't get excited easily, seemed to pace himself well during his year tour. Two months earlier, he watched Charles Kuhlmann roll into a steep dive and crash. Kuhlmann was still missing and O'Connor had very little hope of his survival.

Back in 1967, O'Connor was stationed at Clark AB in the Philippines working in a command post. The war in Southeast Asia was getting larger all the time, and O'Connor was disappointed that he was just handling frag orders. "A dull job in a screwed-up war," he said. Anxious to get into combat, O'Connor asked to talk to Chuck Yeager, the famous test pilot who first broke the sound barrier in 1947. At this time Colonel Yeager was the wing commander of a group of two B-57 squadrons at Clark. O'Connor convinced Colonel Yeager that he could fly combat and joined the squadron. Every other month, pilots went on temporary duty and spent thirty days at Phan Rang AB in South Vietnam flying night strike missions. O'Connor had flown about fifty combat missions in the B-57 when the Air Force disbanded the squadron. Anxious to complete a combat tour before he was ordered to fly in an aircraft he didn't care for, O'Connor volunteered to train in the A-1 as a Sandy rescue pilot.

On December 8, 1968, O'Connor was Firefly 34 on a strike mission in northern Laos with 1st Lt. James Beggerly as his wingman, Firefly 35. Beggerly, a young officer full of piss and vinegar, was an excellent pilot for someone with limited flying experience. O'Connor was flying an A-1J model, serial number 142033. Four months earlier I had completed an FCF on that particular aircraft. It was one of the best aircraft in the squadron, a real jewel.

Laotian General Vang Pao was still trying to retake Lima Site 85, the site that had been lost eight months earlier when North Vietnamese soldiers scaled the steep, rocky incline and captured the secret radar gear. A FAC reported to O'Connor that there were a lot of North Vietnamese troops in the area and cleared him in for a weapons pass on the southeast side of the mountain.

While he was flying his first pass and firing the Skyraider's 20-mm guns, the left wing exploded. The gun access panel blew off, and a solid column of flame came out of the hole. O'Connor knew the fire must be coming from the hydraulic system powering the left landing gear, since there was no fuel tank in the Skyraider's wing. He struggled to grab a handle to dump hydraulic pressure and also to turn to a safe heading in case he needed to get out of the A-1. He thought, "Which way should I go? I'm already at the edge of China!" The left wing continued to burn. O'Connor still thought that if he could jettison his ordnance and put out the fire, he could fly home. Ironically, the engine was still running fine. Then the whole left wing exploded.

O'Connor ran out of options. He pulled the ejection handle between his legs, and the next thing he knew he was dangling in his parachute. His helmet was twisted 90 degrees on his head, causing the oxygen mask to cover his eyes; and the chin strap badly bruised his throat. Looking up, he saw several severed risers and that a couple of parachute panels were missing. O'Connor did not see his disabled Skyraider again or hear where it went down, but he did observe that he would be landing in a fog-covered jungle.

He landed in bamboo on the side of a steep hill and rolled some distance down it. He took his helmet off and climbed back up the hill to a dirt trail. Afraid that enemy soldiers might be on the path, he moved another 150 feet up the hill. He got down in the weeds, put mud on his face and removed the survival radio from his vest. He carried a special microphone connected to the radio by tubing. This mike would allow a pilot to talk without being heard by people around him. Anxious to report his position to wingman Jim Beggerly, he looked for his compass. It was gone. Someone had borrowed it just when he needed it most.

In the distance O'Connor could hear gunfire in the fog, but without a compass he could not tell the rescue force from which direction the gunfire was coming. O'Connor called to Beggerly on his survival radio and said he was alive. Beggerly said that he had seen the bailout and crash and would alert the rescue forces.

O'Connor now saw three people in civilian clothes, each carrying a bolt-action rifle. He realized he was in Laos and that these people were not North Vietnamese soldiers; they were probably Pathet Lao. Pathet Lao were known to be very unfriendly to Americans. Intelligence officers told us the Pathet Lao were mad at Americans for dropping bombs on them. They would probably just immediately execute a pilot. On the other hand, if a pilot was captured by the North Vietnamese, he would be treated roughly but kept alive. An American had value for the North Vietnamese either for tactical information or for trading.

Overhead O'Connor could hear two helicopters but could not see either one because of the fog. It was still early morning, and he hoped the fog would clear soon. Over the survival radio he heard they were Air America choppers and one would try to pick him up.

Ron Furtak and his wingman had just completed a Firefly strike mission in northern Laos when they heard that O'Connor was shot down. They had already expended their bombs and rockets on enemy positions but still had white phosphorous marking rockets and 20-mm ammunition. Furtak flew toward Lima Site 85 and planned to assist the Air America rescue attempt. Unfortunately, within a few moments the Air America pilot reported his plane had been shot, so both choppers left with O'Connor still on the ground.

About an hour and a half after O'Connor was shot down, the fog started to lift, and he heard from the FAC that the Sandy and Jolly rescue armada was on its way. He was hidden in thick bamboo that was approximately fifteen to twenty feet high. As the fog cleared he could hear enemy gunfire from the direction of Lima Site 85, although he could not see the site itself.

The rescue force was set up as follows: Sandy 1—Capt. Jerry J. Jenkinson; Sandy 2—Lt. Col. Richard Walsh; Sandy 3—Lt. Col. Walter Steuck; Sandy 4—Capt. Robert "Wild Bill" Coady.

Because Lima Site 85 area was so dangerous, four more aircraft were put on Sandy orbit. Major Palank, whom I had seen eject from a Skyraider during the rescue of Streetcar 304, would be Sandy 5 and Capt. Joseph Pirruccello his wingman. I would be Sandy 7 and young 1st Lt. Jon Ewing my wingman. All of the wingmen were new to the squadron and inexperienced in rescue operations. Of the eight pilots in the rescue force, three would be killed on rescue missions in the next three months and one would be shot down and survive. A fortune-teller could predict that real bad days lay ahead for the 602nd squadron.

After spending six weeks flying nothing but night combat missions, I was happy to get back to day flights. Since flying in Southeast Asia, I had rescued a Navy A-7 pilot and two Air Force F-4 pilots; O'Connor's rescue would be my first rescue of another Sandy pilot. Tom O'Connor was a close friend. It made the war seem very personal to me to see him down in the jungle.

After the fast movers worked over the area, O'Connor was told that a rescue attempt would be made soon. He had been on the ground about three hours by then. O'Connor had three Mark 13 flares and got them out ready to use. A Mark 13 flare was a metal cylinder about six inches long and two inches in diameter. It was fired by pulling a metal ring similar to those used on soft drink cans back in the 1960s. It had a "day end" with orange smoke and a "night end" with an intense white flame. Every combat pilot in Southeast Asia carried the flares. As he heard the Jolly Green on its way in, O'Connor pulled the wire on his the first flare. The rusty wire broke, and the key came loose in his hand—no orange smoke. He then tried to alert the Jolly on the radio that his flare had failed, but he was too hoarse from both fear and the chin strap injury to his throat. No words came out of his mouth! Fortunately, he carried a plastic canister of water to drink or he would not have been able to talk to the rescue force at all. Even though he had torn ligaments in his right knee, he felt no pain, probably because of his adrenaline pumping.

O'Connor popped his backup flare, and the Jolly Green started in for the rescue. As the chopper arrived overhead, the downwash from the blades pushed the bamboo over, exposing his position. He said that he felt like the Statue of Liberty, standing in the open, holding a torch high in his right hand. With the bamboo blown down, he could see the river below and a nearby village with people yelling and dogs barking. From his position on the cliff, he could see across the valley to Lima Site 85.

The Jolly came into a hover, started lowering the penetrator, but then took a couple of hits and pulled off. Now the enemy knew O'Connor's precise position. He had been exposed and had also used up the second of his three flares. A couple of mortar rounds came in close to him, less than a hundred yards away.

Now O'Connor felt it was too dangerous to stay in his present position. He moved along the cliff about fifty yards to the east and hid again. The Sandys pounded the area more. With only one flare remaining, O'Connor knew his situation was getting critical. He was positive that the Pathet Lao would kill him if he was captured. At that moment he came up with a unique plan. He told Sandy lead that if he was about to be captured, he would put his survival radio on solid beeper and throw it in the bushes. It would be a signal to place ordnance directly on his position. If he got killed, he wanted to take some of the enemy with him.

As the Skyraiders continued to put ordnance down around him, he heard less and less firing from the enemy. Sandy lead told him that an HH-53 Super Jolly (sometimes called a Super Buff) from Udorn was on its way in for the rescue. The Jolly crew was Capt. James Miers, aircraft commander; Maj. Barton Libby, rescue copilot; S. Sgt. Ralph Frazier, flight engineer; Sgt. William Johnson, PJ; and Sgt. Dennis O'Connor, also a PJ but no relation to Tom. Finally the HH-53 arrived, and O'Connor popped his last flare. Again he held it in the air, but this time he held it in his left hand and had his .38 pistol in his right hand. He did not plan to get into a firefight with the Pathet Lao but decided that he would shoot an enemy soldier if one came running out of the bushes at the last moment. The Jolly lowered the penetrator attached to the hoist cable. O'Connor could hear two Gatling guns shooting out of the sides of the chopper. Normally, the survivor would pull the three leaves down on the penetrator, sit on one, and attach himself with a strap around his waist. Instead, O'Connor dropped his gun and flare and used both his hands and arms to grab the penetrator. He gave the flight engineer a thumbs-up, and off they went. "What a view," O'Connor said to himself, suspended about seventy feet below the helicopter. O'Connor told people afterwards that it was like being shot up in a rocket.

As soon as he was reeled into the HH-53, O'Connor wanted to shake the helicopter pilots' hands, but the PJs strapped him in a seat and put a headset over his ears. The Super Jolly needed to find a C-130 tanker and pick up fuel on the way home. Just when O'Connor was starting to relax, a new problem surfaced. The HH-53 could not get hooked up with the tanker. The pilots tried and tried—O'Connor lost track of how many attempts they made. Finally they made a successful hookup and got enough fuel to get back to the chopper's home base at Udorn.

After landing, O'Connor saw a bunch of military brass on the ramp ready to welcome him back, but he wished he had returned to NKP where all of the Sandys would be there to greet him. As he stepped out of the helicopter and onto the ramp he practically fell down. O'Connor told the medics, "My knee hurts like hell!" The doctors immediately took him to the hospital, not to a rescue party. O'Connor took a shower, and the doctors placed his knee in a cast and gave him a sleeping pill. He spent several days in the hospital at Udorn and then was transported back to NKP in a Helio U-10 Courier.

When O'Connor returned to the hooch at NKP, his roommate, Pete Brown, seemed to be acting strangely. After a while O'Connor found out the cause. Brown was acting as an instructor pilot for a new pilot, who was flying his second combat mission. Brown heard over the radio that Tom O'Connor was down, and he and his student diverted from their assigned mission to join in the search-and-rescue effort. By mistake, the student dropped CBU directly over O'Connor. Tom said the CBU had been going off all around him, leaves were flying, but he didn't get hurt. Meanwhile, Brown was afraid that his student had killed O'Connor and was so depressed he couldn't speak about it. It was a close call for both of them.

O'Connor was off flying status for many weeks while he waited for his knee to heal. Once he could walk with a cast, he was made duty officer for the 602nd. O'Connor said he felt foolish trying to walk wearing a cast under his flying suit. He thought he looked like a German Gestapo officer doing a goose step. He was afraid that other airmen would think, "What kind of act is this officer trying to pull?" With his injury he realized how vulnerable he would be if he were ever shot down again. He was so stressed out that he started smoking again.

On December 8, 1968, Tom O'Connor had a bad day but not a really bad day. Captain Pirruccello, on the other hand, had a really bad day on Dec. 8. Joe Pirruccello, age twenty-seven, was a graduate of the Air Force Academy class of 1963, father of two children, and son of an Air Force colonel. He was very tall and kind of a quiet person. But then most of the new guys were quiet and unassuming—they had a lot to learn before becoming assets to our unit. Pirruccello came to the squadron only a few weeks earlier with two other new pilots, Captains Robert Coady and Clyde Campbell. All three roomed together and soon would be faced with the trials of their lives.

On Tom O'Connor's rescue, Pirruccello was Sandy 6 in A-1J, serial number 142035, and wingman for Bill Palank. Pirruccello's A-1J on that day was a very special aircraft to me. Four months earlier, on August 23, 1968, I had ferried the aircraft from Cam Ranh Bay, South Vietnam to NKP. Earlier that morning I was a passenger in a C-123 Provider being transported to Cam Ranh Bay for the purpose of acquiring another aircraft for our squadron. We had lost so many aircraft in the previous four months I had flown combat that we were badly in need of replacement Skyraiders. A-1J serial, number 142035, had just come off the boat from the United States. It had originally been in the U.S. Navy inventory, then retrieved from Air Force storage at the boneyard in Davis-Monthan AFB, Arizona and completely refurbished.

After many weeks on the boat crossing the Pacific Ocean, it was off-loaded at Cam Ranh Bay and prepared for flight. During my preflight inspection, in which I walked around the aircraft checking every exposed part for anything unusual, I noticed patches of white plastic preservation material peeling off the camouflaged surfaces of the Skyraider. It reminded me of skin peeling off my arms and legs when I got sunburned as a child in Nebraska. I was told that the material would not affect the flying qualities of the A-1. Other than the preservation material, the refurbished plane looked like a new aircraft, right off the factory floor.

As soon as I completed my inspection I took off for NKP. I would be flying over South Vietnam and crossing the Ho Chi Minh Trail in a newly restored, but unarmed A-1J. All I had was my web belt with emergency radio, knife, .38 pistol, and a standard mesh vest with survival items. I climbed to 10,000 feet and followed my map to NKP. Compared to the old, worn-out A-1E models we were flying, this A-1J was a superb aircraft. I couldn't wait to fly 142035 on a combat mission.

On the morning of December 8, 1968, the day Tom O'Connor got shot down and rescued, Gene McCormack briefed Joe Pirruccello on the high-speed stall characteristics of the single-seat H and J models. The planes were very unforgiving of pilots who manhandled them during a steep dive and rapid pullout low to the ground.

Squadron commander Colonel Stueck was also flying on O'Connor's rescue. Stueck said there was a village about two miles from where Tom O'Connor was shot down. He observed natives coming out of the village toward O'Connor. The Sandys were strafing the trail, trying to prevent the enemy from capturing O'Connor. Jet aircraft were dropping bombs on the perimeter of the rescue scene.

Stueck watched Joe Pirruccello make strafing pass after pass, each one at a lower altitude than the previous one. During one pass Pirruccello did not pull out in time to prevent the Skyraider from pancaking into a small hill. Stueck later said, "Pirruccello's A-1 exploded on contact with the ground, then careened back in the air and ran smack into a karst mountain about five hundred feet high." Colonel Stueck didn't see Pirruccello eject or parachute to the ground. He had no doubt in his mind that Joe Pirruccello was killed. Even after thirty-two years, he can still vividly see Pirruccello's Skyraider crash into the mountain. Whether Pirruccello was hit by ground fire or simply pulled too many Gs in the stall-prone J model was never known.

Gene McCormack, who had briefed Pirruccello only hours earlier about the J model's stall characteristic, grieved over the loss. He said, "I guess I wasn't a good briefer—the high-speed stall got Pirruccello." McCormack felt

Pirruccello's loss greatly, but Joe Pirruccello was flying the plane and made his own decision on dive angle and pull-up point. We were individually responsible for our own flying techniques and the risks we took in attempting to save another pilot. That fact still didn't lessen the pain and frustration we felt in losing a squadron pilot and good friend.

Nine days after Tom O'Connor was shot down near Lima Site 85, Capt. Jerry Jenkinson got hit in the same area and had to jump out of his A-1. Jenkinson, who had led the rescue for O'Connor, was twenty-eight, a tall, slender bachelor, who had been in the class behind me at Hurlburt. He was very handsome, our unanimous selection as the person we pilots would have selected to play the part of a Sandy pilot if a movie was ever made about A-1 rescues in Vietnam. He had very unusual green eyes; the Thai maids called him "Sweet-eyes."

Maj. Harry Dunivant remembered Jenkinson as quite a cut up; he considered him the star of the Sandy Box. Jenkinson would get up on a table and dance a jig to the applause of his fellow pilots. Many pilots let their hair down after flying combat missions and enjoyed several beers and a few laughs. Being young and vigorous, and under the stress of daily combat, we looked for ways to entertain one another.

Since Jenkinson was also shot down near Lima Site 85, Tom O'Connor was anxious to hear his rescue story. Unlike O'Connor, Jenkinson had more time after he was hit to fly away from Lima Site 85 before ejecting from his A-1H. He flew south a few miles and then jumped. But similar to O'Connor, Jenkinson came down and saw people on the ground. He didn't know whether they were enemy or friendlies. Jenkinson said to O'Connor that his thoughts were, "Do I shoot at them, or are they going to shoot me?" Lucky for Jenkinson, they were good guys. The Jollys made an unopposed rescue, returning him to NKP. Jerry Jenkinson had been lucky; he completed his year tour and returned to the States.

12 PANDA 1

It was practically a perfect mission. On December 24, 1968, I was leading a strike mission in northern Laos using the call sign Firefly 36. My wingman, "Wild Bill" Coady, was Firefly 37. Wild Bill was twenty-nine years old and from Tampa, Florida. He was one of the new guys in the squadron and had only a few combat missions under his belt. He was overweight, had an outgoing personality, and a can-do attitude. While he was jovial and fun to be around, I thought he was quite inexperienced and had a long way to go before he would be a good Skyraider gunner. He had flown quite a few missions as my wingman and something bad seemed to happen to him on every flight.

One time he got a chip light, a red warning light in the cockpit that indicated metal flakes from the engine were sticking to a magnetic plug in the engine case. The light could indicate impending engine failure, a bad omen if you were over enemy territory. I joined in formation and followed him back to NKP, making sure he got home safely. Another time, he had a rough engine, and again I escorted him home. Then still another time, he called out that his flight controls were jammed. Again I escorted him home to NKP.

I remembered once we were flying back home after delivering all our bombs and rockets with Wild Bill flying my wing. He yelled out on the radio that he spotted a tank and wanted permission to roll in and fire his 20-mm guns at it. I cleared him in and followed behind him. I didn't see a tank. We were many miles from enemy country, and, besides, I had never seen a tank in Laos in the 132 missions and 450 hours of combat flying time that I had flown to that point. I thought the tank was a figment of Bill's imagination; however, he was positive it was a tank. We never found the tank.

But our flight together on December 24 was near perfect. Each of us carried eight 500-pound general-purpose bombs, two pods of rockets (nineteen rockets per pod), and two pods of white phosphorous marking rockets. We got airborne from NKP that Christmas Eve day just past noon. Visibility was clear, not a cloud in sight. We were briefed to strike two targets in the southern half of Barrel Roll. I found the first target at 2:05 p.m., and each of us made two passes, on the first dropping four bombs and the next firing nineteen rockets. We pulled off at 2:12 p.m. and flew a short distance to target number two. This time we started bombing at 2:22 p.m. and ended up with a rocket pass at 2:30 p.m. Wild Bill's bomb delivery looked accurate, as did his rocket passes. The mission was normal, using standard squadron tactics.

Afterwards, I was scheduled to FAC in three flights of F-105 Thunderchief bombers (called Thuds). No Trump, a flight of two F-105s, each carrying two AGM-12 Bullpup missiles, three 750-pound bombs, and a rocket pod, arrived at 2:52 p.m. The Thuds fired their Bullpups exactly into the entrance of a cave, severely damaging it and causing one secondary fire. Their bombs and rockets were on target too. As they departed at 3:02 p.m., I told them they put 90 percent of their ordnance in the target area and covered 50 percent of the target. At 3:09 p.m. the next two F-105s arrived, Metric flight, each carrying six 750-pound bombs and one pod holding nineteen rockets. In just five minutes they each made two passes and put 100 percent of their weapons on a different target than that of No Trump flight, covering 60 percent of their target. Finally Calico flight, the last two F-105s with the same ordnance as Metric flight, arrived at 3:18 p.m. Likewise, they each made two passes on a third target putting 100 percent of their ordnance on target and covered 40 percent. They completed their strikes at 3:25 p.m., and we all headed home. It had been a picture-perfect mission.

During the jet strikes, Wild Bill flew a loose wing formation on me and

watched for enemy ground fire. Our mission went like clockwork, very professional, no extraneous radio communications, all strikes on target, and no air
emergencies. Finally I had flown a ho-hum mission with Wild Bill. We landed
at NKP at 4:20 p.m. after three hours and forty-five minutes of flying time.

When we taxied into our parking area we noticed that the Skyraider
ground crews had decorated the planes that would fly strike missions on
Christmas the next day. They painted all the ordnance red for the holiday.
It didn't seem like Christmas; it was so warm the ground crews were working bare chested.

I was anxious to get back to my room in the hooch and listen to the radio.
Six years earlier, I had been stationed in the 84th Fighter Interceptor
Squadron located at Hamilton AFB in northern California flying the Mc-
Donnell F-101B Voodoo. While there I met Bill Anders, a pilot two years
older than I and a graduate of the Naval Academy class of 1955. He was interested in getting into the NASA space program as an astronaut. Bill Anders
had a serious and proper demeanor; he was more straight-arrow than most
of the rowdy fighter pilots of that era. Captain Anders seemed to be a man
with a mission, knew where he wanted to go with his career, and was always
plotting how to get there. Through Anders I learned about the Air Force Test
Pilot School at Edwards and became interested in flight test myself. Anders
was accepted as an astronaut by NASA in 1963 and was now aboard Apollo
8 circling the moon. His flight was the first space mission to leave Earth's
gravitational pull.

Back in my room, I tuned the radio to the Armed Services Thailand Radio
Network to get updates on the Apollo 8 mission. Bill Anders's role in the mission was to photograph possible lunar landing sites for upcoming space
flights. It was a critical task, somewhat similar to our strike missions. It was
very difficult for us to find some of our pre-briefed enemy targets hidden in
the jungle among the winding rivers and numerous bomb craters. Anders
would be looking for a variety of small meteor craters on the lifeless moon
surface to guide him to the proper area to photograph.

Suddenly, there was a knock on the door. Wild Bill came in to tell me he had
looked at the flight schedule for December 25, and we would be flying together
again as Sandy 1 and 2 on rescue alert. Also, he heard that Bob Hope was giving a Christmas show to the troops down at the flight line. Did I want to go?

We walked a few blocks and stood in the back of the crowd to watch Hope's performance. Bob Hope had been performing for GIs since World War II; now he was touring both Vietnam and Thailand. Bob Hope joked about our base by saying, "NKP is so secret the planes have to land backwards!"

Hope was accompanied by star performer Ann-Margret and a group of beautiful females. This year they were the Gold Diggers; they were dressed in fancy pink outfits and looked absolutely gorgeous. The Caucasian women were called "round-eyes" (in contrast to Asian "slant-eyes") by those of us in the military.

One of our young bachelor pilots had thought that he would miss the Bob Hope show. A couple of days earlier, Lt. Jon Ewing was on a rescue mission in southern Laos. Jon Ewing was fresh out of pilot training but a very good aviator for being so new to aviation. During a rescue he was hit in the left gear well by 37-mm ground fire. The canopy was blown ajar and the cockpit filled with smoke. Ewing manually jettisoned all his ordnance and blew off the canopy. He saw fire in his left wing and aimed his Skyraider for a karst mountain in preparation for ejection. Then he realized the engine was still running, so he kept flying. No one answered his calls for help on the UHF radio. At that instant he surmised that ground fire had probably blown off his radio antenna. Even though his fuel gauge showed empty and the fire was still burning, the engine continued to run. Ewing got the fire out by "slipping" the A-1, that is, by putting in full rudder so as to shield the fire from intense airflow. His next objective was to get to the Mekong River and then the Thai base at Ubon. With his Skyraider still staggering, he tried to lower the landing gear, but because of the location of the fire he realized it wasn't going to work. Since the flaps wouldn't extend either, he landed gear up at Ubon using his tail hook to stop the A-1. After his crash landing he said half jokingly, "Who needs flaps and a landing gear?" The aircraft was a complete loss. Jon Ewing was awarded the Silver Star for that flight.

When Ewing was hit, the first thing that came to his mind was that he was going to miss the Bob Hope show and Ann-Margret. Since he survived the crash landing he did get to attend the show and was invited backstage to interview Hope. Ewing got a photo of himself with one of the Gold Digger entertainers sitting on his lap. Ironically, her name was Sandy.

During the show I slipped down the aisle to within a couple of rows of the stage and shot a few photographs with my Pentax camera. When I returned to the back, the Sandy alert pilots who had been relieved of duty for the day joined us. The off-duty Sandy pilots reported to me that an F-105 had been shot down and a first-light effort was planned for the following morning.

Coady and I returned to the Intelligence Office to get an update on the situation. A briefer explained that an F-105 from the 355th Tactical Fighter Wing at Takhli had been hit by hostile ground fire. The aircraft, call sign Panda 1, was flown by Maj. Charles Brownlee, age thirty-five. Major Brownlee was leading a flight of four F-105s when his aircraft caught fire and he ejected. The other members of his flight saw him in his parachute descending into the jungle near Route 911 between the village of Ban Phaphilong and Ban Karai Pass. The location was reported to me as the 102 radial at 68 nautical miles from our TACAN station at NKP. This was near Tchepone again, bad country for a rescue.

That afternoon Jolly Green 17 had been flying an airborne orbit in the vicinity of NKP when they were alerted for a possible search-and-rescue mission. They flew out to a safe position and were joined by Jolly Green 15. The weather in the entire area was clear. Sandy 1 and 2 and a Nail FAC were searching for the survivor without success. A chute was spotted at the approximate location where the survivor went down, but it was thought to be from another source, since the survivor had been seen to disappear into the trees a short distance away. Because no radio contact could be made with Major Brownlee and the sun had set, the search-and-rescue forces returned to NKP. Jolly Green helicopters did not have a night combat rescue capability.

Wild Bill Coady and I were directed to go back to our rooms, get a good night's sleep, and arrive at 3:30 a.m. for briefing on a first-light effort. Seven months earlier, I had a hard time sleeping the night before I went out to rescue Streetcar 304. The same sleep loss occurred back in July for the rescue of Roman 2A and Roman 2B in North Vietnam. This time I spent another night tossing and turning, getting a twenty-minute nap every now and then. Finally, I just got up, took a shower, and dressed.

This upcoming mission had all the makings of a difficult rescue. Crew assignments were: Sandy 1—Capt. George Marrett; Sandy 2—Capt. Robert "Wild Bill" Coady; Sandy 3—Maj. John Shacklock; Sandy 4—Maj. Anthony DeCarlo.

As a backup, Majors Watts and Campbell would stand ground alert as Sandy 7 and 8. We completed our briefing, preflighted the Skyraiders in the darkness, and got airborne at 5:30 a.m. The plan was to arrive in the rescue area nearly an hour before sunrise and conduct an electronic search for Major Brownlee using our standard UHF emergency frequency. We hoped Major Brownlee would hear my A-l circling overhead and call me to report his physical status, his location in the jungle, and the nearness of enemy troops and guns. Once the sun rose, we would then plan a rescue using the safest route over the jungle, attempting to keep the Jolly Green helicopter clear of enemy guns.

After I got airborne in the darkness, I turned eastward and climbed to 6,000 feet. The stars were bright and clear. I could not see any lights on the ground in Laos; as usual, it was as dark as the ocean at night. Sandy 3 and 4 led the two Jollys to a position ten miles south of the survivor's position and set up an orbit.

As I was flying, I began to think about astronaut Bill Anders and his trip to the moon. He was flying over a dark and barren, inhospitable environment on the backside of the moon. Similarly, I felt like I was on the other side of the earth, also flying in an inhospitable environment but this one also full of enemy troops and guns. Anders was relying on the capsule pressurization and oxygen supply to care for him; I was relying on my single radial engine to keep me safe from the enemy. He was looking for small potential landing sites on the surface of the moon; I was looking for a single downed pilot enclosed by thick jungle. We were both looking for the proverbial needle in a haystack. I was sure Bill Anders was tired and fatigued from his cramped quarters in the space capsule. I was tired and fatigued from the seven months of daily combat and the small cramped Skyraider cockpit. We were both on a long voyage, sailing into the great unknown, miles and miles from home and our loved ones.

Gradually, I saw a slight reddening of the eastern sky over North Vietnam. As I could make out the rivers and streams over Laos, I slowly descended and continued to call on our emergency frequency, "Panda 1, this is Sandy 1." I called and called with no answer. Wild Bill was instructed to stay above me, keep me in sight, and call out enemy ground fire. I flew back and forth over many, many square miles of jungle. I avoided the nearby roads, as Major Brownlee had been reported to descend into trees before he disappeared.

Even before the sun rose in the east, my dark-adapted eyes could make out individual trees. It was hard to tell where I had flown or areas I might have missed; the jungle all looked the same to me. I got down to about a hundred feet over the trees and flew at 200 knots; the Skyraider was still full of fuel and ordnance. Back and forth I continued to fly until I thought I spotted a white parachute lodged in a tree some twenty to thirty feet below some taller trees. I was positive it was a pilot parachute and not a smaller flare chute. This area had been hotly contested for years and probably thousands of flare chutes were used in the previous battles at night. All I could see was a parachute, and then only for a split second, as I roared overhead. I needed more light to make a positive determination.

About that time I heard the strangest call I ever heard on the UHF radio. Wild Bill Coady called, "Sandy lead, I'm in an inverted spin!" In my wildest imagination I couldn't conceive of a Skyraider pilot in an inverted spin, full of fuel and ordnance, at dawn over enemy territory. Could any situation be worse? Just when I had placed faith and confidence in Coady, he had found another bizarre problem. I could do nothing but try to spot him in the sky above me and at least determine if he had ejected from his A-1 or where it crashed. After several seconds he called, "Sandy 2 recovered, I'm going home." I spotted him at low altitude heading westbound back to NKP. I added full power to my Skyraider and tried to close on him. Slowly, he climbed back up to 2,000 feet as the sun rose behind me. I joined in formation on his right side and looked to see if I could determine what had happened to his plane. The Skyraider looked normal; I didn't see any hanging ordnance, bent flight controls, or landing gear or flaps hanging down. I slipped under him and took a look at the left side. On the top of his left wing I spotted a twelve-by-twelve-inch metal plate flapping in the breeze. This plate was designed to cover the left 20-mm internal gun inspection port, was hinged on the front, and attached to the top surface of the wing with multiple Zeus fasteners. Evidently, Coady had missed locking the plate on preflight, and, being loose, it acted as a spoiler on his wing. When he attempted a rapid left turn, the plate lifted up in the air stream and the drag it produced rolled the aircraft over. He was fortunate to recover from an inverted spin; I had never heard of that happening in a Skyraider. But if it happened to anyone, it would happen to Wild Bill Coady. Now it was important to get him back to NKP and a safe landing before he lost control again. I passed my Sandy lead to Sandy 3 and followed Coady all the way back to NKP. After thirty minutes, he landed on the runway and slowed to a stop. Seeing he was home safely, I added power to my Skyraider and climbed back toward the location of Panda 1. Sandys 7 and 8 were scrambled to replace Coady and me. At this time I had been airborne for nearly three hours.

While I escorted Coady back to NKP, Sandys 3 and 4 continued electronic and visual search for Panda 1. They were not able to make contact with Major Brownlee.

Back in the area where I had first seen the parachute I reassumed my status as on-scene commander and started searching again. After several passes back and forth, I found the chute. Since the sun had risen higher in the sky, I was now absolutely positive it was a pilot's parachute and even thought I saw a person hanging in a harness below it. Again it was a fleeting sight, a chance encounter; I only had a split second to evaluate what I observed.

It was now time to transfer Sandy lead to another pilot and think about returning to NKP. I asked the new Sandy pilot to get about a hundred feet in my trail position while I flew directly over the parachute and dipped my right wing at the very moment I flew over it. He followed my advice, and we did as I suggested. He could not see the chute. We repeated the maneuver several times with the same results. Even though the sun was higher in the sky and the weather clear, it was not easy to spot the parachute. We tried it one more time with the same results.

I was now presented with the most difficult decision in my year of combat. If I passed the lead to Sandy 3 the rescue attempt would be over; he couldn't see the survivor hanging in the tree. Obviously he couldn't lead the Jolly in for a pickup if he didn't know where the survivor was located. If I flew home we would never know what happened to Major Brownlee. His white parachute would be an image forever branded in my memory.

I had been flying for nearly four hours by then, at low altitude with the mixture rich. I was still hauling a full load of ordnance under the Skyraider's wing. Now my own fuel state was becoming a limiting factor. I had only a few minutes to consider the possibilities and the options open to all of us. If I led the Jollys in for an attempted pickup, it could be very hazardous not knowing if enemy troops were under the tree cover. On the other hand, I had now flown for hours directly over his parachute, and no one in my flight had spotted ground fire. I had not taken any hits.

If I flew home, Major Brownlee would surely be lost. I reasoned that the best choice was to bring the Jolly Green over the survivor and let them analyze Brownlee's condition from a closer distance. It was very hard for me to make that determination skimming over the treetops in a Skyraider at 200 knots.

There is a code among warriors that they always bring out their casualties, living or dead. It was a feeling common to all combatants, offering a form of comfort when we were in combat. We felt assured that we wouldn't be left behind on a field of battle, slowly dying. "If you're down, we'll get you out," we told the jet fighter pilots. "And if you're dead, we'll bring you out anyway. At least you'll be dead among friends."

As Skyraider rescue pilots we took the decision to call the Jolly Green helicopter in for a rescue very seriously. We argued, analyzed, and discussed every possible combat situation we might be confronted with in a rescue as we drank beer in the Sandy Box. Some A-1 pilots felt we were not in the body business. They said, "If you're dead, you're dead. Leave the dead behind, don't risk the living."

We also discussed what we would do if we were shot down and confronted by an overwhelming number of enemy soldiers and still had a loaded pistol. Would you shoot it out to the end? Would you throw the gun down and get captured? Would you shoot yourself? The results were mixed. It seemed to be a function of the actual circumstances. There were no set rules; each man had to decide for himself what he would do. We had a big unknown on the Panda 1 rescue. Was Major Brownlee alive or dead?

As far as the rescue of Panda 1 was concerned, it was a perilous decision for me to make, whichever way I decided to go. If I returned to NKP, the rescue was over. If I called in the Jolly for a rescue attempt, it would be extremely dangerous without the survivor helping by relaying information on what was going on beneath the trees.

Finally I called Jolly Green 17 and said we were going to try a rescue attempt. My four Sandys flew out to meet the Jollys in their orbit. Jolly 17 dropped his external fuel tanks and moved from his holding point and crossed Route 911 to high karst northeast of the downed pilot. The rescue force of five Sandys and Jolly Green 17 followed me at fifty feet above the trees toward Brownlee.

Then I couldn't find the elusive parachute. The other aircraft followed me as I zigzagged once again trying to find the hidden pilot. Back and forth I flew, frustrated that I couldn't find the parachute again. It was extremely difficult to locate. The Jolly Green 17 pilot felt uncomfortable being so low over enemy country and said he was climbing back to altitude until I could relocate the missing airman. Just after Jolly Green 17 started his climb back to the safety of the former orbit, I spotted the parachute again and asked him to return.

Within a few moments, Jolly Green 17 reported seeing a man hanging in his harness, not moving and helmetless. The Jolly crew didn't report any ground fire and could see no enemy troops. A twenty-two-year old PJ, A/1C Charles King, volunteered to descend on the jungle penetrator to recover the pilot. As the hoist started down, Brownlee's parachute was dislodged by rotor blast and he fell to the jungle floor. Jolly Green 17 was hovering in the tree tops approximately 125 feet above the ground. The area of hover was covered by a double jungle canopy with dense jungle undergrowth, allowing only occasional glimpses of the ground. The flight engineer, T. Sgt. Jerome Casey, stated in the official report that after Airman King was lowered to the ground, he asked for more slack and dragged the penetrator about thirty feet through the underbrush and under a large branch to the pilot. He released the parachute and attached Major Brownlee's harness to the penetrator. Then King called for the hoist to be raised and was using it to drag Brownlee over to an area directly beneath the helicopter. With still about ten feet to go, automatic weapons fire broke out and King was heard to say, "I'm hit, I'm hit! Pull up, pull up!" At the same time, Jolly Green 17 started taking hits in the forward part of the main cabin from directly beneath the helicopter. The Jolly pilot immediately initiated a climb out of hover. Normally, the airman on the penetrator would be hoisted clear of the trees prior to the rescue helicopter resuming forward flight. But in this instance, enemy troops were hosing the helicopter with 30-caliber small-arms fire. Out of options and now battle damaged, the Jolly pilot was forced to leave his hover. He elected to ascend and start forward flight, at the same time hoping this maneuver would lift Major Brownlee and Airman King clear of the trees.

At this moment, my Sandy flight was in a left-handed orbit around Jolly Green 17, flying approximately two hundred feet above the trees. We were waiting for the Jolly to relay the status of the rescue. I clearly remember the Jolly starting to climb and transition to forward flight. The cable holding the penetrator started to arc over when the helicopter moved forward. That image is still vivid in my memory thirty-three years later.

As the helicopter gained altitude, either the hoist cable or penetrator caught on a tree and the cable snapped, dropping Major Brownlee and Airman King to the ground. The seriously damaged helicopter was forced out of the area because of the intense ground fire. Three bullets penetrated the front fuel tanks, and one struck under the copilot's seat. The armor plating in the floor under his seat saved him from a serious wound. Three more bullets lodged in the space between the fuel tanks.

Major Brownlee and Airman King were left on the ground. As I saw the Jolly Green lift into the air dragging the cable without the penetrator, it was obvious to me that the rescue attempt had failed. I stared at the jungle tree where Jolly Green 17 had hovered but couldn't see Brownlee's parachute any more. No reference point remained to separate that tree from the rest of the trees in the jungle. I started firing 20-mm ammunition in a circle around the point fixed in my sight hoping that my bullets would prevent more troops from moving in on Airman King and Major Brownlee, allowing them to escape if at all possible. After a couple of circles, I wasn't positive which tree they were under any more—one tree looked like another. Multiple calls were made on our UHF emergency frequency, but it was still as quiet as it had ever been. My fuel was now extremely low. I headed home and arrived back at NKP after nearly five hours of flight.

The next day several beeper signals were picked up in the area. The search-and-rescue forces were dispatched that afternoon and proceeded to the area where Panda 1 had gone down. On arrival all beeper signals ceased. The Jolly Green returned to NKP and two Sandys continued further electronic and visual search. They had no success and returned to NKP. Major Brownlee and Airman King were never heard from again.

Bill Anders returned safely from his orbit of the moon. I never flew with Wild Bill Coady again. He was killed twenty-four days later on another rescue.

Three days later, disaster nearly struck the 602nd again. This time Maj. Albert Roberts Jr. got hit by ground fire while helping General Vang Pao attempt to retake Lima Site 85. After he and his wingman, Capt. Clyde Campbell, dropped their bombs on an enemy position, Al Roberts set up to fire a white phosphorus marking rocket for a jet flight just entering the area. On his first pass he took two hits in the Skyraider's right landing gear. The shells went through the main wing spar and ended up in the trailing edge of the flap. The wing and hydraulic system caught fire and Roberts watched the paint on top of his wing blister. He dumped the hydraulic pressure and climbed south toward Thailand. Eventually, the fire burned itself out, and he was left with a fully functioning engine and flight controls, just no hydraulic pressure for his landing gear.

Roberts decided to fly back to Udorn rather than NKP since it had a better runway and crash facilities. The hour flight back to Udorn gave Roberts time to calm down and the crash rescue forces time to prepare for his arrival. He made a practice approach down the runway and returned for a full stop. His Skyraider was a newly refurbished A-1J model, one of the best planes in the squadron. Al Roberts dropped his tail hook and made a perfect engagement with the arresting gear. He survived the crash landing, but his A-1 was a total loss. It ended up in the fire pit at Udorn.

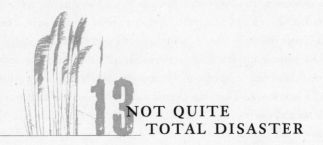

13
NOT QUITE
TOTAL DISASTER

On the morning of January 17, 1969, Gene McCormack and I were scheduled for a midday Firefly strike mission in Barrel Roll. We completed our attack and while returning to NKP heard on the radio that an active search-and-rescue mission was in progress.

At 11 that morning, Capt. Victor Smith and backseater 1st Lt. James Fegan from the 390th Tactical Fighter Squadron at Da Nang, South Vietnam, took off in their F-4D Phantom using the call sign Stormy 2. Their mission was to act as a FAC on an active 37-mm antiaircraft artillery site located in rugged jungle-covered mountains approximately twenty-three miles west-northwest of Khe Sanh, three miles southeast of Muang Xepon, and seven miles west of Tchepone.

Tchepone had become center court of the war in Steel Tiger (southern Laos). All of the trails coming out of North Vietnam converged at Tchepone. Likewise, south of Tchepone the main trail broke up into numerous roads that led into South Vietnam. We were putting pressure on the North Vietnamese to stop men and equipment moving on the Ho Chi Minh Trail into South Vietnam. The North Vietnamese fiercely defended that part of the trail with a giant inventory of weapons ranging from hand-held rifles to 37-mm antiaircraft artillery guns.

At 2:05 p.m., as Stormy 2 commenced an attack pass against the artillery battery, it was struck by antiaircraft artillery fire. Unable to control the F-4D, Captain Smith ordered Lieutenant Fegan to eject at very high speed. He complied with the order and his fully deployed parachute was seen descending to the ground by a flight of Navy A-4 aircraft that were also operating in this area. Lieutenant Fegan, who was twenty-four years old and a graduate of the Air Force Academy, landed in the jungle alive but had eleven fractures in his arms and left leg.

Captain Smith, who was twenty-seven and from Silver Spring, Maryland, was also a graduate of the Air Force Academy. The other pilots in the flight did not see him eject or parachute from his stricken F-4D. In addition, no beeper was ever heard from his survival radio. He was confirmed killed in action years later.

Immediately the search-and-rescue force standing alert at NKP was called upon to rescue the crew of Stormy 2. Flying as lead Sandy was Capt. Jerry Jenkinson, who had been shot down himself just a month earlier. Lt. Col. Lurie "Pete" Morris, Sandy 2, was his wingman. At the time, Pete Morris had been in the 602nd for only a couple of months and had completed fewer than fifty combat missions. Although a lieutenant colonel with thousands of hours in jet aircraft, he was rather inexperienced with the Skyraider to be flying on a rescue mission in an extremely dangerous area like Tchepone. Since no radio contact was made with Captain Smith, Sandys 1 and 2 concentrated their efforts on Lieutenant Fegan, Stormy 2B.

Within just a few minutes of flying over Tchepone, Morris reported to his lead that he felt his Skyraider take a hit from ground fire. Shortly thereafter, his cockpit filled with smoke and he lost his flight controls. In a dire condition and close to the ground, Morris ejected from his A-1. Now three pilots were thought to be on the ground in separate locations in hazardous Tchepone. To add to the complexity of the rescue, dusk was rapidly approaching. It would be impossible for the remaining search-and-rescue forces to effect a rescue that late in the day. Separate first-light SAR teams would be formed overnight and ready to launch early the next day. Stormy 2B was told to lay low for the night; the rescue forces would be back for a first-light effort the next morning. In reality, no one thought Stormy 2B would be there the next morning—there were too many bad guys in the area.

At 6:25 the next morning, January 18, 1969, however, Lieutenant Fegan made radio contact with the rescue force. Because of the stress of his ejection, he did not remember any details from the period shortly before or during the time his Phantom was shot down. Lieutenant Fegan did not know what had happened to Captain Smith. He did report that on the previous evening he heard a beeper signal on his survival radio but could not identify who initiated it. If it was Captain Smith, the signal was of too short a duration to obtain any useful information.

Sandy rescue aircraft found the wreckage of the F-4D on a 1,200-foot-high ridge in an extremely rocky and densely forested area that communist forces had heavily fortified. Because Lieutenant Fegan was seriously injured, PJ Leland Sorenson rode the penetrator down on the hoist and provided medical assistance. The Jolly successfully departed Tchepone without the loss of any more search-and-rescue aircraft. That could not be said for our guy, Sandy 2, Pete Morris.

Pete Morris spent the night high in a jungle tree. After the sun rose, he could clearly see a dirt road very near his position. While strapped to a tree to prevent his falling out, he saw six soldiers wearing North Vietnamese uniforms with pith helmets on their heads and rifles slung over their shoulders. The soldiers were coming down a road directly toward his position. If they looked up, he would be seen since he was fully exposed. Fortunately, they were looking down at the road, which made a 90-degree turn just before his tree—they did not see him. He also had heard vehicles during the night and other noises he described as cooking sounds (pots and pans hitting each other), which convinced him he was in a military containment area. The town nearby appeared to be deserted.

While Sandys 3, 4, 5, and 6 were rescuing Stormy 2B, another search-and-rescue force was being assembled to rescue Pete Morris. Leading that rescue was: Sandy 9—Capt. Donald Dunaway in an A-1H; Sandy 10—Capt. Robert "Wild Bill" Coady in an A-1H; Sandy 11—Maj. "Smilin'" Jack Watts in an A-1H; Sandy 12— Maj. Anthony DeCarlo in an A-1J.

Sitting on the ground and held in reserve, I would be Sandy 13 in an A-1H with my wingman, Maj. Harry Dunivant, as Sandy 14. I wasn't superstitious, but using the call sign Sandy 13 and flying a rescue over Tchepone sounded as bad as I could imagine!

Don Dunaway and Wild Bill Coady took off at 5:23 a.m. and arrived over Pete Morris's position at 6:05, but because of low stratus clouds and fog they could not visually pick up his location. Around 9 a.m. the fog burned off, and they saw Morris's chute in the top of a tree. Both Dunaway and Coady started trolling the area and picked up ground fire, which Morris called out to them. They were getting fired at from both south and southeast of Morris's position.

Both Sandy 11, Smilin' Jack Watts, and Sandy 12, Tony DeCarlo, were holding at 8,000 feet a couple of miles south with Jolly Greens 17 and 37. Two additional Skyraiders from Da Nang were orbiting, also at 8,000 feet. A few miles away, but close enough to get a clear view of the two Sandys flying low over Pete Morris, were Spad 7, flown by Lt. Col. Alexander Corey, and Spad 8, flown by Lt. Frederick Butler.

At 9:32 a.m. Colonel Corey saw ground fire directed at Captain Coady and called out on the radio, "He's getting it. Sandy just went in." Lieutenant Butler saw a fireball erupt from a tree area and then an unidentified voice said, "What in the world was that?" The effort to rescue Sandy 2 was momentarily halted and effort expended to investigate what had just happened. Don Dunaway was just pulling off after a weapons pass and said, "I imagine that's my wingman!" Dunaway saw a white phosphorous cloud and black smoke from burning aircraft fuel rise into the clear Laotian sky.

Orbiting with the two Jolly Green helicopters, both Jack Watts and Tony DeCarlo also saw billows of white and black smoke from what they thought must be an aircraft crash and not simply ordnance drops from a single Skyraider. However, neither of them actually saw an A-1 strike the jungle.

Maj. William Warwick, commander of Jolly Green 17, had a clear view of both Dunaway and Coady making firing passes over Pete Morris. Bill Warwick watched Dunaway pull off the target, and then his attention was drawn to Coady. Coady was approaching the target from the west over a heavily populated area four miles south of the town of Muang Xepon. He saw Coady's Skyraider in a very shallow dive, with wings level, impact the jungle and explode at the 2,100-foot level of a 2,500-foot hill. He thought the canopy was still on the A-1. Warwick said he did not observe a chute or hear an emergency beeper. No one else in the rescue armada of seven aircraft could offer any hope that Coady might have ejected at the very last moment and survived. Attention returned to the rescue of Pete Morris.

By then the original rescue aircraft had been airborne for over four hours. Most pilots were low on fuel and headed home to NKP. Two more Jolly Greens were scrambled, but now they would be HH-53s out of Udorn. At the same time, my wingman Major Dunivant and I took off and aimed for Tchepone. I dreaded another rescue over Tchepone; both my best and worst rescues had been there.

It wasn't until I got airborne that the command post reported to me that Wild Bill Coady was down. We never used words like "killed" or "dead" for our own sake or with the other pilots in the squadron. Those words sounded too final, too horrible a tragedy to comprehend. We usually said our squadron mate simply "went in" or had "gone down." Those phrases gave us some hope and faith that we would still see our buddies again.

Flying the HH-53 Jolly Green 67 was aircraft commander Maj. Paul Darghty; copilot Maj. Barton Libby; flight engineer S. Sgt. James Purdue; and two pararescue specialists—Sgts. Thomas Pope and Donald "Surfer" Johnson. The Jolly had just refueled and was ready to make the pickup of Colonel Morris. After beating up the area, we started in for the rescue, firing rockets, our 20-mm guns, and laying down CBU bomblets. The Jolly made visual contact with Morris's parachute, and, as they approached, he uncovered himself from the foliage he had been hiding behind. It was decided with the flip of a coin that Don Johnson would be the number-one PJ, meaning he would be designated to ride the penetrator down the hoist and recover Morris if he were too injured to help himself. Tom Pope, the second PJ, was stationed at the rear of the Jolly and manned the number-three minigun position on the tail ramp; it was a fully exposed and vulnerable position. Jolly Green 67 came into a hover over Morris. He did not require assistance, so Johnson positioned himself at the number-two minigun on the left side, returning fire as North Vietnamese troops opened fire on them. The Jolly started to take small-arms hits as Pope fired out the rear. Flight engineer James Purdue operated the hoist and kept a running commentary on the intercom while bringing Morris on board. Once Morris was inside the chopper, the flight engineer moved to a minigun place on the right side and fired out the doorway. Major Darghty turned his Jolly 180 degrees and started to lift up and accelerate away from the enemy-defended position.

As they pulled away, enemy gunners found their mark. PJ Don Johnson yelled into the crew intercom, "Tommy's been hit!" He threw off his helmet and ran the length of his safety harness until it jerked him to a stop. Johnson then unhooked his harness and continued to rush to the rear of the helicopter. Hot, viscous, pink hydraulic fluid, under high pressure, gushed out in streams all over the interior of Jolly Green 67. Tom Pope, his left leg practically severed, was drenched in blood and hydraulic fluid and nearly slipped out over the tail ramp to a three-hundred-foot drop because his safety strap was cut in two pieces by ground fire. Johnson reached out to save Pope and also slid on the slippery floor, starting to follow him into the void outside the helicopter. Desperately, Johnson grabbed Pope with his right hand and stretched the other arm out to grab a retainer strap, preventing both of them from falling to their deaths. Johnson has a vivid memory today of Pope using both of his legs to struggle for safety. Meanwhile, the two Jolly pilots valiantly fought the unresponsive flight controls to try to maintain forward flight. Johnson told me the HH-53 started to roller coaster.

At that very moment I was escorting the Jolly Green 67 flying in its five o'clock position. Jolly Green and I were approximately five hundred feet above the jungle, heading for NKP. Then I heard a strange call on the UHF radio. The desperate pilot did not identify himself, but stated in a calm voice, "I have lost my hydraulic system. I can't hold the flight controls." Even though the pilot didn't identify himself, I knew the radio call was from the Jolly pilot. The Skyraider did not have hydraulic-powered flight controls; it simply had wire cables from the control stick to the aileron, rudder, and elevator. It had to be the Jolly in trouble, not one of my Sandy aircraft. The HH-53 started to descend, flying straight ahead. I saw a clearing in the distance.

On board the Jolly, Don Johnson remained in the rear of the helicopter with the seriously wounded Tom Pope. Frantically, he applied a battlefield dressing, using the tails of a rectangular bandage as a makeshift tourniquet. Using his survival knife as a turning key, Johnson succeeded in reducing the spurting of blood from the artery of Pope's left leg. He then ran over to the medical kit and obtained a legitimate field tourniquet and secured it so tight above Pope's knee that it caused Pope to scream with pain. They were still taking ground fire, and James Purdue, the flight engineer, fired back with the only minigun still operating. Pete Morris came over to help Johnson when Purdue yelled, "We're gonna crash!"

I was helpless to assist the Jolly; the chopper pilot continued to keep forward motion, and it appeared to me that he planned to land in the clearing. I stayed in his five o'clock position and descended with him to around two hundred feet. Then I saw him contact the ground, but unfortunately his forward motion continued. I said, "Stop, stop!" to myself, but he passed through the clearing and into the surrounding tree line. As the Jolly's rotor beat up the trees the helicopter finally came to a stop and rolled over.

Inside Jolly Green 67 the five crew members and survivor Pete Morris were having the ride of their lives. It was the second crash landing for Pete in two days. For some reason, either a broken servo mechanism, bad indicator light, or simply not enough time, the Jolly pilots didn't jettison their exterior fuel tanks. They impacted the earth on a downhill slope and skidded into the trees. The tanks acted like an outrigger on a canoe, slowing the Jolly's forward motion. Johnson felt the Jolly lurch over on its left side, the rotor blades chopping up trees in its path.

When they came to a stop after their crash landing, Pope was on top of Johnson. Pete Morris was trying his best to keep a tight grip on both of them. Though shaken, they were still alive. That was the good news; the bad news was that they immediately started receiving more enemy ground fire.

As a Sandy rescue team, we had little ordnance remaining because we had expended most of it in the first rescue of Pete Morris. The situation was getting desperate. Over two days we had lost an F-4D, two Skyraiders, and now a Jolly Green helicopter. Evidence indicated that Wild Bill Coady was lost. (At the time I didn't know that Tom Pope, the PJ on board Jolly Green 67, was critically injured.) The backup helicopter, Jolly Green 70, was called and requested to be ready for another pickup.

In the crashed Jolly, Pete Morris helped Johnson place Tom Pope on a litter, and they started for the exit. The two Jolly pilots were attempting to retrieve secret documents from the weapons locker, preventing the enemy from obtaining classified information. Even though Pope's flak vest had protected his vital organs, he was showing signs of irreversible shock. Johnson grabbed his M-16 rifle, inspecting it to make sure it was locked and loaded. All six of the survivors were safely out of the chopper waiting to be rescued. Johnson ran back into the destroyed Jolly for extra ammo and Pope's survival kit. He couldn't find it and said to Pope, "I can't find your kit." Pope replied, "Well, you're going to have to do the job with yours." Johnson knew what he meant; he would have to defend them as best he could with the ammo they possessed but save some rounds to use on themselves. Both Johnson and Pope agreed they would not be captured alive. Major Darghty, the Jolly commander, interrupted them to report that a rescue helicopter was inbound. Johnson then injected morphine into Pope to ease his pain.

Our Sandy aircraft were now out of ordnance and practically out of fuel as Jolly Green 70 lifted the six survivors away from the wrecked aircraft. With no backup now, we turned toward NKP. The radio was quiet on the way home; silence felt good after what we had been through.

During the flight back, I couldn't get Wild Bill Coady out of my mind. Although I had only known him for a couple of months, he had made quite an impression on me. I came to enjoy his aggressive behavior and good humor. He had unbridled enthusiasm for the Sandy mission and desperately wanted to get into combat. If anything, he needed to rein himself in and make sure he studied the threat area and flew a weapons delivery pass where he wouldn't risk exposing himself to more ground fire than was absolutely necessary. One time he came back to NKP with tree leaves lodged in the Skyraider's pylons. He was cutting it very close, I told him; one slipup and he would be gone. I briefed him on correct procedures over and over again and thought he understood the hazards he was taking. But regardless of what I said he threw caution to the wind. He was like a bull in a china shop and acted like his namesake, "Buffalo Bill" Cody, a Wild West rodeo entertainer from the turn of the century.

When Don Johnson arrived at NKP he was both physically and emotionally drained. An Air Force doctor gave him a quick checkup and allowed him to visit Tom Pope. He walked down the hospital corridor, unsure of what he would find at the end. Looking through a glass window, he saw a white-sheeted figure lying on a hospital gurney. At least the white sheet was not over Pope's face. Johnson opened the door, walked to the gurney, and placed his hand on Pope's shoulder. Pope's glazed eyes opened; he recognized Johnson and smiled. "How are you?" he asked, his words thick from narcotic stupor.

Johnson replied, "Not bad considering what we've just been through." "Hey," Pope said, "you want a laugh?" "Yes," he responded, trying to remain light-hearted amid the recognition of Pope's severe injuries. Pope continued, "Two doctors examined my leg," his words slow and difficult to pronounce with his uncoordinated tongue and cotton mouth. "One of the doctors said, 'Look at the tourniquets on this guy's severed leg, he must have been a real bad medic to have to use two tourniquets.'" Pope was incensed at the doctor's comments; "I'm alive, aren't I?" he yelled at them. The doctors left in embarrassed silence. Pope looked directly at Johnson and said, "Listen, Surfer Johnson, you did good work. Always remember that! I'm alive, aren't I?" Pope faded off to rest before the doctors would amputate his left leg. Later he got his last ride in an HH-53 as he left for stateside. As the chopper arrived, he raised his bandaged stump of a knee in a salute and held his fingers up in a *V* for victory sign. Tom Pope was the ultimate symbol of PJ tenacity.

Show Business: The Rescue of Honda 3 A and B

Exactly a week after Wild Bill Coady was killed, I was sitting alert again as Sandy 1 in the Jolly Green operations building. The last six weeks had been a very difficult time for our squadron. In early December Tom O'Connor had been shot down and rescued near Lima Site 85, but we lost Joe Pirruccello in getting O'Connor out. Then, two days later, Jerry Jenkinson was also hit near Lima Site 85 and ejected a few miles south. Jenkinson was rescued without the loss of another plane or pilot. On Christmas day we failed to get Panda 1, Richard Brownlee, out of the jungle near Mugia Pass and lost a PJ in the process. Al Roberts crashed at Udorn just after Christmas. Then in mid-January Pete Morris was shot down in the attempt to get Stormy 2B out of Tchepone. We successfully got Morris out of the jungle but lost Wild Bill Coady and a Jolly Green helicopter in the process. All in all, we had lost six Skyraider aircraft, a Jolly Green helicopter, two pilots, and a PJ in the last six weeks, a tremendous casualty rate in the rescue business. It had been close to a total disaster.

On the morning of January 24, 1969 I was scheduled for Sandy alert. The lineup was: Sandy 1—Capt. George Marrett; Sandy 2—Maj. Alvin Moreland; Sandy 3—Maj. Ronal "Bud" Cass; Sandy 4—Maj. Harry Dunivant.

Because our loss rate was so high, two more Skyraiders would sit Sandy alert with us. Sandy 5 was Maj. Robert Kraus and Sandy 6 was Maj. Thomas Hipps. I was the only captain in the group, leading five majors. In the 602nd, Sandy leads were selected by experience, not military rank.

Our low Jolly for the day was an HH-3, Jolly Green 17, with Maj. Lance Eagan as aircraft commander. Major Eagan served in the U.S. Coast Guard and had been given the nickname "Coastie." Eagan's copilot was Capt. Roger Gibson. Flying as flight engineer was M. Sgt. Arthur Krum, and, because of the losses the Jollys had sustained, two PJs were aboard. The number-one PJ was A/1C Douglas Horka, and number two was T. Sgt. Dal Widner.

Doug Horka was just twenty-one years old and had completed two years at the University of Massachusetts when he decided he wanted to go off to war. He started the fifteen-month PJ training with three hundred other airmen and was one of only four who finished the program. He then volunteered for a twenty-four-month tour of duty and got picked for Detachment 1 of the 40th Aerospace Rescue and Recovery Squadron at NKP, a choice assignment in his estimation.

Horka told me that Coastie, Lance Eagan, was the finest aviator with whom he had flown. He was an extremely skilled pilot, the helicopter equivalent of Top Gun of that time. Capt. Roger Gibson, his copilot, was a capable pilot. But Gibson was shy, quiet, and studious, unlike Coastie, who was very outgoing—a command type of person.

Doug Horka had previously roomed with Airman King, the PJ lost a month earlier on the rescue attempt of Major Brownlee. Horka still had a year and a half to go before completing his two-year tour, and it was beginning to look like an impossibility that he would get out alive with the loss rates we were incurring. On the other hand, I was only about seventy days away from completing my year tour and becoming a civilian. I was beginning to hope that with a little luck I might make it.

In mid-afternoon we got a call from rescue command that an F-4D Phantom from the 433rd Tactical Fighter Squadron, 8th Tactical Fighter Wing at Ubon RTAFB was hit in the fuselage by 37-mm antiaircraft fire during a dive on a target. Capt. J. A. Nash, Honda 3A, and Lt. Col. R. W. Clement, Honda 3B, ejected about twenty nautical miles northeast of Saravane, Laos. Other pilots in their F-4 flight reported that both crew members got good chutes and were descending close together near Ban Bak, a small village near Route 92 on the Xe Kong River.

At 2:45 p.m. my Sandy flight of four Skyraiders got airborne from NKP and turned southeast, crossing the Mekong River. We had 140 miles to go to get to the two survivors' position. The Skyraider cruised at 165 knots true airspeed. At that speed, it would take nearly an hour to get on station; I hoped the F-4 crew would still be there and not captured by the time we arrived. From a distance I heard an F-100 FAC, Misty 51, talking on the UHF radio to both men on the ground. He was attempting to determine their identity (authentication) by asking them questions that only they knew the correct answers to. I heard Misty 51 ask one of them his favorite car and the other a friend's name. I was too distant to hear the answers, but Misty 51 confirmed for Crown and me that they answered the questions correctly.

When I arrived overhead, I took over as on-scene commander and made radio contact with both survivors. They were not far from each other and were surrounded by river scrub brush. Although they were exposed and not far from the river, we could also see that there were not any antiaircraft artillery guns or enemy soldiers close by. I called Jolly Green 17 and requested that he follow my four A-1s in for the pick up. By 4:20 p.m. Jolly Green 17 went into a hover over the survivors. They were uninjured so Doug Horka, the lead PJ, did not have to go down on the penetrator to assist them. Both pilots got on the penetrator together, which was very unusual, according to Horka. He had never picked up two crew members at once; most often they were some distance apart. In this case Horka said, "It was like getting two fish on one line." Both crewmen were ecstatic. Horka told me the colonel was especially relieved to be rescued. Horka also said that when he secured the crew to the red nylon seats on the inside of the helicopter, their grins lit up the entire cabin. Horka always carried survivor rations that he shared with the aircrew. In this particular case, he had a hip flask full of scotch and one unopened pack of cigarettes. The rations were gladly accepted.

Because we were closer to the F-4's home base at Ubon, I decided to take the survivors there instead of back to NKP. We joined up with the C-130 so Jolly Green 17 could take on some fuel. With the rescue completed, we started to relax, although my armada was still over enemy-held Laos until we could cross the Mekong River again and be back in friendly Thailand.

Flying in a loose formation on the HH-3 as it tanked with the C-130, I got an idea. Ubon was an all-jet fighter base. We were a conglomerate of dissimilar aircraft—the Skyraider had a reciprocal engine; the C-130 was a turbo-prop; and the Jolly was a twin-engine jet helicopter. I figured we needed to return the survivors in style. I asked Coastie if he would fly his HH-3 on the right wing of the C-130 in close formation so we could make a pass down the Ubon runway. He agreed and even said he would keep his fuel probe extended to add his own special touch to this made-up show. I asked the C-130 pilots to descend to five hundred feet above the ground and fly directly over the Ubon runway. I would fly a close wing position on the Jolly's right wing, and my wingman, Sandy 2, would fly a close wing formation position on the C-130's left wing. At this point we would be in a standard jet fighter right-hand fingertip formation.

The more we talked about our show pass, the more excited we all got. We were like little kids about to pull off a fast one. To add an extra flair to this rescue, I requested the pilots of the C-130 to fly down the centerline of the runway at 170 knots and start a shallow climb at midfield. At midfield, the helicopter would drop out of formation and descend, make a 90-degree right turn and come into a hover directly in front of the Ubon VIPs who were awaiting their comrades' return. Both of the Sandys would fly to the end of the runway with my wingman making a 180-degree turn to the left. I would make a 180-degree turn to the right, and we would each circle around to the approach end of the runway. At that time both of us Skyraider pilots would make another 180-degree turn and line up with the Ubon ramp. I would then join up on my wingman's right wing, and we would fly close formation over the two survivors at fifty feet just as they got off the helicopter. This was going to be show business at its best, returning the crew members in grand and glorious style.

The plan worked like a charm. Horka said he dropped Colonel Clement and Captain Nash without the Jolly Green shutting off their engines. My wingman and I could see the celebration taking place as the F-4 crewmen shook hands and hugged their fellow pilots. I figured they would probably have a great rescue party in the Officers Club within the hour. If my wingman and I were to land at Ubon, I thought we would be entertained royally. Two of our single-engine propeller Skyraiders sitting on the ramp surrounded by the twin jet engine F-4s would be quite a sight. Some Phantom pilots probably had never seen a Skyraider before, and I would have bet that Al Moreland and I wouldn't have to buy a beer the whole evening.

We started a climb northbound to NKP, and I called our command post to report that the survivors were home at Ubon. I also asked if we could land and spend the night. It didn't surprise me when the command post ordered us to return to NKP—the two Skyraiders were needed for combat missions the next day. For a moment I thought about making up a story that I had low oil pressure and needed to land as soon as possible. The command post would certainly see through my falsehood, especially since I had already asked permission to land.

My wingman and I continued home happy that we had saved two more F-4 crew members from capture by the enemy and that no one in our rescue flight had been hit by ground fire or shot down. After what our Sandy and Jolly Green squadrons had been through the last six weeks, a successful rescue would cheer up everyone. No rescue party for us, but we were pleased that our slightly illegal formation flyby looked spectacular to the crowd at Ubon. That's show business for the Sandy and Jolly team.

VALENTINE'S DAY CARDS

Three weeks later, on the morning of February 15, 1969, Lt. Col. Richard Walsh III got up very early, around 3 a.m. In preparation for leading a rescue as Sandy 1, Colonel Walsh spent time in his room before he left for the squadron building. He spread out a batch of family photos and Valentine's Day cards he had received the day before on his bed and stared at them, one by one. His roommate, Maj. Harry Dunivant, recalled, "He looked at them for a long time—maybe an hour or more."

Dick Walsh had just returned from R and R, meeting his wife in Hawaii. In fact, we had traveled there together. My R and R would normally have been the previous December; but the squadron had lost so many pilots they couldn't afford to have me gone then, so my R and R was delayed until mid-February.

While five days of peace and quiet at Army Fort DeRussy on the sunny shore of Waikiki was extremely pleasant, I had found it hard to say good-bye to Jan and my boys again. Some pilots had a hard time getting back to the routine of combat flying after spending time with their families. It seemed that their minds wandered and they lost the concentration needed to keep alive in an extremely hostile environment. Both Bat Masterson and Charles Kuhlmann were lost immediately after they returned from R and R. It was difficult for me to return to NKP, but I was only six weeks from becoming a civilian.

Dick Walsh and his wife had five children, all under the age of thirteen. At age forty-one, Walsh had spent nineteen years of military service in the Air Force; he had only one more to go before retirement. Although a 1950 graduate of the U.S. Naval Academy, Walsh chose the Air Force for a career. He attended flying school and flew jets for a while until he got into the technical side of the Air Force. Before flying the Skyraider at NKP, he was stationed at the North American Air Defense Command headquarters in Colorado tracking satellite payloads with new computer technology. As a mathematician with an MBA, he also taught part time at the Air Force Academy in Colorado Springs.

But on February 15, he would be leading a flight of four Skyraiders and two Jolly Green helicopters in the rescue of two downed pilots. Walsh and a classmate of his from the Naval Academy, Lt. Col. Daryle Tripp, made small talk with each other at breakfast. Colonel Tripp wondered if Walsh, with only eighty hours of combat time under his belt, was ready to lead a rescue. Walsh had never led a rescue before.

In the 602nd, a Sandy lead was not selected by rank. The most important factor in deciding who should lead a rescue was combat experience. Jet flying time was not important, instrument time was not important, flying time at night was not important, military rank was not important—the only real measure of capability was the number of rescues a pilot had flown. One time Colonel Tripp even flew wing on a first lieutenant. He remarked in a comical tone, "In the 602nd, the only difference between a colonel and a first lieutenant is about $800 per month."

On the previous day, late afternoon of February 14, 1969, two F-4D Phantoms from the 497th Tactical Fighter Squadron departed Ubon for a mission in southern Laos. Before they reached their original target, an F-100 Misty FAC diverted them to an alternate target near the Ho Chi Minh Trail, a highway river ford about twenty-four miles east of Saravane, Laos. The plan was to destroy the ford and create a traffic jam of enemy trucks on either side of the river, setting up an even better target for later missions.

Lt. Col. Stanley Clark, the F-4D commander, and his backseater, 1st Lt. Gordon Breault, were using the call sign Pintail 1. "We had gotten hosed pretty good on the first pass," said Breault, who watched tracers from antiaircraft guns fly over their wing. "On the second pass, we took two or three hits. Both of us were on the flight controls to maintain control," he said, when their wingman, Pintail 2, called on the radio, "Your plane is a ball of fire!" As the two pilots tried to pull up, Breault prepared to eject. Pintail 1 was a wounded duck as it leveled off about 8,000 feet and then went into a slight roll. Clark shouted on the intercom, "We've got to get out! Get Out!" At Clark's command, Breault jettisoned his canopy and ejected. As he floated down in his parachute, he scanned the sky for Clark. All he saw was their F-4D crashing and burning. Fortunately, Breault's survival radio was not damaged and he made contact with the Misty FAC. He had no radio communication or beeper contact with Colonel Clark.

"Misty, I'm coming down on the bad guys," Breault said as he watched puffs of smoke come from the enemy position. Though he made it to the ground in one piece, it was too dark to rescue him that night. Pilots in the other F-4Ds marked his position. They suggested he climb a tree and say his prayers; they'd send the Sandys and a Jolly Green after him at first light the next day.

Breault freed himself from the orange, white, and olive-drab parachute and ran for what seemed to him like miles and miles, hoping to elude the enemy. Once he felt he had run far enough into the jungle, he climbed a tree. "I heard the enemy," Breault recalled. "They had dogs, trucks, and at first I thought they were coming to get me." But then he had a more ominous thought, "The enemy knew I was in a tree. They were just setting up so they could have a turkey shoot the next day."

The next morning at 5:00 the rescue armada took off. It included: Sandy 1—Lt. Col. Richard Walsh III; Sandy 2—Lt. Col. Walter Stueck; Sandy 3—Maj. Eugene McCormack; Sandy 4—1st Lt. Clarence "Larry" Howerton Jr.

Colonel Stueck, from the Ozarks in Missouri, was the squadron commander. He had been flying missions in Southeast Asia for about two months. On the rescue of Pintail 1, his job would be to fly a couple of hundred feet above Walsh and call out ground fire to him.

The night Breault spent in a tree, he did not sleep at all. During that endless night his life passed before him a dozen times. He recalled conversations he had with other F-4D pilots about what they would do if they were captured. "We believed the enemy had bounties on our ears," he recalled. "Most of us made the determination that we were going to get rescued, not captured. Everyone had a sidearm with about ten rounds. We always said we'd never be taken alive."

When it got light enough to look around, Breault could see where he left his parachute; it was much closer to his tree than he thought. He was more convinced than ever that the soldiers around him were not as interested in him as in the flock of aircraft that was about to circle overhead.

Early in the morning the rescue armada showed up and Walsh made a radio check with Breault. "Hang loose. We're going to get you out of there," Walsh said. Walsh's voice was reassuring; for the first time Breault believed he might get out. Col. Walsh descended to a couple of hundred feet above the jungle trees and attempted to determine Breault's exact position as well as any potential guns nearby.

Stueck and Walsh received about ten rounds of 37-mm ground fire on one of their early passes. Walsh had seen Breault's parachute on the ground but needed to pinpoint his exact position. Breault climbed down from his tree and moved into a small clearing so he would be easier to spot. On one of Walsh's passes, he finally saw him. "I've got you, Tally Ho," Walsh said, dipping his wing to confirm.

Just seconds later, Stueck noticed flashes on the canopy of Walsh's Skyraider. "I thought at first they were reflections from the sun," said Stueck who was in a perfect position to witness the event. Then he realized that the flashes he'd seen were either 12-mm or 37-mm antiaircraft rounds striking Walsh's canopy.

From the ground, Breault saw Walsh's A-1 flying a couple hundred feet in the air. He heard guns fire and saw that Walsh had been hit more than once. He saw smoke streaming from the Skyraider, heard the Pratt & Whitney engine race, and then watched parts of the A-1 scatter into the air.

Gene McCormack also saw Colonel Walsh get hit. Even thirty-plus years later, he can still visualize the gun placement around the karst shooting at Walsh. McCormack said he watched Walsh get hit, roll over, and hit the ground. "The gunners ate his knickers," McCormack said, meaning that Walsh had been hit square on with no chance of recovery.

Stueck later explained, "Walsh's aircraft began a level roll to the left, rolled 360 degrees, then continued rolling, going from a horizontal position to a vertical—and crashed after about two and a half rolls." He added, "In other words, he rolled several times and went in vertically."

Breault lost sight of Walsh's Skyraider as it fell into the trees, but he heard the explosion of hundreds of gallons of fuel and a full load of ordnance. Then there was silence. It was followed by some of the most disappointing words ever heard on the UHF radio: "Sandy . . . is down."

Colonel Stueck called Crown and requested that the backup aircraft, Sandys 5 and 6, be scrambled and then turned the rescue command over to Sandy 3, Gene McCormack. McCormack called in flights of fast movers to neutralize the area.

"They blew up every piece of real estate all around me," Breault said. After a while McCormack's fuel state was "Bingo" (just enough fuel to fly home). He passed the lead to another Sandy and later told me, "I was glad to go back to NKP. It was a hot area."

Finally, at about 10:45 a.m. Capt. James Jamerson led the Jolly Green in and they dropped the penetrator. Breault climbed on and held it tightly as the chopper made a hasty ascent. Though exhausted and in shock, Breault later remembered being hoisted aboard. He took a nip from a bottle of Old Crow and then a long drag on a cigarette.

On the flight back he asked about his front-seat pilot, Colonel Clark. There had been no word, no contact at all. Breault did not have to ask about Sandy 1, who had gone down during his rescue. Though Breault did not know Walsh, he knew he had placed his life on the line to attempt his rescue.

The Jolly Green landed at NKP, where that evening we had our traditional rescue party at the Officers' Club. It was a bittersweet affair—we gave a toast to Dick Walsh and Stanley Clark, two more pilots claimed by the "secret" war in Laos. For Breault every Valentine's Day since 1969 has been difficult. His memory of the loss of Clark and Walsh remains very fresh.

On February 19, 1969, four days after we lost Dick Walsh, I was scrambled to rescue Pancho 2, an F-105 pilot. For this rescue I was Sandy 3 and escorted the two Jolly Green helicopters to a safe area. We launched at 5:30 a.m. and headed for North Vietnam to a location where Pancho 2 had been seen in his chute the previous afternoon. When we arrived, both Nail 43 and 71 were already orbiting overhead. They had seen the pilot and a parachute late the day before and confirmed that the chute was no longer in the same position. No radio contact or emergency beeper was established with Pancho 2 that morning. The area where he had last been seen was only fifty yards from a road in an area loaded with guns and enemy troops. Evidently Pancho 2 had been captured—if he was alive—or his body had been removed from his chute if he was dead.

After orbiting for over an hour and attempting to make radio contact, it was apparent the situation was hopeless. Reluctantly, the search-and-rescue force returned to NKP, knowing another pilot was lost somewhere in the jungle below. It was always sad to depart knowing we were the last hope of recovery.

Jeep Racing

I heard a strange noise outside my door. It was mid-morning in early February. I was sitting at the desk in my room in the hooch. Since I had decided to get out of the Air Force when my Southeast Asia tour was over, I had printed a résumé and planned to mail it to aerospace companies that might need a test pilot. I was preparing a cover letter to be sent with the résumé. Within a few moments I heard the same loud noise again. It now sounded like a motorized vehicle. I got up to investigate.

When I opened the door to my room it was easy to see the reason for the unusual sound. Our squadron commander's jeep was being driven between the hooches. Each squadron had a separate hooch. They were about 150 feet long and spaced seventy-five feet apart; there was enough room to easily maneuver a jeep. Except that this particular area between the hooches had recently been sodded by Thai women. For several days the women had carried the sod in large wicker baskets balanced on their heads. Each piece was neatly pressed in place and watered to accelerate growth. The sod had been in the ground for only a few days, certainly not long enough for the roots to get a foothold and support a jeep.

The Sandy Box was at the end of our hooch, and some of the Skyraider pilots who had flown combat missions the night before were still partying. A Skyraider pilot dressed in a flight suit was driving the jeep around in circles. I went back inside my room and continued writing my letter.

Trying to concentrate on the details of my writing, I was still aware of the jeep's noise. After a few moments I opened the door again. This time I saw a second Skyraider pilot driving the jeep but much faster than the previous one. Now sod was flying out behind the jeep's spinning wheels. Several Thai maids, who washed our clothes and shined our boots, were standing outside watching the crazy American pilots.

Earlier that morning, I passed the Sandy Box on my way to the post office. Several drunken pilots were shooting water from a fire extinguisher at passing airmen. Everyone was fair game at NKP it seemed. Gradually this game escalated, causing the Air Police to arrive and issue a warning.

I went back inside my room and started to write again. I would be returning to the States in just two months and wanted to set up a couple of job interviews before I arrived home. All military mail went by air, but even so it would take five days to arrive in the States. While two months meant I had a lot of combat missions still in front of me, it didn't give me much time to look for available test pilot jobs before I got home.

The continual noise interrupted my concentration. I got up for the third time to see what was happening. This time another Skyraider pilot was driving the jeep even faster than the previous two pilots. Two more pilots were sitting on the back of the jeep, holding on for dear life. As the jeep circled to the left, with more and more sod being thrown out behind, it lifted up on its two right wheels from centrifugal force. All the pilots were drinking beer, laughing, and having a great time. Quite a few airmen from other squadrons were now assembled watching this show and shouting encouragement.

I thought to myself that if I had consumed a few beers I would probably have given the jeep a try myself. But I was stone cold sober and scheduled for a combat mission later in the day. The Skyraider pilot gunned the jeep's engine—fun and games at NKP.

I went back to my desk and sat down again. My past test pilot training and mental thinking took over. It seemed that each Skyraider pilot who drove the jeep drove faster than the previous one. If that cycle continued, eventually the centrifugal force of the turn would overpower gravity and the jeep would turn over. There was even a mathematical formula called geometrical progression that could be used to calculate these forces. If I could solve the equation, I could predict the exact time when the jeep would roll over. I printed out the equation.

As I started to put numbers in the formula on my page, I heard the Thai maids scream. Before I even opened the door, I knew what had happened. I opened my door and saw the jeep about fifty feet away completely upside down. I ran over to it as fast as I could and grabbed a bumper. Two passengers were already up and limping around. A third passenger, a female Air Force officer, was laying face down in the sod completely unconscious. She had wet her pants—some of the drunken men were pointing and laughing at her. The driver was trapped under the jeep and also unconscious. Gene McCormack and I, lifting together, managed to pick up one end to allow others to pull the Skyraider pilot to safety.

The driver was Capt. Clyde Campbell, a twenty-five-year-old from Longview, Texas. Clyde Campbell graduated from Texas A&M, went through Air Force flying school, and had been in our squadron for only a couple of months. He had roomed with Wild Bill Coady and Joe Pirruccello, both of whom had been killed weeks earlier.

Someone called the base hospital, and in a few minutes an ambulance arrived. Both Campbell and the female officer were awakened and departed in the ambulance.

Clyde Campbell physically recovered from this senseless accident but was required to explain to the squadron commander why he had upset the jeep. Obviously, there was no way he could justify his careless driving. As a penalty, he was grounded for two weeks. He had taken the jeep beyond its limit, a bad omen for a pilot flying combat in a complex and dangerous Skyraider.

On March 1, 1969, Captain Campbell led a flight of two Skyraiders on a strike mission in northern Laos. Campbell flew an A-1J using the call sign Firefly 24. His wingman was Maj. Harry Dunivant flying as Firefly 25.

Dunivant was also checked out to be a Firefly lead but had been in the hospital a few days. Ironically, he had hurt himself getting out of the squadron commander's jeep. But his injury occurred after the jeep had been repaired following Campbell's accident. The operations officer thought Dunivant should fly a couple of wingman flights again before leading a combat mission.

On that day both Campbell and Dunivant were carrying eight 500-pound general-purpose bombs with fuse extenders. A fuse extender was a four-foot-long metal rod screwed into the front of the bomb with the arming fuse on the front. The extender would cause the bomb to explode above ground as an air-burst, creating an increased blast effect on enemy troops and war matériel.

Campbell checked in with a Raven FAC and was given a target very near Lima Site 36. It was near the end of the six-month dry season and a time when the in-flight visibility was less than two miles because of haze and smoke. During this season the farmers burned the rice stubble remaining in their fields. The Raven marked the target with a white phosphorous rocket and cleared Campbell in for a dive-bomb pass. The plan was for each Fire-fly pilot to make four passes, dropping one bomb off the left and one off the right wing per pass. That technique would keep the Skyraider laterally balanced during the high-G pull off target.

Dunivant was orbiting overhead when he heard the Raven transmit on the radio, "That A-1 just went in!" Dunivant looked down at the target area and could barely see a ball of fire because of poor visibility. Campbell's Skyraider hit the ground in a clearing very close to the area marked by the FAC. Neither Dunivant nor the Raven saw a parachute or heard a beeper on the emergency frequency.

Dunivant didn't know whether Campbell was hit by ground fire during the dive-bombing pass or whether he didn't pay close enough attention to his minimum release altitude and flew the A-1 into the ground. Campbell could also have stalled the A-1's horizontal tail. Dunivant said that Al Roberts had previously briefed him to trim the horizontal tail nose-down prior to a high-G pull-up in the H and J models. This technique would make the horizontal tail more effective and give better dive recovery because more Gs could be pulled. The method was not a briefing and training item at Hurlburt since only the E model was flown there. When the E model was trimmed, only the tab moved, unlike the H and J models where the entire horizontal tail moved.

Dunivant flew back home, and Col. Edwin White Jr., the wing commander, was waiting for him when he landed. Colonel White had already talked to the Raven FAC but still wanted Dunivant's first-hand report on Campbell's crash. Dunivant agreed with the Raven—Clyde Campbell did not get out of his Skyraider.

14 INSTRUCTOR PILOT

During the first couple of months of 1969, a group of new Skyraider pilots, fresh out of training at Hurlburt, arrived at the 602nd. Quite a few of these pilots were first lieutenants only a few months out of Air Force flight school. These pilots were low on flight experience; some had fewer than three hundred total flight hours. In contrast, most of the existing pilots in the squadron had years and years of experience. At one time we had six lieutenant colonels in the squadron, one with combat experience in World War II. Most of the flight commanders were majors, some with up to 8,000 hours flying time and combat experience in Korea.

Capts. Ron Furtak, Don Dunaway, and I each had about 3,000 hours and had been flying in the squadron for about eight months. The three of us were designated as instructor pilots (IP) and assigned to check out these new pilots. Every new pilot to the squadron, regardless of rank or previous combat experience, was required to fly five combat missions with an IP sitting in the right seat of either an A-1E or G before they were cleared to fly solo. As IPs we had great difficulty getting some of these pilots combat ready. Most of the first lieutenants had the desire to learn the complex rules of engagement that controlled our operation. They studied maps showing locations of enemy gun positions and were briefed by the intelligence office about the order of battle. They were given exhaustive presentations on our combat tactics and the secret codes used in flying combat. In my estimation, their biggest problem was simply flying and controlling the tail-wheeled Skyraiders.

Some of the new pilots I flew with had directional control problems on takeoff. The A-1 required a healthy amount of right rudder at brake release to counteract the engine torque of the big Pratt & Whitney engine. Pilots would snake down the PSP trying to get back on the centerline. Some were very rough on the flight controls when flying in formation. Also, the lead Skyraider pilot kept his engine at a high cruise power setting. This setting left the wingman very little excess power to stay in formation. He had to cut the leader off on every turn or run the risk of falling too far behind to be of any value. Some new pilots also had a problem staying in formation as the flight flew in and out of clouds.

Most of the first lieutenants were poor at keeping their heads on a swivel. Flying combat required a pilot to watch for ground fire, protect his lead's six o'clock position, navigate over the dirt roads and winding rivers of Laos, keep a continuous watch on his engine instruments, fuel supply, and electrical power, and still fly a loose formation position. When FACing in F-4s and F-105s, we needed to keep the jets in sight to prevent a midair collision and also to call out ground fire aimed at them. We flew so far north in Laos that there was always the possibility a MiG would dive down from higher altitude and make a pass at us. Some of the new guys seemed like their heads were in a cloud.

But not all the first lieutenants had difficulty flying the Skyraider. Both Lts. James Beggerly and Jon Ewing were excellent pilots. Back in December, Jim Beggerly had been Tom O'Connor's wingman when he was shot down near Lima Site 85. Beggerly called in the search-and-rescue forces and performed well in O'Connor's rescue. Jon Ewing was my wingman on that rescue, and he also performed well for a young inexperienced pilot.

A month later Ewing completed enough missions to be upgraded to a Firefly lead. During his evaluation flight he made a mistake in switch settings and instead of firing his rockets he "bombed off" his rocket pods. Ewing failed the check flight and was rescheduled for another evaluation. For his second evaluation I reviewed his performance. Ewing bombed off his rocket pods just as he had done the first time. I could have failed him. Instead, I passed him knowing that in December he had saved one of our Skyraiders when it was struck by ground fire and he was able to crash land it at Ubon. I knew Ewing would be a great asset to the squadron's combat capability as a Firefly lead.

During this time, another young pilot, Capt. Richard Hall, arrived at the squadron. I first met Rich Hall five years earlier when he was a radar observer flying in the backseat of the F-101B Voodoo. Hall flew in the Voodoo for a couple of years when he was assigned to the 322nd Fighter Interceptor Squadron at Kingsley Field, Oregon. Then he attended Air Force flight school. It was good for me to greet someone from my past. He had a big smile and a generous amount of vitality and humor. Even though Hall was a captain, he had limited pilot experience. Still he flew the Skyraider extremely well. Unfortunately, the A-1 night strike squadron was short of pilots and Hall was transferred to that unit.

Some pilots had a problem remembering what ordnance was aboard their Skyraider. The A-1 had fifteen weapon stations besides the four 20-mm wing guns and carried bombs, rockets, napalm, and cluster bombs. It was important to fill out your mission card with the location of each weapon and keep track of what you expended on each pass. To place weapons on target, the correct mil setting needed to be selected on the gun sight. The correct dive angle would have to be flown and compensation made for surface winds, a difficult task, especially if the enemy was shooting at you. The most important factor to remember was the minimum release altitude and the need to jink back and forth during pull-up. I realized this was a lot of information for a new guy to learn, but all of these procedures were critically important. Any error could lead to crashing into the jungle or getting shot down.

Even some of the more-experienced captains and majors had trouble adapting to combat flight. In my opinion, these pilots had learned the skills required to fly a Skyraider, but they lacked the will and desire to fight. One major who flew my wing was a case in point. He was short with a round face. One of the experienced pilots said he looked like an alcoholic, looked worn-out, and was absolutely worthless. When flying my wing, he would slowly drift away until he couldn't see me anymore. Then I would have to look for him and rejoin formation. Within a few minutes he was out of position again. He obviously didn't want to "mix it up" in combat. I thought he was a hazard for both of us; but he outranked me.

Another pilot reported that the major went to Bangkok in a party flying suit. Party flying suits were made in Thailand by Indian tailors. They were the same size and fit as our Air Force cotton flying suits except these were bright orange and decorated with numerous combat-related patches. The major arrived at the party in Bangkok in a party suit with Sandy and A-1 rescue patches sewed on it, as if he had participated in some rescues. In fact he had not even checked out in the Skyraider yet. Many of the pilots in the squadron were very ticked off at him and happy when he was finally transferred out of the squadron.

One captain developed an unusual quirk. He was quite vocal about not wanting to fly combat. As time went by, he complained to the flight surgeon that one of his legs was starting to atrophy. The flight surgeon did not ground him. Once he pulled up one leg of his flight suit and showed me his small leg. He was correct—for some unknown reason one leg was getting smaller and smaller. The senior officers in the squadron were not sympathetic to his physical status, and he was ordered to continue flying combat missions. It would be bad for morale in the squadron if he were allowed to sit out the rest of his year. Under the circumstances, I preferred he not fly my wing, but the duty officer placed names on the scheduling board. I flew with whoever was assigned.

In the end, the short-legged pilot came back from one combat mission as a wingman in a flight of four. Because the weather was poor, the Skyraider leads asked the ground approach controllers to let their wingmen land first. He was first to land at NKP and came out of the clouds with his landing gear up. A T-39 Sabreliner was holding on the taxiway awaiting takeoff clearance. The T-39 pilot observed an A-1 on final approach with its gear up but mistakenly thought it was a normal procedure. The short-legged captain landed gear up, severely damaging the Skyraider. At a time when we needed to keep a maximum number of A-1s ready for rescue missions, this aircraft had major damage and would be out of service for a long time. After that incident I never saw the captain again—he was sent away.

Another captain also gave us a lot of grief. Until the first lieutenants arrived, he was the youngest pilot in the squadron and therefore nicknamed "the Kid." When he flew he experienced more emergencies, more air aborts, and less time on target than anyone else in the squadron. Some pilots complained that he was ineffective in the target area but still was always running off at the mouth in the Sandy Box. They thought he was a hazard as a wingman, simply unreliable and not pulling his weight. Others said he was a pain in the butt and wanted to get rid of him. Finally, the squadron leaders sent him to a T-28 unit that trained Thai pilots. The idea was to get rid of him, although he happily departed thinking the new assignment was a promotion.

Maj. Robert Kraus, one of the more courageous Skyraider pilots in the squadron, was gruff and argumentative. He reminded me of sportscaster Howard Cosell—he always called it the way he saw it. Bob Kraus came up with an expression for some of our problem pilots. He said they "turned tail."

Thirty-Seven-and-a-Half Gallons of Oil

We all made mistakes; no one was immune from making an error flying the Skyraider. I made a stupid mistake one time even as an instructor pilot. Fortunately, I wasn't hurt and didn't damage an A-1. I simply embarrassed myself in front of one of the airmen who serviced the Skyraider.

After I had flown several flights as an instructor pilot I was scheduled to fly with one of the new pilots. Our flight was late in the afternoon; the A-1 would be "turned around," that is, flown a second time on the same day as it had been used for a mission.

The new guy and I sat through an intelligence briefing; we talked over the flight and put on our life support equipment. Unfortunately, we arrived early at the aircraft and all the ordnance was not yet loaded; the Skyraider even needed to be fueled. The new guy checked the aircraft records and started to do a walk-around inspection. My responsibility was to monitor everything he did without interrupting him unless he made a mistake. "It would be nice to fly with someone who didn't make mistakes," I thought to myself. As he was checking out the left side of the aircraft, I walked over to the right side by the tail and waited. It was one of those rare moments when I had time to simply look around at the hustle and bustle of life on the flight line. Aircraft were taking off and landing. Some were taxiing out for takeoff and some were taxiing back in from a mission. The flight line was a beehive of activity. Airmen were driving trucks pulling trailers of ordnance, some pulling up under our Skyraiders' wings. Other airmen would lift the bombs and rocket pods by hand and secure them to the A-1. I stepped aside to keep out of the way. My new guy pilot was still over on the left side of the aircraft.

It was at this time when I noticed a yellow truck pull up in front of and perpendicular to our Skyraider. The driver, an enlisted airman, got out of the truck and pulled a long, black rubber hose out of the truck and laid it down under our A-1's right wing. He wrote down some numbers off the dial of the truck, threw a couple of switches on a panel, and returned to pick up the nozzle at the end of the black hose. He stepped up on the bottom of the Skyraider's right wing root, where the wing attached to the fuselage, and removed a cap from the side of the fuselage. I knew engine oil was added to the A-1E's engine through that opening.

I thought to myself, "Why would this airman add aircraft fuel to the engine oil tank?" I rushed up, trying to prevent him from damaging an A-1E aircraft that I would soon be flying in combat.

"Don't put fuel in the oil tank," I shouted to the surprised airman. He looked at me in amazement and replied, "Sir, this is oil I'm pumping into the tank."

I countered, as a veteran combat pilot with about 150 missions under my belt, "Airman, oil comes in quart cans." I even held both hands up about eight inches apart to display the dimensions of the quart-sized oil cans I carried with me when I was a jet pilot. A jet engine only held about two to three gallons of oil and hardly ever needed more than a quart added, and then only after quite a few flights.

The airman put me in my place when he said, "Sir, the Skyraider's engine holds thirty-seven-and-a-half gallons of oil, and for that we use a truck."

At that moment I felt very stupid and said meekly, "Carry on!" The airman was absolutely right. Thank God the new guy didn't see me make a fool of myself. Later, I got in the right seat of the cockpit and asked the new student how many gallons of oil were in a Skyraider engine.

Mr. Volunteer

While I was struggling to get the first lieutenants combat ready, suddenly an experienced fighter pilot was assigned to the 602nd. Capt. Wayne Warner, Air Force Academy graduate of 1963, came aboard and was greeted warmly. Warner would be placed on a fast track of training to become a Sandy lead because of his previous combat credentials. He had flown a two-year tour in C-130s out of Okinawa. While there he went on temporary duty to South Vietnam, flying in and out of Cam Ranh Bay, Tan Son Nhut, and Da Nang. During the last six months of the tour he flew out of Ubon and completed eighty-two missions in North Vietnam as a Blindbat and Lamplighter flareship pilot. After completing his first combat tour, he volunteered to fly the F-105 Thunderchief. From October 1967 to October 1968 he flew with the 357th Tactical Fighter Squadron, 355th Tactical Fighter Wing out of Takhli RTAFB. At the time, if a pilot flew 100 missions over North Vietnam, he was eligible to rotate back to the United States. After flying his 100th, Warner volunteered to stay at Takhli for an additional four months as a maintenance test pilot and to ferry battle-damaged Thuds from Ubon, NKP, and Udorn back to Takhli.

The Air Force then assigned him to be an instructor pilot at Williams AFB in Arizona. There he would be training South Vietnamese pilots to fly the F-5 aircraft. Warner turned down the assignment and volunteered to become a Skyraider pilot. He deeply wanted to get into the 602nd and become a Sandy pilot so he could rescue downed aircrew.

After finishing the A-1 training at Hurlburt, Warner was sent to the 56th SOW at NKP. By this time, graduates of Skyraider training at Hurlburt who were transferred to our wing were not given squadron assignments until they arrived and checked in with the wing commander. Warner met Colonel White, who wanted to use him in the 22nd SOS because of his previous night-combat experience. Warner convinced Colonel White that he had flown enough night missions in the C-130, was tired of flying at night, and wanted to be a Sandy rescue pilot.

Wayne Warner arrived at the 602nd in February 1969, anxious to get into action, but he was still required to fly five dual combat flights in the A-1, just like every other new pilot. On February 28, 1969, I was scheduled to give

Warner his fifth and last flight before he would be declared combat ready. I especially remember the flight with Warner because of what I didn't have to do. After so many flights with the first lieutenants where I always had to take over the controls of the aircraft on takeoff, rejoin in formation, level the A-1 out flying through weather, or point out the target area, for the first time I sat back, put my hands in my lap, and did absolutely nothing. Warner flew the entire mission without any assistance from me. I passed him with the highest grade I ever gave to a new pilot. We were short of pilots since so many of the men in the squadron had been shot down and were either missing in action, killed in action, or injured. Everyone was anxious to get Warner into action as soon as possible.

Because he had never flown a single-seat A-1H or J model, the next day Warner was scheduled for a training flight in the squadron commander's aircraft, nicknamed *Maggie's Orange Blossom Special III*. Lieutenant Colonel Stueck had flown combat in World War II, Korea, and Vietnam. In each war he named his aircraft after his wife Maggie. *Special I* was a P-38 in World War II, *Special II* a P-51 in Korea, and now *Special III* was a Skyraider in Vietnam.

Warner took off from NKP, and, while he was flying about fifteen miles north of the base, the Pratt & Whitney engine failed. Being too far from the field to deadstick the Skyraider back home, Warner jumped out of the A-1 and landed safely in Thailand. Colonel Stueck was not happy to lose *Maggie's Special III*, but there was nothing Warner could have done to prevent the accident. Stueck said that *Maggie's Orange Blossom Special III* was the third aircraft he had named for his wife that had been lost. He had no desire to name another Skyraider after her.

Wayne Warner started flying strike missions as a wingman. A couple of flights later he had another engine problem. This time he managed to get the Skyraider back to NKP, although thirty-six gallons of oil out of the thirty-seven-and-a-half-gallon oil tank leaked out of the engine. This oil covered both the outside of the A-1 and the interior of his cockpit. Warner had oil all over his hands, face, and flight suit. He was beginning to feel uneasy about the A-1. The aircraft were old and practically worn-out, and he seemed to have more than his share of problems; he had not even flown a rescue mission yet. Warner, like some of the other fighter pilots, was superstitious. He recalled that "bad things always happen in threes."

On the morning of March 14, Warner was scheduled as Sandy 4 on rescue alert. His plane for that day was an A-1H, serial number 134562. Ron Furtak, one of the other instructor pilots in the squadron, had named that aircraft the *Fightin' Polish Eagle*. By this time Warner had flown twelve combat missions; this upcoming flight would be number thirteen. With everything that had gone wrong so far in the previous two weeks, Warner was dreading his thirteenth combat mission. His premonition was correct.

While he was checking the magnetos on run-up, the engine started to backfire. Warner taxied back to the ramp and shut down. Anxious to get the problem corrected and get airborne again, he stayed strapped in the cockpit while mechanics pored over the engine. After the ground crew removed the cowling and made adjustments, Warner fired up the engine and taxied back to the runway. He was in a hurry to get airborne, so he checked the engine out while taxiing. All indications were that the engine was performing normally.

Our PSP runway was being replaced. The new runway would be made of concrete but was not expected to open for some time. For several months we had used an asphalt taxiway as a temporary runway. Warner lined up on the end of the runway and started takeoff heading to the south. At fifty knots, he pushed the stick forward and raised the tail wheel off the asphalt so the Skyraider would accelerate better. The A-1 "charged down" the asphalt, bouncing back and forth in both pitch and bank on account of the uneven surface. Eventually, the airspeed moved up to eighty knots and hesitated there. This was a very common condition in the A-1. I remember that the airspeed would kind of stagnate in that range for a few moments and then continue to accelerate. It seemed to Warner that his A-1 just stayed at eighty knots. He rechecked the engine instruments and all indications were normal. He thought the aircraft must be traveling close to takeoff speed of 110 knots and tried to get it airborne by coming back on the control stick. Instead, the Skyraider floated and skipped along the asphalt taxiway but stayed on the ground. Warner thought about jettisoning his fuel tanks and ordnance but was concerned about all the A-1s and Jolly Green helicopters just off to his left. Because he was taking off on our taxiway, which was very close to the ramp, and because all the A-1s and HH-3s were lined up parallel to the taxiway and not in revetments, he was afraid his ordnance might skid into the planes and aircraft mechanics and cause a catastrophe.

His first thought was to retain his fuel tank and ordnance and simply drop the tail hook and engage the wire barrier crossing the far end of the taxiway. He dropped the tail hook and called the control tower on his UHF radio, "Sandy 4 aborting." Then he remembered, "Oh, man, the taxiway doesn't have a barrier!" Seeing the end of the taxiway coming up fast, he decided to retract the landing gear. With the aircraft bouncing up and down so much, he couldn't get his hand on the gear handle. As it turned out, having the gear down was probably a blessing. Unknown to Warner or any of the pilots in the 602nd, an eight-to-ten foot ditch was just off the end of the taxiway. Had Warner been able to collapse the gear, he might have slid nose first into the ditch and either upset or exploded. Had the Skyraider nosed over, he would have been trapped in the cockpit. If the A-1 exploded, he probably would have been killed instantly.

As the A-1 crossed the ditch, the landing gear was sheared off and the plane skidded to a stop. Warner used his jettison handle to blow the canopy off and saw flames over his left wing. He attempted to pull the ground egress emergency handle to release himself from his parachute, survival kit, and both the shoulder harness and lap belt. Even though he squeezed the handle so hard he thought he bent it, the release mechanism didn't open. Knowing he was in imminent danger of a full-scale aircraft fire, he chose to use the manual release for the four Koch fittings that were still securing him to the Skyraider.

As he reached to undo the fittings, the squashed 300-gallon centerline fuel tank blew up, with flames erupting through his rudder pedals. Warner was wearing a standard Air Force cotton flying suit; he watched it catch fire and burn off his body. He was also wearing the newly issued Nomex flight gloves, which were designed to protect a pilot from just such a fire. The gloves had leather palms and Nomex on the outside part of the hand and fingers. The Nomex didn't give him the protection advertised—the backs of his hands were badly burned.

Meanwhile, I was scheduled for a strike mission later in the day. At the time Warner's Skyraider blew up, I was sitting on the toilet in the 602nd squadron building. I heard a massive explosion and figured something terrible had happened; either a plane had crashed on the field or two planes had collided. I hurried back to the scheduling office to find out from the duty officer that an aircraft had crashed on takeoff. At the time, no one in our squadron knew what kind of aircraft it was or who was flying it.

Warner managed to release both shoulder harness Koch fittings and the lap belt on the right side. Because of flames in the cockpit, he rolled over the left side of the canopy bow onto the Skyraider's left wing and was upside down struggling to get loose of the last lap belt fitting. Warner was being burned alive as his Skyraider ordnance started to cook off.

Finally, after all the bad things that had happened to Warner, his luck started to change. First Lieutenant Ewing was on Sandy alert and sitting in the Jolly Green squadron building when he heard the explosion. Ewing ran out the door to lend assistance to a fellow Skyraider pilot. Two Jolly Green PJs were jogging nearby and also headed in Warner's direction.

Maj. Stuart Silver had just taken off in a Jolly Green HH-3 to perform a functional check flight. Seeing the Skyraider in flames off the end of the asphalt taxiway, he flew over to the crash site and hovered in order to blow the flames and smoke away from the struggling pilot. On board was a female intelligence officer, up for a joyride. Some of the 20-mm ammo from Warner's Skyraider blew up and hit the helicopter. The female officer got more of a ride than she bargained for. Two months earlier she had nearly been killed in the jeep joyriding accident with Clyde Campbell. It seemed that no one at NKP was immune from death and destruction while living on the base, either from combat or partying a little too hard.

Jon Ewing was the first to arrive and assist Warner. He removed a knife from Warner's canvas belt and cut his lap belt, releasing him from the flaming Skyraider. Ewing and Warner started to run down the left wing of the A-1 toward safety. After twenty feet Warner fell face down in the dirt and passed out. Ewing lifted him up by the back of his harness and yelled, "Run, we're not out of the fire yet!" All of the Skyraider's ordnance was now fully on fire; the *Fightin' Polish Eagle* was a total loss. Major Silver landed his HH-3 helicopter near the Jolly Green alert shack, picked up Warner, and delivered him by air to the front door of the dispensary.

Meanwhile Jon Ewing returned to the Jolly's alert shack to find everyone gone. He feared that the other Sandys had been scrambled for a rescue and had left him behind. Later, he found out that an order was given to evacuate the building on account of Warner's exploding ordnance. Ewing was not injured, so he ran over to the dispensary to check on Warner's condition. When he arrived he found the medics were preparing Warner for an immediate move to Korat on one of the C-130 klong flights.

Wayne Warner arrived at Korat and was then transported by C-141 to Clark AB in the Philippines where he spent a couple of weeks in intensive care. From there he was transferred by air to the Army Far East Burn Center at Tachikawa, Japan. Doctors there attempted to stabilize his condition for several weeks before he could be flown back to the States. Finally, he arrived at Fort Sam Houston, the Army Burn Center in San Antonio. Warner would spend practically a year in the hospital.

For his part in saving Wayne Warner's life, Jon Ewing was awarded the Airman's Medal, the highest award given for noncombat bravery.

COMMANDER'S CALL

Printed in large bold letters on a bulletin board in the hooch was the message: MANDATORY PILOTS' MEETING 1900 HOURS. This pilots' meeting was to be held at our squadron building that evening. I looked forward to the meeting, thinking it would be valuable for all the pilots to assemble and discuss some of the critical issues concerning the war. We could talk about the shortage of white phosphorous bombs, the difficulty we had in getting some of our first lieutenant pilots combat ready, and the continual engine problems we were all experiencing. We were overdue for some serious discussions.

Leaving the Sandy Box in a flourish of empty beer cans, several of us jumped in one of the squadron's jeeps and drove to the building.

"Room—At-ten-shun!" Everyone stood as the leaders of the squadron marched into the room. "Be seated," said the senior officer. It was unusual for all of the pilots to be in one room at the same time. With the requirement for night-strike missions and some pilots on Sandy alert, we were usually scattered all around the base. The colonel must have something very important to report. Looking at his face, I certainly detected a degree of seriousness.

"Gentlemen," he started, "our squadron has lost a lot of pilots and aircraft from enemy ground fire." Maybe he is going to change our combat tactics, I thought to myself. "Also," he continued, "during the past five months of the dry season, the enemy has regained a lot of the territory lost earlier. We are losing ground in this new offensive. The war is going poorly." All eyes were on him. . . . Then he said, "We are instituting a new program in the squadron." It was dead quiet in the room. Any new program would greatly affect each of us.

Sitting next to me was another captain, Don Dunaway. Dunaway was one of the better gunners in the outfit. Both of us had been in the squadron for about nine months but still had many combat missions ahead of us. We had started as strike wingman and during the last months upgraded to Firefly and Sandy leads. In addition, we were on official military orders as functional check-flight pilots, instructor pilots, and senior flight examiners. Any new program or tactic would greatly influence how we trained the new guys and flew combat missions ourselves.

The colonel continued, "Starting tomorrow, every time you fly a combat mission with myself or one of the flight commanders, we will rate your bombs and rockets. The operations officer will collect the information from each flight and keep the totals." I heard shuffling of feet and clearing of throats. This new program didn't sound like it was addressing any of the really critical problems we were experiencing.

"Each month we will add up the score of every pilot and determine the winner," he added. "A trophy will then be given out to the Top Gun of the squadron."

I could not believe what I was hearing. None of us thought we were winning the war. After each mission we debriefed with intelligence, and they kept track of the tons of bombs, rockets, and napalm we fired in Laos. If we had an airborne emergency, like an engine problem, and had to jettison our ordnance over the open jungle in Laos, it was still listed as ordnance dropped on target. Even Secretary of Defense Robert McNamara spoke about body count as a method of determining how U.S. forces were doing—a questionable method in our estimation. Now another stupid statistic or numbering system was being instituted to determine how well American forces were conducting the war. I shook my head in disbelief, trying to remember that I would be a civilian in just a couple of months.

Don Dunaway glanced over at me. He also had a look of disbelief on his face. He leaned over and whispered in my ear, "Winning the trophy would mean that you were the best of the losers."

15 PAPAYA 2 B

On March 10, 1969, with just three weeks remaining in my one-year combat tour, I was scheduled for rescue alert duty as Sandy lead. My crew consisted of: Sandy 3—myself, Capt. George Marrett; Sandy 4—Maj. Alvin Moreland; Sandy 5—Capt. Jerry Jenkinson; Sandy 6—1st. Lt. Rex "Little Rex" Huntsman.

In the early afternoon, my flight of four Sandys and two H-3E Jolly Green helicopters was scrambled to rescue two airmen who ejected from an F-4 Phantom in southern Laos. The F-4D aircraft, from the 435th Tactical Fighter Squadron at Ubon, was on a strike mission working over a petroleum, oil, and lubricant storage area and truck park. During its fifth pass at the target, the F-4D was hit by ground fire.

A cold chill crept over me as I thought about what a long year it had been so far. During the past months I had been involved all three days with Streetcar 304, which was the largest successful rescue to date. I had deadsticked a disabled Skyraider into a dirt strip in Laos. I had been hit by ground fire flying a rescue in North Vietnam. Leading another rescue with only a couple of weeks left in my tour was cutting it damn close.

But when a pilot was down, he was more than a stupid McNamara statistic to us. He was a fellow American, with a family at home, with hopes and dreams and a potential that could not be measured. From our perspective, he was a man in trouble; he needed help fast. It might be me shot down the next time. So, even though my stomach churned and my mouth was dry, I shouted hoarsely to my rescue crew, "Let's go."

Both crew members of the F-4D, had ejected safely, landing about three hundred feet apart near the intersection of two dirt roads. The two crew members were seen in their parachutes by other members of their F-4 flight. A FAC, Nail 24, reported that he had seen both of Papaya 2s parachutes on the jungle floor. He made radio contact with the crew on their emergency UHF radios, and they stated that grass and ordnance fires were around them and enemy ground troops were in their immediate vicinity. The road intersection was level, at an elevation about nine hundred feet above sea level. As a rescue force we preferred hilly jungle, which allowed us to use terrain-masking (flying so low that terrain denied the enemy clear vision of the Skyraider and Jolly Green) when we brought the chopper in for the pick up. We would not have that advantage in this rescue, but fortunately the nine-hundred-foot elevation was in our favor—the heavily fueled Jolly Green could hover better at low altitudes than at high.

As I got airborne from NKP, I could see that it was a cloudless day in southern Laos. We were near the end of the six-month dry season; it had not rained for a long time. The smoke from the farmers' burning of the rice stubble rose to around 10,000 feet. After the better part of an hour I approached the pickup area and could see that smoke and haze had reduced the in-flight visibility to just a couple of miles. This required me to get down on the deck within the range of enemy gunners. Fortunately, the Skyraider could take a real beating and still make it home.

The A-1 was rugged in another way too—it was able to stay in the air for more hours than a pilot's bladder. It could also carry a wide variety of fuel tanks and weapons needed to rescue pilots from the jungle. For this particular flight I carried a 300-gallon fuel tank on the centerline of the fuselage and a 150-gallon fuel tank on the right stub station. Counting the 380 gallons in the self-sealing fuselage tank directly behind me, I had 5,400 pounds of gas. That was enough fuel for nearly ten hours of flight if the Skyraider's weight and drag were reduced by expending ordnance and jettisoning empty fuel tanks. Our flight limit was actually determined by engine oil. Even though we started with a full tank of 37.5 gallons of oil, the Skyraider would spit out a lot of oil from the engine stacks, making it the limiting factor on long-duration flights. No wonder oil was added by a truck.

For this special rescue mission I carried four 20-mm internally mounted wing guns, each holding 200 rounds of armor-piercing incendiary ammunition. Because the 20-mm guns jammed frequently, I also carried a 7.62-mm minigun on the left stub station. On each of the outer wing stations, I carried a pod with seven white phosphorous rockets. Two CBU pods loaded with antipersonnel bomblets (each pod contained six tubes) were installed on the inner wing stations. I also carried two white phosphorous smoke bombs left over from World War II. Many times we dropped them unarmed so that they would hit the ground, break apart, and send a cloud of white smoke billowing in the air for around half an hour. This smoke cloud could be seen for miles and miles and became a reference point for explaining the survivor's position in the jungle to all arriving strike aircraft. The big radial engine and great amount of weapons we carried allowed a Sandy to make a tremendous amount of noise and dribble a small amount of weapons on each pass over the survivor. We needed to keep the enemy's heads down to prevent them from moving in to capture our survivor.

As I approached this survivor's position, Nail 24 transmitted on his UHF radio that the frontseater, Papaya 2A's parachute had disappeared. He had also lost voice contact with him. Crown advised me that several flights of jets loaded with heavy general-purpose bombs were orbiting a short distance away and available as soon as I needed them. I took over as on-scene commander and asked Nail 24 to point out the location of the backseater, Papaya 2B's parachute. From the air I could see a couple of gun positions slightly east of his parachute and several small foot trails along with troop foxholes.

From other rescue missions I had been on, I knew that the clean-up job, suppressing enemy ground fire, wasn't always easy. Sometimes a pilot ejected and came down very near the gun that hit his aircraft. He could also land close to one of the major trails in Laos used by the North Vietnamese to transport supplies into South Vietnam. In this case, we knew the jungle would be swarming with enemy soldiers and the trail would be defended at all costs.

In jest, I suggested we design a Honda-type minibike that could be dropped to the survivor attached to a parachute. If the jet pilot was stupid enough to get shot down close to a road, he could retrieve the bike and drive on the enemy trail to a safe area. This would save our rescue team from a deadly all-out slugfest over a dangerous segment of the trail, during which we would probably have several of our rescue aircraft hit or shot down.

But as lead Sandy I had a few aces up my sleeve. If enemy defenses were really heavy, I would contact Crown and ask for maximum jet support. By this time in the war, Crown could divert any jet fighter flight from their assigned target to help the rescue effort. Nothing was more important than getting one of our own fly-boys out of the jungle. And more lucrative targets would sometimes appear during rescue efforts as we observed secondary explosions.

During the last eleven months I had observed that if a plane was hit by ground fire and the pilot could continue to fly for even a few seconds before ejecting, it was possible for him to parachute in a remote area away from populated towns and trails. In that case we could get in fast, make our rescue, and get out quickly without the enemy having time to mobilize their forces near the survivor. We classified those rescues as being unopposed, and thanked the survivor for his precision flying or good luck. At the Officers' Club, the survivor would buy a round of drinks for everyone involved in his rescue, and we would celebrate his good fortune. The next day he would look for a ride back home in one of the C-130 klong flights that circled the Air Force bases in Thailand each day. By then we would have forgotten about his rescue and begun preparing for the next one.

But unopposed rescues had been in the minority. Most of the jets started coming apart as soon as they were hit. These pilots had only a few moments to prepare for ejection and, as a result, usually landed near enemy positions. We went into each rescue expecting the worst and hoping for the best.

I gave Nail 24 the job of FACing the fast movers in on the gun positions, leaving me free to work with the survivor. Unfortunately, a few minutes later Nail 24 developed flight control difficulties and headed back to his home base. I took over again as FAC and worked the jets in on the gun positions. With the guns silenced, I made multiple low passes over Papaya 2B's position, trolling for ground fire. He told me the guns had stopped firing.

By this time in the war, another tactic had been added to our Sandys' bag of tricks. For some reason unknown to those of us who were Sandy pilots, Air Force headquarters directed that we use CBU-19 disabling gas on all rescues. It was commonly called tear gas and code-named Juicy Fruit, and we could dispense in the air from a CBU-19 pod. Hundreds of small bomblets, about the size of a D flashlight battery, could be dropped and would emit white smoke as they crisscrossed over the ground in a random manner. When inhaled by the enemy, or our survivor, the smoke would cause stinging eyes and uncontrollable vomiting. This effect lasted about ten minutes, long enough for our stagecoach robbery. However, the gas had several major disadvantages. We needed the survivor to help us as much as possible—if we gassed him he couldn't help us. The rescue could proceed faster and safer if the survivor could call out enemy ground fire to us, direct the Jolly Green through the final maneuvers, and grab the penetrator by himself.

While flying the Skyraider, we wore standard Air Force oxygen masks, which gave us protection from fire and fumes in the cockpit and allowed for better communication using the UHF radio. Flying through the CBU-19 gas cloud would be a hazard for us also, so we carried special gas masks. But they were difficult to put on in flight, had poor visibility through the oblong eyepieces, and had no UHF radio communication capability. For these reasons, we only used disabling gas as a last resort. If enemy soldiers were directly under the tree the survivor found himself hung up in, disabling gas made sense.

Two A-1s from the 1st SOS, our sister squadron at NKP, with call signs Hobo 52 and 53, were already airborne carrying the gas. As on-scene commander, I took a little liberty with the military rules. While the regulations stated that gas would be used on every rescue, it didn't say how it would be used. Under the circumstances I found myself in, I thought it made more sense to use the gas as a smoke screen downwind of the survivor. That's what I directed them to do. Ed Leonard, my Skyraider instructor months earlier, who always had a unique outlook on how to plan a rescue, would have been proud of me.

While the Hobos were placing gas in the jungle, my Sandy flight led the Jolly Green in for the pickup. My heart rate raced as I called for Papaya 2B to pop his Mark 13 flare. We formed a firing circle around the helicopter as he hoisted Papaya 2B up the cable and into the door opening. I led the chopper through our planned exit corridor while two or three enemy antiaircraft guns fired at us from a river valley. No one got hit; the rescue force got out in one piece. Jolly Green headed back to NKP with the survivor on board; the stagecoach robbery had been a success.

My Sandy flight climbed back up to 8,000 feet and orbited over the pickup area while I continued to call Papaya 2A on our emergency radio frequency. When our fuel state got low, we went home. The F-4 pilot had either been captured or killed; I would never know. His loss still haunts me. It's a feeling common to every Sandy lead who has had to leave a flying buddy stranded in the jungle.

From official Air Force reports I found that Papaya 2B was Capt. Aldis Rutyna. For the three hours he was on the ground in Laos surrounded by enemy troops, he had done an excellent job of assisting in his own rescue.

The front seat pilot, Papaya 2A, was Lt. Col. Carter Luna. He was born September 28, 1928 in Hazlehurst, Mississippi, and continues to be listed as MIA to this day. His aircraft was one of 444 F-4s lost in the war. Overall, 2,254 American planes were destroyed.

16 LAST FLIGHTS

By early 1969, Colonel Jones was assigned as commanding officer of the 1001 Flying Training Squadron at Andrews AFB, Maryland. In March of 1969, I received my last letter from him.

Dear George:

I am writing chiefly to keep in touch with the "Fighting 602nd," and to find out how things have been going as I haven't heard much since December. . . .

At Andrews . . . we have T-33s, 39s, C-131s, 54s, 118s, and even Goons but nothing nearly as good or near to my heart as the old A-1. . . . I wanted to stay in the [D.C.] area until I could be cleared to go back to SEA [Southeast Asia]. I got back on flying status in January with the restriction that I not be stationed in tropical climates until I get a medical recheck in April. Actually I am in fine shape—played 4 games of handball to celebrate getting out of the hospital but the skin on my left elbow just finished completely healing last week. It took some exercising to regain complete motion in my left arm.

Now that I have this job and so much time has passed I have about decided that I won't ask to go back [to the 602nd]. I can't in good conscience leave this position until I have had it for a while and fixed some of the things I was put here to set right and by that time all the people I know will be gone home and I wouldn't be sure of getting back to the 602nd. . . .

I got the party recording that Gene McCormack sent me. John Carlson [stationed at Wright–Patterson AFB, Ohio] sent me a scrambled egg Sandy [baseball] cap. . . . When my stuff came in I finally got the orange Sandy party flying suit I never had when I needed it but had ordered. I would like some insignia to put on my flying suit for reunions and some for my L-2 [flying] jacket so I'll look as good as [Charlie] Flynn, so I am asking you to get and send to me if available some A-1H, Sandy, 602 patches and Yankee Air Pirate—what $5 will get me. . . .

Buice . . . is retiring on a medical disability due to his injury—OK but not fit for combat flying—and is getting a Govt job at Hurlburt. A good thing to know—a reg off [a regular officer] can take a govt job and not lose pay if he retires as a result of enemy action. . . .

I have heard nothing on any decoration which is not surprising considering the devious way I came back, but I did find an order on an Air Medal and Purple Heart in my folder at Randolph when I checked out of the Hospital. Nothing has followed me here—they even lost my Pay Record—so I would appreciate any order numbers or info on anything the Squadron my have gotten back. . . . I should have orders on some more Air Medals, probably a DFC . . . plus whatever finally came out of my last mission—it went in as an Air Force Cross. Incidently, I did get a well done so they tell me, but they forgot to send the award—the Safety people I reckon. . . .

I really want to thank you for your last long letter which was much appreciated and which I have attached to my Diary of events in SEA. Some day when I have a chance I intend to write a book. You would have much better material having seen so much more. I read in the paper of the capture of Na Khang—LS [Lima Site] 36. The 602 really had some hard luck last fall—I hope it has been better lately though I heard by the grapevine that you had lost a couple of airplanes. . . .

Well, best of luck—say hello to the fellows in the [Sandy] box who still know me and to the FNGs [Fucking New Guys].

Sincerely,

Bill

On March 29, 1969 back in the States, former President Dwight D. Eisenhower died. He had been a symbol of America's victory in Europe during World War II. I wondered what he had thought of the quagmire in Vietnam.

On that same day I flew my next to last combat flight. On that mission I would give a lead check-out evaluation to 1st Lt. Neal "Clint" Ward. Clint Ward was a recent graduate of Texas A&M, just like Capt. Clyde Campbell, who was killed just twenty-eight days earlier.

Ward went to flight school at Webb AFB near Big Spring, Texas. After flight school, he went through Hurlburt to train to fly the Skyraider in the same class as our squadron commander, Colonel Stueck. While there, one day after a flight together, Ward and Stueck were filling out military forms and Stueck remarked, "Today is a special day for me." Ward asked him why it was special. "Today is the twenty-fifth anniversary of the day I received my Army Air Corps flying wings," Stueck answered. Ward said it was a special day for him also. He told Stueck it was his birthday—he was twenty-three years old. Stueck remarked, "You sure know how to make a guy feel old." Ward was young enough to be Stueck's son. Stueck took a special liking to the aggressive young pilot. He was happy Ward was assigned to the 602nd, and they both arrived at NKP in December of 1968.

On the flight with me on March 29, Ward was flying an A-1H, serial number 139738, and using the call sign Firefly 20. I was in an A-1E as Firefly 21. Six months earlier Colonel Jones had been flying 139738 when he got hit by ground fire in North Vietnam during his attempted rescue of Carter 2A. Even though 139738 was substantially damaged, the maintenance crews were able to repair the Skyraider and return it to combat action. I had flown the aircraft twice back in February. It seemed odd to fly the plane in which Colonel Jones had received such a direct hit from enemy gunners. In one sense it seemed to be an unlucky aircraft to have taken such a direct hit in the extraction rockets. On the other hand, it was a lucky ship to have survived the assault and make it back home to NKP. The plane flew as well as it did before getting hit, a tribute to the airmen who labored on twelve-hour shifts every day, seven days a week to keep all of our Skyraiders operational.

It also seemed strange to fly on Ward's wing and see 139738 from the air while giving him a lead checkout evaluation. I could practically imagine that

Colonel Jones was still in the cockpit, getting ready to finish his tour just like me. He would have a sense of accomplishment in putting in a full year of hard-fought combat as well as rescuing many of the jet jockeys who ejected over the trail. His plane, 139738, was a resilient old buzzard now, still in the thick of battle. My recent letter from Colonel Jones, who also seemed like a resilient old buzzard, indicated that he was anxious for his burns to heal but would not be coming back to fly the Skyraider at NKP. I wondered if 139738 would be hit again and maybe shot down.

But on the morning of March 29, I briefed Ward on our mission to upgrade him to a strike lead. If he passed he would be qualified to lead other pilots on Firefly strike missions. I briefed Ward long and comprehensively just as Leonard had briefed me, covering every possible situation that could happen. During my previous 186 missions, I had seen first hand some brilliant successes, but also some incredible failures. We talked about every abnormal event that could occur and what we would do if it happened. I felt that talking about it might keep it from happening. Now I realized how Leonard felt as he came to the end of his tour.

Ward and I flew a standard strike mission in Barrel Roll. Ward followed our pre-briefed procedures and found the target area. Unlike most of the other pilots I had flown wing on, I found Ward to be very rough on the flight controls. With a full load of ordnance and fuel, a pilot needed to be smooth in handling the heavyweight Skyraider. It was good to be an aggressive pilot, but not necessary to rack the Skyraider's flight controls like he did. It looked to me like Ward's mind was working slower than his hands, not a good sign for a combat pilot.

But what concerned me the most was that Ward broke all the altitude limitations imposed by the squadron for a standard Firefly strike mission. If we were on a rescue, a pilot could fly at any altitude or airspeed he needed to get ordnance on enemy guns opposing the rescue. A search and rescue was so important that we simply briefed the pilots to just use good judgment in determining the flight maneuvers that would work to silence the guns threatening the rescue. For a Firefly mission, however, it seemed to me that Ward was flying too low and was subjecting himself to extra risk of getting shot down or colliding with the ground. I cautioned him over the UHF radio and again when we got back to NKP. I passed him but still had the uneasy feeling he was too inexperienced and too willing to take unnecessary risks. Ed Leonard probably thought I was too inexperienced ten months earlier.

On June 16, 1969, two and a half months after I completed my tour and returned to the States, Ward led another two-ship flight up into Barrel Roll. Ironically, he was again using the call sign Firefly 20, just as he did with me months earlier. This time he was flying an A-1H and scheduled to make a strike near Ban Ban, Laos. Ward spotted a convoy of twelve trucks on a road east of Ban Ban. Some of the convoy's trucks had been destroyed by flights days before. He strafed the lead truck and stopped the column. That was a good tactic since the other trucks were now blocked on the road and an easier target. Ward returned for a second low pass and crashed. His wingman, Lieutenant Moore, did not see a parachute or hear a beeper signal. In nine more days Clint Ward would have been twenty-four years old. A very young Skyraider pilot had bit the dust.

LAST FLIGHT

It had been a long year and I was dead tired from flying combat missions. I viewed my last flight with mixed emotions. On one hand, I would really miss the other Sandy pilots and flying rescue missions. On the other, I had dodged bullets for 187 missions, surely using up my share of luck.

My last flight, on April 1, 1969, would be a standard Firefly strike flight in Barrel Roll near the PDJ, the same area where I had flown my first combat mission eleven and a half months earlier. A new guy from our sister squadron would fly my wing and gain experience from me, now an old veteran.

Because of a mix-up in the flight schedule, my going-away party was held the night before my last flight. The pilots in the 602nd put on their party flight suits and joined me at the NKP Officers' Club for an evening dinner. I didn't purchase a party suit, since I was planning to get out of the Air Force. I could see no reason why I would ever wear one in civilian life. In California, where I hoped to live, prisoners wore uniforms of the same orange color. I simply wore a pair of slacks and a short sleeve shirt. I was now only a few days from becoming a civilian again.

Even though I wore civilian attire, I still partied like the best of my good friends and squadron mates. They all wanted to buy me a farewell drink, and I couldn't turn any of them down. Full of drink, my comrades at arms toasted my good fortune and embellished my aviation heroics. We spent hours in laughter; we gripped each other with a firm handshake and an arm around the shoulder, embracing. As the crowd thinned, a few of us wandered over to the Sandy Box for a final nightcap. We continued to celebrate into the late evening and early morning. The party continued on and on and took on a strange twist. Another Skyraider pilot and I were lying on the floor of the Sandy Box, and other pilots were popping Mark 13 flares and throwing them in at us. Orange smoke filled the room. But by keeping low to the floor we could still barely breathe and drink. At three o'clock in the morning, in a drunken stupor, it dawned on me that I had only a couple of hours before briefing for my last flight. The party ended for me.

A few hours later I was airborne again, motoring north into Laos. It was the end of the dry season; no clouds were in the sky, only haze and smoke reaching up to 10,000 feet. My head was pounding; I was paying dearly with a tremendous headache for the good time at my going-away party the night before. My headache sounded louder than the roar of the engine. It seemed so strong that I feared the Skyraider's huge radial engine might even quit and I wouldn't notice it. I made a mental note to watch the four-bladed propeller. If I saw only one blade suspended in space it would be the only way I would know that the engine had stopped!

In one sense it was going to be a big letdown to never again climb into the cockpit of a single-engine prop fighter, canopy open, the wind spilling through like an ocean. I would really miss the other Sandy pilots and the rescue mission. But then, it was going to be ever so nice not to get shot at day after day, night after night. The odds against survival were bad if one elected to stay on. Many pilots, as they got to the end of their tour, began to believe they were invulnerable. If they had survived that long they began to get bolder and bolder, often taking wild and dangerous chances well beyond what was necessary. Several volunteered for another tour and went back into battle armed with thoughts of their invincibility. Some never returned. Ed Leonard had extended for six months. Now, ten months after the rescue of Streetcar 304, he was still listed as missing in action.

One could hope to fly through thousands of rounds of ground fire for only so long. The odds would eventually catch up with you. The decision to pack up, get out of the Air Force, and go home was the right decision for me . . . but it was bittersweet as well. Ever since deciding to resign from the Air Force six months earlier, I had given a lot of thought to how I would fight during the end of my tour. As a citizen-soldier, awards and decorations would be of little value to me, and chalking up flying hours in a tail-wheeled prop would not enhance my résumé as a jet test pilot. I was returning to the United States unemployed, married, and the father of two small boys. Similar to combat, another great unknown lay ahead of me.

If I chose to do so, I could back off from combat missions. If I felt ill, tired, or disinterested, I could decline to fly. If I did fly, I could choose to be removed from the battle, take the safe course. I saw it happen to one of our pilots on a rescue. But even if my squadron mates didn't detect I was hanging it up, I would know it myself and never be able to forget it. After hours of mental anguish and indecision, I decided to fight as hard as possible, get my bombs and rockets on target, and give it my all to the very end. I wanted to keep rescuing every fly-boy down in the weeds who was waiting for voice contact with a Sandy.

I couldn't help but remember a humorous philosophy I had heard about when I was playing high school football. If your team was behind in the score late in the fourth quarter, you should feign injury after a play and lie on the field. You would get carried off the field in a stretcher to the locker room to the applause of the whole stadium. Then the plan was to take a fast shower and arrive at the Friday night post-game dance early. Everyone would come up to you concerned about your injury. You could say, "If I had played the rest of the game, we would have won!" On the other hand, if your team was winning, you should make sure you were on the field for the last play. Then you could take off your helmet, hold it high in the air, and dance around acting like the team won because of you.

This war looked like a loser to me. Without our government's will to bomb Hanoi and the shipyards of Haiphong, and to cut the Ho Chi Minh Trail once and for all, this terrible skirmish that was causing the loss of a generation of pilots and planes was hopelessly doomed.

One of the new Skyraider pilots, Lt. Col. Daryle Tripp, made an interesting observation on the state of the war. He said, "The Air Force is using a fifteen-million-dollar jet aircraft, flown by a five-hundred-thousand-dollar trained pilot, to attack a five-thousand-dollar truck, defended by a five-hundred-dollar AAA gun, operated by a five-dollar-a-month 'Gomer'." ("Gomer" was a degrading word we used to describe the enemy.) Tripp said this type of attack was not a very fair economic exchange. The approach was just the opposite of Secretary of Defense McNamara's cost-effectiveness theory.

We flew north, still in the haze and smoke, getting nearer to the PDJ. My wingman maintained the correct formation position; the UHF radio was quiet. My stomach tossed and turned, reminding me again that I had partied too hard the night before. Having flown over this enemy area many times before, I easily spotted our target. We turned east and rolled in to drop our bombs and fire our rockets. It wasn't a spectacular mission; we finished the strike in just a couple of minutes. It was time to head back home to NKP.

We continued east over familiar landmarks. For the last time I looked at Arrowhead Lake, Roadrunner Lake, and the soccer field near the Chinese Embassy that Colonel Jones had bombed six months earlier. It had been a haven for Pathet Lao gunners who knew we weren't allowed to strike it. Jones hit it anyway. He said we didn't have a handball court at NKP, so why should the Chinese have a soccer field?

Off to the left was Lima Site 36, an area of intense battles during the previous year. As we neared the town of Ban Ban, I armed my four 20-mm guns. As a gesture of farewell I put a few unofficial rounds into the town; it was a payback for all the times they had fired at me. We turned back south and crossed the highest mountain of northern Laos while banking back and forth in the lightly loaded Skyraider, now smooth to the touch with all the ordnance expended. I watched the dense jungle trees stream by as we started a long descent toward the Mekong River. The airspeed picked up as the P&W radial purred. I opened the canopy, took off my flight gloves, and allowed the warm air to soothe my tired spirit and upset stomach.

Leveling off around five hundred feet above the river, I saw a flock of large white birds flash by. Several small boats also swept by, undisturbed by the war miles away. The river looked peaceful and serene, although one of my flying mates had seen a body floating in it when he visited the town of Nakhon Phanom a short time before. It was not yet time to let my guard down.

I applied power to climb back to pattern altitude for landing at NKP. The field was in sight about ten miles distant. With my upset stomach I chose to make a straight-in approach. I thought about what would happen to my wingman in the months to come. What would be the fate of the 602nd squadron and all the Skyraider aircraft still flying? What would be the final chapter in this "secret" war in Laos?

I lowered the landing gear, then the flaps. The sound of rushing wind diminished, but my head was still pounding like the engine in front of me. The throttle was slowly retarded to idle and back-stick pressure applied. The tail wheel touched first, then the main gear kissed the asphalt. At that moment I realized the enemy's plan to shoot me down, to capture and imprison this flyboy, was foiled. The enemy had had their chance. If there was a bullet with my name on it, it had not been fired.

A crowd of pilots and mechanics waited for me on the ramp. As I pulled the mixture control off, the fourteen-foot prop stopped, and the instrument gyros spun down. As soon as my feet touched the ground, water from a fire extinguisher blasted away at me. It was refreshing to be on the receiving end this time. I shook some of the same hands I had held the night before, detecting envy and sadness. I would be one of the few to walk out of NKP in one piece—neither killed, captured, injured, nor burned. Would they be so fortunate?

It was a short walk to the Intelligence Office to debrief this last mission. In a matter-of-fact fashion, I wearily relayed to the officer in charge my time on target, ordnance expended, and bomb damage assessment. During the debrief my breathing became irregular and perspiration formed on my forehead. Though I should have been happy and excited to have completed my last mission, I was feeling sick. I excused myself and went to the latrine. In the next few minutes I returned most of my going-away party back to the klong of Thailand. It was a fitting end to my year of combat. I always thought of it as a throw-up war.

"The Green, Green Grass of Home"

It was a late afternoon in early April when the Boeing 707 engines were started on the ramp of Tan Son Nhut AB just outside of Saigon. My year of combat was over and I was going home. Just as the aircraft started to taxi, one of the stewardesses noticed that a soldier had passed out in his seat. Soon, all four engines were shut down and military corpsmen carried him out to an awaiting ambulance. It was only a short delay; nevertheless, we were all anxious to leave Vietnam. The engines were started again and the airliner stopped just short of the runway. We would be the next plane to depart.

Another soldier passed out. Many had been drinking and celebrating since they left the jungle only hours before, and it was also extremely hot and humid. The stewardess and copilot tried to awaken the soldier while the rest of us chanted, "Go, go, go!" This time only the two engines on the left wing near the entrance door were shut down, and the ambulance returned. Off went another combat veteran who was going to be extremely disappointed when he woke up.

As the wheels left the ground, one guy let out a cheer. He was immediately stared down by the GIs around him. We weren't out of Vietnam yet, and no one wanted to tempt the gods. Everyone was silent during the climb to altitude. The States were still thousands of miles away. We settled back for the long flight across the Pacific Ocean. As the sun set back of the clouds I took my last photograph of Vietnam, looking deceptively peaceful from high in the sky.

My thoughts turned to my year spent in combat. Now on my way home, it seemed both the longest and shortest year of my life. I remembered going to sleep each night exhausted from long combat missions, wondering if the next day would be my turn to get shot down and captured.

As I looked around the airliner, I saw some of my fellow passengers were U.S. Army ground soldiers who had probably experienced more first-hand losses of their buddies than we had as aviators. By the looks on their faces and their blank stares, I could tell they didn't yet believe they were finally going home either.

I couldn't help but feel badly that some of my fellow pilots, missing in action in Laos and Vietnam, were not going home too. Ed Leonard, whom I had seen parachute into the trees, was still listed as MIA. Bat Masterson, who went down on a night mission, was still missing. My crazy wingman Wild Bill Coady had crashed on a rescue mission. Both of Wild Bill's roommates, Clyde Campbell and Joe Pirruccello, were lost. Charles Kuhlmann was lost up in

Barrel Roll. Dick Walsh was lost as a Sandy lead. Although I could not know it at the time, James East, a pilot I met just a week before I left, would crash and be killed only three weeks later. And Clint Ward, only a young first lieutenant, would be lost a couple of weeks after that. Wayne Warner was severely burned and in a hospital back in the States. Bill Jones, who had been shot up badly on a rescue mission, was also burned and not expected to return to Southeast Asia. Bill Buice was injured so badly the Air Force retired him. Because of battle damage, fifteen pilots, out of around fifty in my squadron who I knew during my year tour, and twenty-six aircraft did not return to Udorn or NKP after combat missions. We had paid a high price in men and equipment to support South Vietnam. I did not think the war could ever be won with the strategy and tactics then being followed by our government, but I was just a small cog in the huge wheel of war.

I also thought about my wife and two sons, now four and eight years old. Because of the gifts of toys I had mailed back during the year, my youngest son thought I had been in "Toyland." He thought I was near the North Pole with Santa Claus. He couldn't comprehend a country named Thailand. I wasn't sure I ever did either.

In the middle of the night, we refueled in Hawaii; it was my first chance to be on American soil. Between Honolulu and Travis AFB in California I dozed off, dreaming I was back in combat, flying a low-level night mission in the monsoon rains. It was a bad dream that I had experienced many, many times before. The old A-1 would shake and shudder in the turbulence. I'd be fighting to fly on the flight instruments without getting vertigo. I always worried I would get lost and inadvertently fly directly over enemy guns. At night, the tracers from the enemy guns looked like golf balls streaming out of a garden hose. They were weaving back and forth. I was never sure whether the enemy was shooting at me or someone else. It was a nightmare. When I woke and found myself in a plane, I wasn't sure what was a dream and what was reality.

At the moment the airliner wheels touched down on the Travis AFB runway, everyone unbuckled their seat belts, jumped up and down, and cheered. We grabbed one another and danced in the aisle. I didn't know anyone on board, but we had shared and survived a common experience. We were really home at last.

Later, as I was driving home with my wife and sons, the radio was playing a Tom Jones song that was popular at the time, "The Green, Green Grass of Home." In the early morning light of dawn I could see California's green, green hills of spring, so different from the brown dry season of Laos.

The song is about a prisoner who dreams he is set free. He is riding a train home and expects his family will be there to meet him, as my family was there to meet me. As the train stops, he spots his girl, Mary, "Hair of gold and lips like cherries. It's good to touch the green, green grass of home." The song continues as he awakes to find that he is still in prison. At daybreak a guard will be taking him to be executed, and only in death will he again touch his green, green grass of home.

In many ways I felt I had been a prisoner of the war in Vietnam and the "secret" war in Laos. When I was there, I dreamed that eventually I would return to my golden-haired wife. But I also realized that I might return in a box, to be laid beneath the green, green grass of home, like the prisoner in the song.

Once in our house, I immediately took a long, hot shower. I tried to wash away the smell and memories of war. The shower would get rid of the smell. But it would take a long time to forget the war.

EPILOGUE

The biggest surprise of my life occurred in February 1973. At that time I read in the *Los Angeles Times* that, after five years in prison, CAPT. EDWARD LEONARD was one of 591 Americans released by North Vietnam as part of Operation Homecoming. It was against all odds; he was one of only ten to return from Laos. Even though Ed made only one radio call to us from the ground, I was always convinced during my year of combat that he was still alive. But as the years passed and there was no more information or contact with him, his chances of survival seemed slim.

After several phone calls to military bases, I was told I could contact Ed at the base hospital at Travis AFB in California. I called and was instructed by an Air Force nurse to leave my phone number as he was eating lunch. Several minutes later, I received a phone call and instantly recognized Ed's voice. He was really alive. I couldn't believe it. Ed told me how he evaded the enemy the first night, climbed a tree, was spotted and captured. He said, "When I climbed down from the tree, the war ended for me." He was pleased to find out that we had eventually rescued Streetcar 304, Navy pilot Kenny Fields.

Ed said his divorce was finalized while he was in prison and he was starting life anew. He was anxious to get back on flying status but had concerns about his physical health. While he was in captivity the North Vietnamese had knocked out his teeth and cut his neck. He also had injuries to both shoulders and hips from being tied in straps. He said he needed a lot of medical attention. But on the positive side, General Motors had given a new car to every returning POW, and he had five years of military leave (vacation) to use. When he was in prison, each new captive would share news about what was going on in America. Ed said the two biggest events that occurred while he was held prisoner were the Americans landing on the moon and *Playboy* having a centerfold showing everything.

Exactly twenty years after I saw Ed parachute into the trees of Laos, we met face to face in Texas. My sister's daughter was to be married on a Saturday afternoon in the summer of 1988 in Austin, Texas. I met Ed for breakfast that morning; it was a chance to greet the man I felt best represented the spirit and courage of all the Sandy rescue pilots who fought in the war. Ed explained that he got back on flying status and flew the reconnaissance version of the F-4 Phantom out of Bergstrom AFB, Texas for a few years. He retired from the Air Force as a lieutenant colonel and went to law school at the University of Texas in Austin. He said he married the first woman he met after being released as a prisoner of war. That marriage was a mistake and lasted only six months. Then he married for a third time, and by 1988, when we got together, that marriage had also failed. Ed explained that during his five years as a prisoner of war, with most of it in solitary confinement, he had enough time to solve a lot of life problems but he still didn't understand women.

In the fall of 1993 I heard more about Ed from a mutual friend. Ed had written a letter that said the events of the last eighteen months of his life had been fantastic. He had finally gone home to the Pacific Northwest, the place of his birth. It started with what appeared to be a grim event: being fired as a lawyer for the state of Texas with ninety-three other white males who were over forty by Texas Governor Ann Richards. The first twenty-four hours was spent in shock; he had received a merit raise two days earlier. Ed called and asked for an application to take the Oregon bar exam. He was paid accrued comp time and vacation from the state of Texas and qualified for unemployment funds. He studied his law books during the summer of 1992 on the Oregon coast. After the exam he returned to Texas, sold his house, and moved north in February of 1993. If he hadn't been fired, he said he probably would never have made it home to the Pacific Northwest. During this time a friend tracked him down and called to tell him that his old love Suzanne Edgell had breast cancer and that her condition could be terminal. The last time he had seen Suzanne was twenty-five years earlier in May of 1968 when he was in the hospital in the Philippines and she was teaching school. At that time, they planned to meet again the next month; instead Ed was shot down and listed as missing in action. Suzanne waited nearly five years and had been in regular contact with Ed's family. A man she'd met was pressing suit hard. When the first list of POWs was released and Ed's name wasn't on it, she married the man. Three weeks later, the Vietnamese released the names of prisoners held in Laos. Suzanne contacted Ed's sister two years later when her marriage failed. By then Ed was within a week of being married to his third wife. Through the following years Ed lost track of Suzanne. After his third marriage failed he still had a beautiful memory of Suzanne, the woman whose spirit had been with him and sustained him for so many years. After the friend called in 1993, Ed knew that he wanted Suzanne in his life. Calls were made, letters written, and he found her. Her chemotherapy treatments were going well. On his way from Austin to Astoria, Oregon he stopped to see her. He said, "Suzanne was skittish; she wasn't so sure. It seemed entirely too much soap opera." He overcame her concerns, and they were married at Coxcomb Hill in Astoria on August 14, 1993, surrounded by five of Ed's buddies from prison, teachers who had been with Suzanne in the Philippines, and family—lots of family. Today they live on the Pacific coast of Washington state and finally enjoy the freedom and love that had so long escaped both of them. It is a love story that a Hollywood writer could never have imagined.

As is written in Joel 2:25 in the Bible: "And I will restore to you the years. . . ."

While I was attending a flight safety conference at Kirtland AFB, New Mexico in the spring of 1978, a Navy commander by the name of KENNY FIELDS made a presentation. Back in 1968 when I participated in the rescue of Streetcar 304, I did not get to meet Fields as he was returned to the hospital at NKP and I flew home to Udorn. I thought to myself, "Could this be

the same Kenny Fields I rescued ten years ago?" After the presentation, I
asked the short, gray-haired naval officer a question. I said, "Commander
Fields, I believe I know you by a different name." He looked at me like I had
lost my mind. I continued, "Were you Streetcar 304?" His answer was an em-
phatic, "Yes! Were you there?" I nodded my head and responded, "Only for
the three longest days of my life!" We ate dinner together that night and discussed in detail his three days and two nights in the jungle evading the North
Vietnamese. I heard the same stories from Kenny that had been relayed to us
in the Sandy Box by Colonel Jones. I wondered whether Kenny and his wife,
Shirley, ever named a child Sandy as a tribute to the pilots who rescued him.
I took an indirect approach and asked him if he had any children. He reported
that his wife was pregnant when he got shot down. She was notified by Navy
authorities that Kenny was missing but that rescue forces were in radio contact with him. Naturally, she worried that she might have to raise a child
without a father. She was again contacted when he was finally rescued and
told that, although injured, he was expected to make a full recovery. Kenny
told me during dinner that several months after he was rescued Shirley gave
birth to a son they named Todd. I didn't ask whether they had decided not to
call the boy Sandy or if it was just a rumor in the first place. In a strange twist
of circumstances, Kenny said, "Todd is now about ten years old and we are
having problems with him." He added, "Sometimes he is perfectly normal,
and other times it is like he has a loose electrical connection in his brain."
The Navy doctors couldn't find anything organically wrong with him. The
only diagnosis they could make was that Shirley suffered severe emotional
trauma during the thirty-nine hours Kenny was reported as missing. This extreme condition could have affected the embryo she was carrying. Todd was
also a casualty of that "secret" war in Laos.

Kenny Fields said that in October 1969 he returned to Vietnam for his second combat tour, flying the A-7 for 150 missions off the USS *Coral Sea*. On
his first mission he was directed to contact a Nail FAC at the exact target
site where he had been shot down sixteen months earlier. Kenny said, "What
kind of fate is that?" He dropped all his bombs on one pass with precise, de-
liberate aim. The FAC and his wingman thought he made a bad run, that he
had missed the smoke from the marking rocket. But his bombs hit just exactly where he aimed them—in among pots and pans, during the time of day

when he knew the enemy soldiers chanted, smack dab in the middle of a base camp he had seen before from the ground.

Just a few days before Christmas in 1979, my secretary said she was holding a phone call for me. For some reason that escapes me twenty-three years later, I was having a bad day. Some insignificant event in the long history of our personal lives had gotten me down in the dumps. I was feeling sorry for myself. I answered the phone and instantly recognized Kenny Fields's voice. He simply said, "Merry Christmas, thanks for saving my life." In those few moments my attitude changed. I had become bogged down in the small discomforts of human existence and had forgotten what was really important in life. The pilots I served with in the Vietnam War are extremely important to me.

CAPT. PETER LAPPIN, Nail 69, who directed an F-4 Phantom to drop CBU directly on Kenny Fields, left the military to fly for an airline. It's not surprising that a few years later smooth-talking Pete became a stockbroker in Southern California. In 1995 he and his wife went back to Tchepone for a vacation, the trip of a lifetime, he said. Whenever Pete describes his part in the rescue of Streetcar 304, he always starts the story by saying he spent the first two days of the hectic rescue in a massage parlor in Bangkok. It never fails to get a big laugh.

MAJ. EUSTACE "MEL" BUNN JR., my lead on the third day of the rescue of Streetcar 304, flew the last rescue attempt of any of us who served combat together. Mel returned to Hurlburt after his year of combat in Vietnam and became a Skyraider instructor pilot. In May 1970 he participated in the surprise raid on the Son Tay POW camp in North Vietnam. Although no Americans were found at the camp, rumors of the rescue spread widely, reaching other prisoners and the guards holding them hostage. As a result, the North Vietnamese consolidated all prisoners of war in camps in the center of Hanoi, and their treatment greatly improved.

Earlier, in late 1969, I heard through Air Force channels that COL. WILLIAM A. JONES III (he was promoted to full colonel on November 1, 1969) had lost his life shortly before being presented with the Medal of Honor. I was shocked to hear that he died during a crash on takeoff in a small civilian aircraft.

As John L. Frisbee, contributing editor of the Air Force Association's *Valor* newsletter, wrote:

In a supreme irony, Colonel Jones, who had survived more than 20 years of flying high-performance aircraft and nearly 100 combat missions, was killed in the crash of his private plane before the presentation ceremony could be held. President Nixon presented the medal posthumously to Jones's widow [Lois] and three young daughters [Elizabeth, Anne, and Mary Lee]. After the ceremony, Jones's youngest daughter, 9-year-old Mary Lee, gave the President a copy of her father's book, *Maxims for Men-at-Arms*, illustrated with his own pen-and-ink drawings. Jones had received the first copy of the book the day before his death.

According to Jimmy W. Kilbourne, Colonel Jones planned to say to the President, "I consider this great honor and high award to be a tribute not so much to me but to all the Sandy pilots who have flown out of the 602nd Fighter Squadron. I'm honored to represent them in this manner."

In 1972, A-1H, serial number 139738, made its last flight. Colonel Jones had flown the aircraft during the rescue of Carter 2A in September 1968. Somehow he managed to fly back to NKP after the aircraft was extensively damaged by enemy ground fire. On September 28, 1972, while flying no. 139738, Lt. Lance Smith of the 602nd experienced heavy buffeting during a weapons pass and went into an uncontrollable roll. Smith's last transmission on the radio was, "I'm getting out." A Jolly came in for the rescue and a PJ recovered Smith. A-1H serial number 139738 was the last of 202 Skyraiders lost in the Vietnam War.

SGT. THOMAS POPE, the PJ who was shot and critically injured during the rescue of Lt. Col. Peter Morris, had his left leg amputated. When Tom departed NKP he raised his bandaged stump of a knee in a salute and held his fingers up in a *V* for victory. For Tom, victory since Vietnam has been difficult to achieve; the years have been hard for him. He gave up smoking seven years ago and he has been attending Alcoholics Anonymous for fourteen years. Tom says he has given up a lot of things over the years but confesses he still occasionally cusses. He and his latest wife went their separate ways several years ago.

In September 2001 he suffered TBI (traumatic brain injury) from falling on his head and was in a Veterans' Administration hospital in Oklahoma. He is recovering now and has been released. But he has not lost his PJ tenacity.

The doctors and nurses have termed his latest medical recovery fantastic, and his family calls him a miracle child. Tom gets a disability pension from the military, which pays some of the bills. Several years ago he started painting landscapes and portraits in watercolor but felt he had no talent. As a lark he took twenty of his paintings to an art fair and sold fifteen of them. People said, "You are an artist; you have talent." Indeed, Tom Pope has lots of talent and is still an inspiration to those of us who served with him in combat; he's a true American hero.

1ST LT. JAMES FEGAN, Stormy 2B, was severely injured as a result of his high-speed F-4 ejection over Tchepone. Doctors discovered eleven fractures in both of his arms and his left leg. He spent six weeks in traction during a ten-month stay in a hospital while physicians performed ten surgeries. Jim said he was medically retired from the Air Force, his marriage was over, and he started life anew. He went back to college and graduated from medical school, specializing in rehabilitation treatment. Through the years he has treated himself, regaining his ability to snow ski. During our most recent search-and-rescue reunion Jim entertained us by playing his guitar, with mended fingers, while singing a song he wrote about Tchepone. There was not a dry eye in the room.

In 1978 I attended a gun show in Los Angeles. While there I came upon a Vietnam MIA booth. Several veterans displayed MIA banners, brochures, and information about men lost in the war. Being curious, I stopped and was shown a large book that presented information on all the U.S. military personnel still listed as missing. I found a short biographical sketch on each of my missing Skyraider flying mates. As of that time, nothing more was known of their fate. I did learn that Fran, the wife of CAPT. MICHAEL "BAT" MASTERSON, was living in the Los Angeles area. I copied her address and telephone number on a slip of paper and was encouraged by the veterans at the MIA booth to contact her. They said the federal government was not cooperating with families who wanted to know more about the status of their loved ones. I wasn't sure I wanted to open up old wounds so I filed the information away for future use. Several weeks later I summoned the courage to call Fran Masterson. We had a long conversation and I found out that she thought Bat was still alive and being held a prisoner in either Laos or Vietnam. She had become an MIA activist, giving speeches and conducting meetings all around the country. It has become her life mission to seek out the truth about what happened to Bat. She has dedicated her life and resources to unraveling the mystery of his disappearance and to supporting other MIA families who are in a similar situation. To this day Fran still believes Bat is alive and held captive.

In 1995 an Air Force military team from the Joint Task Force–Full Accounting (JTF–FA) found Bat Masterson's crash site. The five-member team consisted of a major as team chief, a medic, a casualty resolution specialist, an explosive ordnance disposition specialist, and a search-and-recovery specialist. They first attempted to interview persons living near the crash site. None of the villagers currently living in nearby Ban Thalin Noi were there in 1968. The village was not reestablished until 1983. All the former residents fled to Thailand in 1975 when the Communists took over. One villager was aware of an American aircraft crash site and led the team to its location. The team found the site covered with vegetation consisting of tall grass and trees located on a 30- to 35-degree slope. The team searched an area measuring one hundred meters by fifty meters and identified aircraft wreckage. They looked closely in a fifty-by-thirty-meter area starting at a crater and spreading down the slope. Numerous pieces of aircraft wreckage were found during the search, including portions of a Skyraider landing gear and two 20-mm internal wing guns. The team believed they had correctly identified Masterson's aircraft; however, no pilot-related equipment, personal effects, or biological evidence was recovered. As a result, Masterson's case was recommended for placement into the "pending" category until such time as new material evidence is discovered. After thirty-three years, Bat's wife Fran and my A-1 squadron mates still don't know what really happened to him. Bat Masterson's disappearance and our nation's effort to resolve the MIA issue is a lingering cause of pain to the families left behind.

CAPT. JERRY JENKINSON, who had led the hostile rescue of Tom O'Connor near Lima Site 85 in December 1968, and had been fortunate to be rescued himself only a few miles away the next week, found that his luck was soon to fail. He returned to the States in May 1969 and was assigned as an instructor pilot in the 3561st Pilot Training Squadron at Webb AFB in Big Spring, Texas. Jerry checked out in the Cessna T-37B and was promoted to major. On December 17, 1969, practically a year to the day he had been shot down near Lima Site 85, Jerry departed Webb AFB on a dual training mission with student pilot 2nd Lt. Robert McCracken in the left seat. The flight was briefed as a mid-phase check ride for the student. Jerry and his student took off mid-morning and completed some flight maneuvers before returning to the Webb AFB flight pattern for a straight-in, no-flap landing. The no-flap landing was part of an evaluation Jerry was giving the student. After a successful landing, Lieutenant McCracken took off again and Jerry requested a closed pattern from the tower controller, to be followed by the student demonstrating a simulated single-engine landing. The landing was completed and Jerry called the tower and requested another simulated single-engine landing. This landing was also completed without incident, and the T-37B departed the aircraft pattern for more flight maneuvers about forty-five miles northeast of Webb AFB. No further radio transmissions were ever heard from the pilots of the aircraft. Military investigators would later determine that Jerry and his student placed the T-37B trainer in a flat spin and did not recover. Neither pilot ejected and both were killed on impact. The official accident report stated that the aircraft accident resulted in minimal damage to one-fourth acre of mesquite and sagebrush located on the side of a canyon about five nautical miles northwest of Fluvanna, Texas. The aircraft impacted the ground at exactly 11:18 a.m. as evidenced by a watch found in the wreckage. Ironically, Jerry Jenkinson survived the rigors of a year of combat only to die in the United States during a student training flight. The pilot called Sweet-eyes by our Thai maids, who we all thought would play the part of Sandy in a smash war movie, was dead. Hollywood never knew they had lost their handsome movie lead.

CAPT. WAYNE WARNER, who was severely burned on an aborted takeoff at NKP in March of 1969, was given a medical retirement later that year. After retirement, he decided to go back to school and get a law degree. Graduating in 1974 as a patent attorney, he went to work at Eglin AFB in Florida, in the area of weapon-system acquisition. Wayne is still working for the Air Force, thirty-three years after crashing on takeoff in the Skyraider. "Working pays the rent," he said in a phone conversation. Wayne hasn't lost his love of flying. He told me that if he ever got rich by winning the lottery, he would like to buy an old World War II tail-wheel propeller fighter and take it to air shows all around the United States. His favorite part of the movie *Flight of the Intruder,* which is about a Navy A-6 shot down in Vietnam, is the part where Skyraiders come in for the rescue. No one volunteered more and tried harder to participate in rescue missions. Wayne Warner is a true Sandy pilot in his heart.

In 1972, my sister's husband, an Air Force doctor, was transferred to Vandenberg AFB in California. They invited my wife and me to a backyard barbecue and said their neighbor, who my sister said knew me from Vietnam, would also attend. When we arrived we met MAJ. MICHAEL MORGANSTEIN, the navigator who flew a night-strike mission with me in northern Laos. Mike didn't seem to show any lasting effects from having a bug fly up his nose at 200 knots. He vividly remembered my screwed-up dive under a flare and still thought I had tried to kill him. The intervening years and a couple of drinks still had not improved his sense of humor; I was reluctant to ask him if he ever applied for the Purple Heart.

The plastic military photo ID of MAJ. CHARLES KUHLMANN, showed up in Hanoi before the war ended. Our government received the badge in a classified exchange with the North Vietnamese. Tom O'Connor, who as Kuhlmann's wingman watched him roll into a steep dive and hit the ground, found out that someone in Kuhlmann's family said, "My God, he is a POW after all." Tom said, "No, his ID badge was probably in the chest pocket of his flight suit, which was zippered closed and covered by his nylon mesh survival vest. It could have survived the crash; Charles didn't."

Many years later, in the early 1990s, Tom O'Connor was contacted by an Army major stationed in Germany. The major was a friend of one of Charles Kuhlmann's two daughters and was assisting the office of JTF–FA in finding missing airmen in Laos. He wanted a physical description of the road, hills, trees, and gully where Kuhlmann crashed. The office sent a map of the crash site to Tom showing several possible locations of the Skyraider's final resting place. After more than thirty years Tom could still see in his mind's eye the Skyraider in a steep dive and impacting large trees in a gully. He precisely marked the location and returned the map. Using Tom O'Connor's very accurate description of the crash site, the search team was able to find Kuhlmann's A-1. When the Air Force sent in a team to survey the wreckage they found most of the Skyraider's ordnance, one boot, a watch, and a St. Christopher medal. Some human remains were also recovered. Tom was correct—Charles was still in the A-1 when it crashed. In 1994 a memorial service for Maj. Charles Kuhlmann was held at the U.S. Naval Academy chapel, and he was buried in Arlington National Cemetery. As was fitting for a former bomber pilot, an eight-engine Boeing B-52 made a flyby.

Within a few days after my return to the United States from Southeast Asia, I was a civilian again. I found it difficult to get information on the "secret" war in Laos. Once I looked for an update in the *San Francisco Chronicle* and only found a small article on page 17. Although the war in Laos was of critical importance to the combatants, it captured little attention from the American public and news media.

After completing several job interview trips, I accepted a position as an experimental test pilot with Hughes Aircraft Company in Culver City, California. I moved my family to Los Angeles, bought a house, and watched the Vietnam War from a distance. By July 1969, our nation's thoughts and prayers were with Neil Armstrong and Buzz Aldrin as they landed Apollo 11 on the moon. President Nixon was starting to scale down the war and bring thousands of troops back from Vietnam.

Ironically, by the fall of 1969 I checked out in the F-4 Phantom again, flying a radar test program in an F-4C model. I also flew F-4D and F-4E models as part of the Hughes Aircraft Company's AGM-65A air-to-ground Maverick missile program. It felt good to get back in a jet aircraft again, but I still remembered how poorly the F-4 performed on the dive-bombing passes I observed as a FAC in Southeast Asia. Learning from our mistakes in Vietnam, the Air Force was now developing "smart weapons," which could be fired from a stand-off position, a capability Sandy pilots did not have during the Vietnam War. These "smart weapons" would be absolutely perfect for future rescue missions.

It was terrible for me to sit in my living room watching television in the spring of 1975 during those last days before Vietnam fell. Seeing what we fought for come undone and thinking about what we had sacrificed there, I was sickened. I was also torn in two directions. There was no sense in more people being killed. Yet, were we just going to pull out? I said to myself, "Is this what all the sacrifice has come to?" I made another drink, stronger than the last one. I was extremely disappointed and irritated, not only for myself, but for the families of Leonard, Russell, Jones, Kuhlmann, Masterson,

Pirruccello, Brownlee, King, Coady, Walsh, Warner, Campbell, Ward, and East. My flying buddies and their families paid a terrible price for what appeared to be nothing. I couldn't believe what I was seeing. South Vietnamese soldiers were climbing into the wheel wells of Boeing 707s as they flew out of Da Nang. Vietnamese pilots crash landed helicopters next to Navy ships in the Gulf of Tonkin. It made me angry at my country to see the loss of so many people and planes. But I didn't have any answers to this final tragedy either. I wiped my face with a handkerchief. In one sense it was like the war never happened. We never went to Vietnam. Pilots and PJs were not lost over there. But in my heart I knew it happened, it really happened. It has been written that men who go to war have been numbed, have lost the capability to feel. That is wrong; they feel too much.

In the spring of 1983, I attended an F-14A Tomcat meeting at the Naval Air Test Center at Patuxent River, Maryland. For my return commercial flight to California, I arrived in Washington, D.C., with a few hours to spare. It was an opportunity to make a fast trip through the National Air and Space Museum. To my surprise, I found my photo on the museum wall. Ten years earlier, I had launched a Hughes Aircraft Company–built AIM-54A air-to-air Phoenix missile from an F-14A flying at Mach 1.6 at 45,000 feet above the Pacific Ocean. My target was a simulated Russian MiG 25 Foxbat fighter heading directly toward me at Mach 2.2 and at 80,000-feet altitude. The Foxbat was the Soviet's equivalent of our SR-71 Blackbird. My launch was called the "Foxbat shot" by the news media and it was an outstanding success. The missile firing was captured by Rudy Vonick, a Hughes photographer, flying in the backseat of a Navy F-4 chase aircraft. His photograph was absolutely spectacular, catching the very moment the missile rocket motor lit off. The photo was used on the front of *Aviation Week & Space Technology* magazine, the cover of one book, and in articles in many other periodicals. While visiting the museum, I was pleasantly surprised to see the photo hanging on the wall behind a Phoenix missile. It was like being in the National Aviation Hall of Fame, surrounded by pilots who had made aviation history. It also showed how sophisticated and accurate weapons had become since I flew in Vietnam fourteen years earlier. In my estimation the Air Force and Navy were now on the right track in developing sophisticated weapons for the future.

During that visit I also had time to visit the Vietnam Veterans Memorial, which had been completed about six months earlier in the fall of 1982. The sun had just set, giving the park a soft golden glow as I searched for my comrades' names. Twelve familiar names were among the 58,209 veterans inscribed on the black granite wall. I was saddened to see my flying buddies' names etched in stone; it seemed to confirm they were actually dead and not missing, as I had thought of them for so long. But I was also pleased that their sacrifice for our country was permanently recognized.

In October 1989 I retired from Hughes Aircraft Company. After spending thirty-one years employed in the military service and aerospace industry, I now witnessed the end of the Cold War when the Berlin Wall came down. It was a tremendous feeling to have played a part in the defense of freedom against what President Ronald Reagan had called "the Evil Empire." Losing the Vietnam War was like having a bad inning in baseball. We lost a generation of pilots and aircraft in that ten-year misadventure; but in the end we won the ultimate game with the Soviet Union without a head-to-head military confrontation.

In 1991 I watched on TV as the U.S. military took on Saddam Hussein in Iraq. I was gratified to see the military had developed a massive armada of weapons, including many of the "smart weapons" I had helped test for Hughes Aircraft Company, and used them to finish off the enemy in just a few days. Unlike the limited war, the war of attrition we fought in Vietnam, our military went in with overwhelming force, went in to win, and quickly defeated the enemy.

In 1995 I decided to write a book about my experiences of twenty-five years as an Air Force and Hughes Aircraft Company test pilot. While doing research at Edwards Air Force Base I met an aviation historian, Fred Johnsen. He had just published a soft-covered book called *Douglas A-1 Skyraider: A Photo Chronicle*. To my surprise I found five photos I had taken with my Pentax 35-mm camera printed in his book. Years earlier, an engineer, who I worked with at Hughes Aircraft Company, had copied several slides I had taken of the Skyraider at NKP. These photos had been given to a third party, who lent them to Johnsen. Fred Johnsen and I shared a love of the history of the A-1 and traded Skyraider stories. He encouraged me to write about my combat experiences in Laos and North Vietnam. But at the time my interest was in writing a test pilot book.

Later that year I invited Dieter Dengler, the author of the book *Escape from Laos*, to give a talk to my local aviation museum. Dengler was a Navy pilot who flew the Skyraider over Vietnam in 1966. On his first combat flight he was shot down and captured. After about five months in captivity he escaped and wandered through the jungle for another three weeks before being spotted by another Skyraider pilot, Air Force Lt. Col. Eugene Deatrick. Gene Deatrick, a test pilot friend of mine, spotted Dengler standing on a rock in the bend of a river. Dengler was subsequently rescued, and both he and Dietrick presented a spellbinding program to my flying friends. Dengler and I exchanged war stories, and he also recommended that I capture my war experiences in print for future generations to read.

A couple of years later I attended an A-1 Skyraider Association reunion in San Antonio, Texas. It was the first time that I had gotten together with other A-1 pilots, even though these reunions had been going on for about twenty-five years. One of the pilots offered to collect a war story from each of us and have it published in a soft-covered book. I promised to write a story. Within a few days I wrote the story about my dead-stick landing on a dirt strip in Laos and sent it to him. Also attending the reunion was Lt. Col. John Carlson, who flew with me out of NKP in 1968 and 1969. After completing eighteen months of combat in the Skyraider, John returned to the United States. He flew a second combat tour in the F-4 and had just completed combat crew training in the F-105 in preparation for a third tour when the United States pulled out of Vietnam. John recalled that I had flown on the rescue of Streetcar 304 and suggested that I contact every pilot who had flown during the 189 sorties on the rescue. He said we could meet to debrief the mission. At that time both John Carlson and I had lost contact with Kenny Fields and Ed Leonard. Although I agreed it would be an emotional experience to gather all these old warriors in one place at one time, finding people after thirty years would be a daunting task. Nevertheless, I thought it was a good idea and started the search.

Six months later, on a Saturday morning in the conference room of a motel in Fort Walton Beach, Florida, eight of us finally debriefed the rescue of Streetcar 304. A videotape recording was made of our three-and-a-half-hour discussion. We drew quite a crowd of aviators interested in search and rescue. Three Air Force pilots from the Weapons School at Nellis AFB in

Nevada listened to our story and were astonished and overwhelmed. They had never heard such a stimulating story. As a result of this debriefing, the eight of us were invited to give our presentation on the Streetcar 304 rescue to the Weapons School students and instructors. The following fall the eight of us gathered before a new generation of Air Force warriors at Nellis AFB. We explained the daring aerial battle that resulted in the rescue of Kenny Fields. Fields told them what it was like on the ground in enemy territory, surrounded by guns and wondering if he would ever get back to freedom again. The young Air Force aviators in the audience were responsible for developing and performing tactics to be used to rescue downed American aircrew worldwide. Our previous successes and failures were explained in a way that would be useful for the decisions facing them on rescues in the future.

As a result of our presentation, we formed a new organization that we called the Society of Combat Search and Rescue (CSAR) with the purpose of meeting on a yearly basis to debrief a hostile rescue that had taken place in Vietnam. We viewed it as an opportunity to pass on our experiences to a younger generation of pilots and also a chance for old warriors to drink a beer and enjoy one another's company. In a sense, we can regain our lost inning of the game if we can transfer our combat experiences to another generation of rescue pilots.

In April 2000 the story I wrote for the Skyraider Association's soft-covered book (which was never published) appeared in *Wings* magazine. Five of my color photos were used, including a picture of *Sock It To 'Em* on the cover. The magazine sold out immediately, and I was in great demand to give talks about flying the Skyraider in Vietnam. Tamiya, a Japanese model airplane company, took information from the magazine article and designed a plastic model of *Sock It To 'Em*. The model can now be purchased in hobby stores and assembled by young people worldwide.

There seemed to be a tremendous interest in the old, battle-weary Skyraider and the rescue mission it performed so well. My older son Randy, a professor of geology at the University of Texas in Austin, encouraged me to capture my war experiences in print. So, in February 2001, I made a decision to interrupt the writing of my test pilot manuscript and concentrate on writing about the Skyraider and the Vietnam War.

It was a hot and humid summer afternoon in San Antonio, Texas, in early

September 2001. I had worked hard for seven months trying to capture my experiences in flying and fighting in the A-1. I had written about all of my flying mates lost in Southeast Asia except for MAJ. JAMES "J. B." EAST JR. The heat and intense sun made it practically unbearable to search for the site where my flying buddy's remains were buried. Noise from construction equipment being used to expand the Fort Sam Houston Military Cemetery competed with aircraft taking off and landing from nearby San Antonio International Airport. I didn't know if I would be able to find the final resting place of J. B. East, age thirty-five, from Oklahoma City, Oklahoma. A cubicle called a "grave locator" held twenty-six books where thousands upon thousands of names of military personnel were alphabetically listed. J. B. East was in section 12, grave number 187. I obtained a free map of the cemetery, adjusting it so north would be up, just like we did with our flight maps of Thailand, Laos, and North Vietnam. Also similar to our flights in Southeast Asia, the cemetery map contained military regulations to follow. Nine floral regulations explained the strict rules on how graves could be decorated.

On April 26, 1969, three weeks after I left Southeast Asia, Major East flew a combat mission over the east side of the PDJ near Lima Site 32. The Pathet Lao had chased General Vang Pao and his troops back toward their last stronghold. The 602nd was asked to launch every Skyraider in commission and keep the enemy from overrunning Vang Pao. Major East took off from NKP in my old plane *Sock It To 'Em*. East encountered ground fire as soon as he arrived in the area. As he was attacking a mortar position, a Laotian soldier saw him fire rockets. Then a fire started in his wing area next to the rocket pod and the wing sheared off. No parachute was observed—likewise, no emergency beeper was heard. Major East was listed as missing in action by the 602nd squadron.

Several weeks later General Vang Pao retook part of the area he had lost during the battle with the Pathet Lao. Some of his soldiers found the crash site of *Sock It To 'Em* and scavenged the remains. A .38 caliber pistol was recovered and transported to the 602nd at NKP. Maj. Harry Dunivant took the gun to life support personnel (the men who took care of our parachutes, survival vests, life preservers, helmets, and the like) to remove the pistol's six live rounds. Dunivant told me the barrel of the pistol was bent practically 30 degrees and showed severe crash damage. A life support specialist placed the gun in a vise and straightened the barrel so the live shells could be removed. Once the gun was safetied, its serial number was read and compared with the gun East was listed as carrying. The number was the same, confirming that East was still in the Skyraider when it crashed. With this information, his status was officially changed from missing in action to killed in action.

Even though J. B. East was killed in 1969, it would be another twenty-five years before a search was allowed by the Laotian government to find his Skyraider crash site and identify his remains. In 1994, a Laotian identified a possible crash site of an A-1. Later that year, the JTF–FA recovery team excavated the site and found A-1 wreckage, pilot-related items, and human bone fragments. DNA testing confirmed the remains were of Maj. James B. East Jr.

I found J. B. East's grave faster than I thought I would. I wasn't ready to be confronted with his name neatly etched on a white marble stone. Every one of the thousands of stones were exactly the same size and design; no individuality was permitted for the fallen veterans. All of the military personnel interred in the cemetery had served our country; East had died for it. Below his name were the letters KIA, looking so stark and final.

In 1997, he was finally laid to rest. His stone marker identified his place of death as Vietnam. Even in death the U.S. government failed to reveal to the public the true location of his loss. In reality, he was a victim of that "secret" war in Laos that was kept hidden from the American people for so many years. Visitors to the military cemetery will never know from the marker the story of his loss and the true location of his death.

During the course of writing this manuscript I have learned a lot about myself and the American fighting man. I now realize I still carry a lot of hostility and anger within me as a result of the way that the Vietnam War was conducted and its veterans treated. I also fully comprehend how much I miss my lost flying buddies and how proud I am of them for their sacrifice to our country.

While I went to war because I was ordered by the Air Force to do so, I also felt it was my duty to fight as a citizen-soldier serving my country. I thought I was protecting my family, my hometown, the American way of life, and the Constitution. I also thought I was giving the South Vietnamese, Laotians, and Cambodians an opportunity to experience freedom.

But as I look back now over the course of more than thirty years, I realize that the main reason I went into battle was to support my flying buddies. The Sandys, Jollys, PJs, and FACs all depended upon one another in combat in a way rarely seen in civilian life. As Darrel Whitcomb, the author of the book *The Rescue of Bat 21*, said, "The rescue armada in Vietnam was the ultimate team sport." Whitcomb was absolutely correct. I expected my teammates to do their duty, to support me and the rescue mission we shared in common. I would give my life if need be to rescue another airman with the full knowledge and faith that he would do the same for me. It was an unwritten agreement, a special bond, felt deeply by each of us.

I was fortunate that the Air Force picked such a superb group of aviators for me to fly with in combat. Some have called us heroes, but Skyraider pilots did not think of themselves that way. To us, the Jolly pilots were heroes. But if you talk to a Jolly Green pilot, he will tell you that the PJs were the real heroes. Likewise, the PJs will say that the Army infantrymen who spent all their time in the jungle were the heroes. And one F-4 pilot told me he spent some time with foot soldiers and they had said the jet pilots who supported them with air strikes were the heroes. Everyone thought someone else was the "real" hero.

My memories of these picturesque and courageous pilots and the dramatic rescues we flew are still crystal clear to me. Over the past year I have interviewed twenty-four pilots who flew with me and could confirm that my memory of these details was correct. They helped me describe the colorful aviators I served with and to write of events that occurred so long ago.

I did not keep a diary or journal at the time, as I didn't think I would survive the year of combat. I didn't want my wife, children, and grandchildren to find out how difficult it was to lose so many friends and how I feared I would be lost also. I did reread letters I had mailed to my wife, wiping tears from my eyes as I did so.

I now know why we who have been to war yearn to reunite. It's not just to tell war stories, look at old photos, and drink beer—although we do all of that. We don't do so to laugh at our past mistakes or dry one another's tears either. Warriors gather because they long to be with buddies who once acted their best, men who suffered and sacrificed, who were stripped raw, right down to their humanity. I did not pick these men to share my year of toil and torment. They were delivered to me by fate and were the best men of my generation. I now know them in a way I know no others. Never have I given anyone such trust. They were willing to guard something more precious than my life. They would have carried my reputation, the memory of me into the future. It was also part of the unwritten code, the reason we were willing to die for one another and our country. So with the words I have written here I have kept the faith, to use an overworked cliché. This book permanently engraves the memory of the lost and injured for future generations. I have fulfilled the bargain we made so long ago. As long as I have consciousness, I will think of the Sandys, Jollys, FACs, and PJs and the sacrifices they made in that "secret" war. When I leave this world, my last thoughts will be of my family and my brothers in arms.

The time in combat was the most intense year of my life, combining tragic losses with unbelievable successes. Not being a professional writer, I have struggled to describe the everyday life of a Sandy rescue pilot as accurately as I can. I have laughed and cried as I put these words on paper. Words that might thrill some and offend others. But, with this book, the Vietnam War is finally over for me. I have told it all.